Praise for *Unraveling Bias*

"Prejudice starts young. In this enlightening book, Dr. Brown explains very clearly how we develop biases as children and how those biases get reinforced over time by policies and institutions. Best of all, *Unraveling Bias* offers actionable steps that parents, educators, and policymakers can take to eradicate bias and discrimination from our society."
—**Lara S. Kaufmann, director of public policy at Girls Inc.**

"*Unraveling Bias* is truly remarkable, timely, and incredibly important. This is a book that parents, educators, and policymakers will highlight, dog ear, and refer back to time and time again. I wish it had existed years ago, but I'm so grateful to have it now!"
—**Dolly Chugh, author of *The Person You Mean
to Be: How Good People Fight Bias***

"In *Unraveling Bias*, Dr. Brown pointedly reveals the subtle and pervasive ways that bias has fundamentally shaped childhood. By combining social history with the most current developmental science, the book traces the history of bias from the perspectives of research, law, and the social influence in the lives of children. It breaks down the forms, experiences, and meanings of bias in the lives of children. This book is crucial for our times not just because it synthesizes the relevant research, but because it provides the pathways for families, schools, and communities to unravel and break the cycle of bias."
—**Stephen T. Russell, Priscilla Pond Flawn Regents Professor
in Child Development at the University of Texas at Austin**

"Given that bias is the root of so many of the world's injustices and ills, it is perhaps the most important issue to understand and unravel today. Christia Spears Brown has given us an invaluable resource with her deeply researched book about how bias develops, how it affects our children, and how we can successfully fight it. This should be required reading for every American."
—**Melinda Wenner Moyer, author of *How
to Raise Kids Who Aren't Assholes***

"This book by Christia Spears Brown is a must-read for anyone who wants to understand the true nature of bias and the many ways it affects our kids. With a compassionate voice, ample research evidence, quotes from youths and parents, and insights from legal scholars and the courts, Dr. Brown charts pathways for breaking down entrenched patterns of discrimination and opening up new conversations about the pervasiveness and effects of bias in our society."

—Linda R. Tropp, PhD, professor in the Department of Psychological and Brain Sciences at the University of Massachusetts Amherst

"A passionate and occasionally harrowing account of the damaging racial, gender, and sexual biases children continue to encounter in schools, with thoughtful suggestions about how parents, teachers, and whole communities can confront them."

—Stephanie Coontz, author of *A Strange Stirring: The Feminine Mystique and American Women at the Dawn of the 1960s*

"Informative and inspiring, Dr. Brown brilliantly weaves history, data, and stories from courts to classrooms in this timely and much-needed resource. *Unraveling Bias* empowers readers with actionable, science-backed tips for improving the lives of children for generations to come. A must-read for every parent, educator, and policymaker."

—Kyl Myers, author of *Raising Them: Our Adventure in Gender Creative Parenting*

"In Christia Spears Brown's fantastic and much-needed book, we'll find both good news and bad news. The bad news is that bias—on the basis of race, gender identity, sexual orientation, and much more—is real, pervasive, deeply consequential, and baked into both our personal practices and institutional norms. If we take that message to heart, then we can act on the good news: as individuals and as members of communities, we can transform our hearts, minds, and institutions, where biases thrive, while raising the children in our lives to do the same. Dr. Brown's arguments are as historically and empirically informed as her language is clear. If we are ever to achieve the full promise of our diversely constituted democracy, it's work like *Unraveling Bias* that will point the way."

—Andrew Grant-Thomas, cofounder of EmbraceRace

Unraveling
Bias

Also by Christia Spears Brown, PhD

Parenting Beyond Pink and Blue (2014)

Discrimination in Childhood and Adolescence (2017)

Unraveling
Bias

How Prejudice Has Shaped Children
for Generations and Why It's Time to
Break the Cycle

CHRISTIA SPEARS BROWN,
PhD

BenBella

BenBella Books, Inc.
Dallas, TX

BenBella Books, Inc.
10440 N. Central Expressway
Suite 800
Dallas, TX 75231
benbellabooks.com
Send feedback to feedback@benbellabooks.com

BenBella is a federally registered trademark.

Printed in the United States of America
10 9 8 7 6 5 4 3 2 1

Library of Congress Control Number: 2021026220
ISBN 9781953295552 (print)
ISBN 9781953295897 (electronic)

Editing by Alyn Wallace and Vy Tran
Copyediting by Ginny Glass
Proofreading by Lisa Story and Kim Broderick
Indexing by WordCo Indexing Services, Inc.
Text design and composition by Katie Hollister
Cover design by Brigid Pearson
Cover image © Shutterstock / Nowik Sylwia
Printed by Lake Book Manufacturing

Special discounts for bulk sales are available.
Please contact bulkorders@benbellabooks.com.

Ruth (Horowitz) Hartley died the year I started graduate school. I was a full professor before I learned her name. What I learned—twenty years after I began conducting research about race and gender stereotypes and discrimination in children—is that Ruth's work played a critical role in the science I practice. Her contemporary, Mamie Phipps Clark, expanded on Ruth's research and helped change race relations in American schools. But the biases of their time prevented both women from getting the credit they deserved. This book is dedicated to them.

This book is also dedicated to every kid who has been marginalized, disenfranchised, and silenced because of their race, class, immigration status, gender, or sexuality. May you live in a world that values your voice, your experiences, and your life.

Contents

PART III—Moving Forward

Foreword

Bias is a slippery beast. Invisible to the eye, hard to name, and harder yet to pin down and fight. It operates in the subtlest ways, through words or glances, in social norms and traditions, and, today, as powerful algorithms and influential data that, increasingly, shape the world around us at unprecedented scales. From schoolyard bullying to workplace inequities to the efflorescence of public violence, bias, stereotypes, and prejudices powerfully govern not only our social interactions, economic lives, and political institutions but our very identities and relationships.

As human beings, we are all subject to biases, which are part of our cognition. We take the lessons we learn as young people, frequently infused with harmful and damaging stereotypes, into the world with us, incorporating them into our sense of self, our sense of our place in the world, our understanding of social roles and relationships, and, ultimately, into how we recognize and distribute power and resources in our society.

As Dr. Christia Brown compellingly shows us here, however, this does not mean that the *content* of our biases is fixed and unassailable. It doesn't mean that we are powerless in the face of our own heuristics or traditions or beliefs. And, as she shows so vividly here, the best and surest way to understand and challenge damaging biases, and to confront the profound harms and influences of stereotypes and prejudices, is to tackle them in early childhood education. Her scholarship and recommendations, grounded in insightful research and analysis, are further enriched by the stories she shares of people who have experienced discrimination and inequality and subsequently dedicated themselves to changing the world around them for the better.

There is immense benefit in tackling a problem of this scope at its root the way she has set out to here. All of our lives are impoverished by biases and the stereotypes and stereotype threats they cultivate. Any genuine consideration of the complexities of living in diverse and increasingly global and mobile societies—from educational inequities and workplace discrimination to fathoming why young boys are killing themselves, or decoding the aggrieved racialized and gendered entitlement at the heart of so much of our social and political violence, leads us back to deeply held biases, learned in childhood. For the most part, however, by the time we come to this conclusion, we are, as a society, fighting a rear-guard action.

Providing adults—teachers, coaches, administrators, parents, doctors—with the information they need to understand biases and stereotypes is essential to addressing all types of inequality and suffering. Brown's writing—from the descriptive to prescriptive—compellingly reveals the ways in which biases can and do influence us all, in our homes, schools, workplaces, and legal system. She explains, in clear and illuminating ways, the nuanced interplay of biases related to gender, sexuality, race, ethnicity, disability, and social class, how they inform one another. The tools that Dr. Brown provides here make it possible for us to be more effective, and as early as possible.

Expanding public awareness and understanding of how biases operate will not eliminate them, but will enable us, as individuals and as a society, to be more creative, better informed, and more successful in efforts to build a more just world. This book provides vital resources that enable us to improve educational environments, institutional behaviors, and social and political outcomes, from the start.

The long-term value to society is inestimable.

—**Soraya Chemaly,**
activist and award-winning author of
Rage Becomes Her: The Power of Women's Anger

Introduction

Bias is everywhere, embedded in almost all human interactions. It's there when a store clerk keeps a watchful eye on a Black teenager browsing a department store or speaks slowly to the Asian American teen at checkout. It's there when a stranger compliments your daughter for being pretty and your son for being big and strong. It's there when a school librarian refuses to stock books featuring gay characters. On a larger scale, the fallout from individual and institutional prejudices splatters across headlines every day. Many trending topics and social movements are direct responses to biased behaviors, discriminatory actions, and structural inequality. Systematic police brutality against and murder of Black people gave rise to the Black Lives Matter movement. Rampant sexual abuse and harassment of women—and men—led victims to come forward and say #MeToo. Decades of homophobia, transphobia, and extreme violence toward LGBTQ+ folks have sparked everything from the Stonewall Riots, to gay and transgender rights movements, to annual pride parades around the world.

There's a reason for these mass demonstrations and protests—people are not responding to the actions of a few racist or sexist individuals. Biases are internalized and enacted by almost everyone, and they are embedded in the media, in institutions, and in laws and policies. Biased policies result in immigrant and refugee children locked in holding cells at the border, in school-funding models that keep kids of color at underfunded and understaffed schools, and in regulations about after-school sports that restrict how transgender student athletes can participate.

Many of the biased policies in the United States directly affect or target children in their homes, schools, and communities, which is particularly alarming since biases and prejudices don't just develop when people become adults (or CEOs or politicians). Rather, they begin when children are very young, slowly growing, becoming more entrenched each year, and becoming harder and harder to erase. Children are being raised in a world in which biases penetrate like arrows from all sides—at times marginalizing them and limiting their growth, and at times being believed, internalized, and passed along to others. Prejudices shape almost every aspect of children's development.

People often say children aren't born hating others—they have to learn it. "Kids learn prejudice from their parents," they say knowingly during conversations about racism, sexism, or homophobia. Prejudice is the result of "poor parenting," everyone agrees, and the discussion ends there. The implication is that *they* aren't biased, so *their* kids can't be biased, and prejudices are other people's problems. Potentially harmful social constructs, such as gender norms or stereotypes, are similarly brushed off. People roll their eyes and dismiss certain actions and behaviors as, "That's just boys being boys," or, "You know how girls are." They blame biology and leave it there.

But these are just convenient ways to point the finger and shirk the responsibility of societal inequalities. As the adults who make decisions impacting children, we need to pay careful attention to how they are affected by stereotypes, prejudice, and bias—the ones that harm them as they grow up and the ones they learn from a biased society. There is enough blame to go around. It also means there are a lot of opportunities to make changes.

The only way to have a more just and equitable world is to take a closer look at the biases beginning in childhood. We have to know how bias affects children from before they are born and lays a foundation for the rest of their lives. We also have to know how those biases have changed over time, a reflection of the policies and culture of the day. Unraveling the causes and influences of bias—in all the ways it plays out in the lives of children—is the only way to make the future more just than the past.

As a developmental psychologist who studies stereotypes and discrimination in children, my goals for this book are to share the research that shows how and why bias runs roughshod through childhood, and delve into how our laws and policies and schools have been changed in the past—and can be changed in the future to make the world more equitable.

In the first part of the book, we'll explore how biased laws and policies affect children—both historically and today; how those laws were fought by advocates and lawyers and changed by judges and policymakers; and how the science of bias played a crucial role. We'll start with the fight to racially desegregate schools and the *Brown v. Board of Education* case, because it is an inspiration for positive (albeit slow and imperfect) social change and represents the first time that social science helped push public policy toward equality. This case served as a template for later legal battles that protected students from sexual harassment in schools and allowed trans teens to use the bathroom that matched their gender identity. Unraveling race bias came first in the courts, so it comes first in the book.

In the second part, we'll dig deeper into the science of bias—how it looks in different forms, how it is influenced by our modern-day policies, and how it has changed over time. We will explore historical and modern research conducted by social scientists in fields like developmental psychology, family studies and child development, education, social psychology, sociology, and economics. Throughout that section, I will not only share my own research but also draw heavily from the work of others who are studying these social problems.

Additionally, in the second section, each chapter features a sidebar that focuses on some of the scientists who pioneered this work, despite themselves facing discrimination. All are women, and, more precisely, immigrant women, women of color, Jewish women, and LBTQ women, whose innovative research asked questions of children no one else thought to ask, whose work started unraveling children's biases and helped usher in more just and equitable policies and laws. Science is a human endeavor, and the questions researchers ask are informed by their life experiences and perspectives. These women laid the foundation for what we know now.

In the final part, we'll look at what we can do to unravel bias within our own families, within our communities, and within society at large.

Whenever possible, I use children's and teens' own words from historical documents taken during the legal battles to desegregate schools to modern studies about sexual harassment and online racism. There are many types of biases affecting children: biases because of class, ability, weight, mental illness, and neuro-development, to name a few. But to keep the book from becoming unbearably long, I will focus on how children are harmed by individual and societal bias because of race, ethnicity, and nationality; gender; gender identity; and sexual orientation. These are the social groups established at birth that give us personal meaning, bind us to one another, and capture children's attention from infancy.

Although this book is written from my vantage point as a researcher, it is, no doubt, shaped by my own biases and privileges. Owning those biases and privileges is an important part of reducing our biases, which is why I'd like to take this time to be forthcoming about my own. I have a PhD in developmental psychology from the University of Texas at Austin, and spend my days as a college professor, where I teach and conduct research with children about their gender and ethnic stereotypes. I am a White cisgender woman married to a White cisgender man. I have two White cisgender daughters. One identifies as straight, and I worry about her internalizing stereotypes that tell girls that their value comes from being sexually objectified by boys; one identifies as gay, and I worry about her experiencing any homophobic bullying as well as how to ensure her rights for marriage and family equality.

I was born in the South to teen parents who quickly divorced, and raised in a town known for a battle of the Civil War where local mascots wave Confederate flags, and I am the first member of my family to attend college. Race and class have always been salient features of my world. I have internalized ethnic and gender biases, biases I picked up by my sheer presence on earth. Overriding those personal biases, checking myself and my assumptions, is my own daily task, a task I sometimes succeed at and sometimes fail at. None of us have emerged unscathed from a biased world. All of us belong to privileged groups and marginalized groups. All we can do is continuously check ourselves: Am I relying on a stereotype? Is my opinion filtered through my privileges? How is that person's lived experience different from my own? That task is an internal one—but it is also one that informs our external responsibilities. Fighting against biases at the societal level and making the world better for the generations that come behind us will take all of us working together—starting now.

1 A Primer on Bias

Not everything that is faced can be changed, but
nothing can be changed until it is faced.
—James Baldwin

lthough we like to think of ourselves as individuals charting our own unique destinies, the social groups we are born into as humans shape much of our lives. There are a variety of groups that exist, from social class to citizen of a certain neighborhood—and all of these groups tell children something about themselves and about others. However, in this book, we are going to focus on three big groupings that are important to children and teens (and which happen to make it into headlines almost daily): race and ethnicity, gender, and gender identity and sexual orientation.

To start, children are born into one or more racial or ethnic groups. From a sociological perspective, race is based on physical differences (such as skin color or hair texture) that "groups and cultures consider socially significant, while ethnicity refers to shared culture, such as language, ancestry, practices, and beliefs."[1] We typically lump these groupings together, and based on someone's skin color or facial features, or the birthplaces of their parents or grandparents, we assign labels like White, Black, Latino, Asian, biracial. These are neither definitive groups nor perfect labels. If this book were written ten years ago or ten years from now, these groups and their labels would be different, but even now, even at this single moment in time, labels are inconsistent. For example, Latino and Hispanic are labels that only have meaning in the United States, where they're used to lump together everyone from Mexico to Chile, regardless of their similarities or differences. In theory, Hispanic is supposed to refer to people either from Spain or from Spanish-speaking countries in Central and South America and the Caribbean, while Latino is supposed to refer to anyone from Latin America. Neither term tells us anything more about a person's race than being told that someone is a New Yorker. In practice, however, those terms—along with Chicano and Mexican American—are often used interchangeably[2] and treated as a racial grouping by adults and children. There are similar inconsistencies across all racial and ethnic designations, but, despite the obvious imperfections of these labels, the associations they carry shape how we think about ourselves and others. Labels take on meanings that suggest unique cultural contributions, family connections, and food histories. They also allow for stereotypes, prejudice, and discrimination.

Beyond racial or ethnic groups, children are also born into other groups that our society tells us are important. For example, humans are born with certain external sex characteristics that a doctor, upon quick inspection, assigns a label: boy or girl. Names, clothing, and hairstyles are differentiated by these labels, children are drenched in pink or blue based on that label, and children recognize these distinctions when they look at others. Those labels teach us how we think others should think and act, and we treat them accordingly. Girls are supposed to be pretty, boys are supposed to be tough, and those expectations perpetuate sexism even by preschool.

While such gender stereotypes and biases target children who fall "neatly" within a girl or boy category, a different set of biases affect children who don't fit so clearly within that binary. Some children may have external sex characteristics that don't align with their internal sense of gender, they may identify as transgender or nonbinary,* and they will likely face prejudices because some people are uncomfortable when they can't easily categorize a person into a tidy box.

When children begin to recognize the gender of whom they are romantically or sexually attracted to (some children seem to know from the beginning, while some have a slower timetable), labels based on their sexual orientation, like straight, lesbian, gay, bisexual, queer, and so on, take on

---

* If they also feel intense and continuous discomfort because of their gender identity, they may be clinically diagnosed with "gender dysphoria."

personal and social meaning. These are also not definitive groups or perfect labels, and as adolescents explore their sexuality and figure out which label fits best, their labels may change. While some youth are open to others about their sexual orientation, other folks may keep these labels private. And just like with race and ethnicity, these terms aren't static: they change as our appreciation of the diversity of people changes. In this book, I'll use LGBTQ+ to represent lesbian, gay, bisexual, trans, and queer youth because it is the most commonly used label at this time, but I am mindful that the "+" is meant to incorporate a wide variety of people who identify as pansexual, asexual, and many others, and this notation has its own set of biases.

In each one of these groups—race/ethnicity, gender, gender identity, sexual orientation—there is a dominant group, either by sheer numerical majority or through greater economic, political, or legal status:

- White people in the United States are the largest single racial/ethnic group and occupy the highest economic position, largely because they have oppressed, disenfranchised, and excluded all other racial/ethnic groups. The result is that White kids have a very different experience than all other children.
- Boys and girls are equal numerically, but women have yet to reach economic parity with men and, in 2021, have yet to reach the highest levels of political power in the United States.
- Youth who identify with a sexual orientation or gender identity that is anything but straight and cisgender (meaning *not* transgender) are in the numerical minority *and* are still fighting for equality within the law.

All of these groups overlap and interact within a single individual, so the biases Black girls and Black boys face are different from one another, as are the biases Black girls and White girls face. The biases don't just add up in a simple equation either. A Black cisgender lesbian will not have the exact experience of a White transgender lesbian plus the effect of being Black minus the effect of being transgender. The unique combination of multiple identities differs from the sum of their parts.

With all of these factors and labels in mind, this book is ultimately about *all* children. It's about children in the marginalized groups—the ones who are harmed by biases, stereotypes, and discrimination. It's also about children in the privileged groups—the ones who hold biases and stereotypes about others (and themselves). It's about two sides of the same damaging and dysfunctional coin. After all, most children have moments of being marginalized and moments of being privileged. To understand bias, we have to examine both when it is pointed at children and when children point it at others.

BIAS TAKES MANY FORMS

To unravel the biases that have restricted generations of children is to make the world more just for all of us. In order to do that, we have to closely inspect the fabric of that bias and understand precisely what it's made of. Bias, regardless of whether it is based on race, gender, or sexual orientation, is a bit like gray fabric. From a distance, it appears to be one color. But a closer look reveals black and white threads woven together so tightly they are hard to disentangle. Bias is similarly made up of two types of thread: one is the stereotypes and prejudices that individuals hold in their hearts and minds; the other is the biased policies and laws that keep some groups disadvantaged and marginalized compared to other groups.

At the individual level, the threads of bias appear in the cognitive distortions, or stereotypes, we hold when we think _____ group of people think or act a certain way. These biases are things like Black boys are troublemakers, Black girls are loud, Latino kids can't speak proper English, Asian boys are gifted in math, girls are more suited for liberal arts and the humanities, boys who like theater are gay—the list goes on. Sometimes bias comes in the form of feeling a sense of discomfort or anxiety when around someone from a different group. Biases can also appear even more overtly when we interact with one another: kids using a racial or ethnic slur during a basketball game at school, police officers harassing a group of Black boys for "illegally loitering," high school boys loudly rating the body parts of a girl as she walks down the hallway to her class, middle school girls spreading a rumor that a classmate is a lesbian because of how she dresses, or school officials not allowing children to use the bathroom that aligns with their gender identity.

At the societal level, the other thread of bias is made up of the structural and systemic racism, sexism, heterosexism, and cisgenderism that are embedded within our institutions, laws, policies, and historically informed practices. This thread of bias acts to infect the institutions where children spend their time. Biases are embedded into how teachers and police officers are trained, how neighborhoods are designed, and how schools are structured and financed. For example, in the United States, on average, schools spend $334 more on White students than on students of color.[3] Because that race-based funding deficit meant calculus and physics weren't offered at their schools, there was no money for a guidance counselor to help with college applications, and no one paid for an ACT prep course, students of color in underfunded schools will leave school underprepared and less likely to attend college.

While these two threads of bias are different, they strengthen and fortify one another. Structural inequalities that force some groups to face poverty at higher rates than others, and allow some groups to more easily escape poverty, enable false individual-level beliefs such as "if they are poor, they must be lazy; if they are lazy, they deserve to be poor." In other words, structural biases lead to group-level educational and economic inequalities, and, by making it appear as though anyone who remains impoverished deserves it, the biases about individuals' intelligence or work ethic are reinforced and strengthened. Relationships like that are why, in this book, I pull at and unravel *both* threads. We cannot reduce individuals' biases without readdressing deeper structural inequalities, and we cannot motivate people to change structural inequalities unless they face their own individual biases. To undo the damage of centuries, we have to simultaneously change biased policies *and* biased people.

BIAS APPEARS AT THE BEGINNING

Nelson Mandela said that "no one is born hating another person because of the color of his skin, or his background, or his religion. People must learn to hate." He was right. Babies aren't born hating others—but they do pay a lot of attention to what people look like, focusing on groups that are visible and perceptually obvious. It is that attention that can eventually develop into the biases that Mandela tells us people learn—but it isn't inevitable. We can change that if we intervene.

Because we literally come in different shades that we segregate into similar groups (which makes the groups take on significance beyond random variation*), and because we exaggerate gender as a category with clothes

---

* It isn't just that we come in different shades of skin, but we also treat the grouping based on race as meaningful through segregated families and communities. In contrast, we have other physical variations that we *don't* ascribe meaning to. For example,

and hair cues, babies develop race/ethnicity and gender categories within a few months and prefer the groups they see most often. In studies where researchers show newborn babies a series of faces of different races/ethnicities, the babies look at people of different race/ethnicities equal amounts of time.[4] But by the time babies are three months old, not only can they differentiate faces by race, but also they gaze longer at people who are the same race as the people raising them.[5]* They have developed a mental race-specific prototype of faces based on what their visual input is (i.e., the face peering over their crib the most often). Because the majority of babies are raised by a primary caregiver who is their same race, this means that most babies show a same-race preference by three months. Since everything in the world is brand-new to babies, they seem to latch onto what they find most familiar—and not just with race/ethnicity. Similarly, babies at this age can categorize people into gender categories and prefer the group they are most familiar with. For babies who spend more time with women than men (as do the majority of babies in the United States), they show preferences for female-presenting faces; for babies whose primary caregivers are men, they show preferences for male-presenting faces.[6] By the time babies are nine months old, they start to associate positive emotions with the racial group they are most familiar with. In one study, babies from same-race families looked longer at same-race faces paired with happy music and other-race faces paired with sad music.[7]

Moving beyond babies, once children can say biases out loud, they do. In an international meta-analysis† of 121 different studies on ethnic,

---

humans can be blond-haired, brown-haired, black-haired, red-haired, or no-haired. Yet because those groups are not used in "functional" ways, we do not develop early biases on hair-color groups. Race and gender are exaggerated in importance to children because they are used in functional ways to sort and organize the world.

* Evidence of this point is supplemented by the counterpoints. Babies adopted by other-race parents prefer looking at faces the same race as their parents (not themselves). Also, multiracial babies who see a mix of races consistently—to the point that all of those faces become familiar to them—have a broader preference for others. For example, multiracial infants raised in multiracial families process faces differently than monoracial children, scanning their faces differently, likely because they have more experience with a diversity of faces.

† Meta-analyses are a really important research technique that collapses hundreds of studies that have been published on a topic into one giant analysis. This approach allows researchers to see the overall effect of something, regardless of the exact way it was measured or the specific sample of kids. It gives us a "take-home message"

racial, and national bias in children ranging from two to seventeen from eighteen different countries, researchers found that explicit biases are present in preschoolers by around age two and sharply increase as children move through kindergarten and begin elementary school.[8] For almost all children, regardless of their own racial or ethnic group or experiences, their explicit ethnic, racial, and national biases (including their stereotypes about groups' traits and preferences for one group over another) are at their strongest when they are seven years old, before becoming less rigid later. Racial and ethnic biases at this age are particularly explicit: children primarily prefer to be friends with same-race kids and assume other-race people are "all the same." I have found, in my research on bias in children, that using a "thermometer rating" reveals a lot about how this explicit bias manifests in children. We show children an individual of a specific ethnic or racial group and a thermometer ranging from 0 to 100. We ask children to rate how warmly or positively they feel toward the individual in that racial/ethnic group, with 100 being the most positive. Almost all children, regardless of their race or ethnic group, rate their own group the best.[9] Over the course of elementary school, children begin to endorse common racial stereotypes about what people in different groups are like, such as who is smart or who gets into trouble.[10]

Gender biases follow the same pattern. By the time children are three years old, they believe gender stereotypes about boys' and girls' abilities and interests and usually show a strong aversion to playing with one another at school.[11] For example, when three-year-olds were asked to sort toys, such as a skateboard figure, a motorcycle figure, a ball and glove, an army coat, a tea set, a baby doll and crib, a ballet tutu, and a white straw hat with ribbons, into piles of "girl toys" and "boy toys," 92 percent of their responses reflected gender-typical stereotypes. By age five, the number had risen to 98 percent.[12] Meta-analyses[13] on gender biases find that, similar to the pattern shown with racial bias, children's endorsement of gender stereotypes peaks around age six before becoming more flexible.*

---

from an entire field. I will use these whenever possible because they give us the most confidence in the findings.

* This pattern of gender stereotype development, in which stereotypes are strongest around the beginning of elementary school, is the same for children who identify with their gender assigned at birth as well as transgender children who identify with a different gender than the one assigned at birth.

Children's limited cognitive abilities drive much of these early biases. Not only are race and gender cognitively easy categories to latch onto, but we also exaggerate the salience and importance of race when we live in families and have friends who are only one race and of gender when we constantly use it to color-code (into pink or blue clothes), label ("what a smart *girl!*"), and categorize people (do you use the boys' or girls' restroom?). So, children interpret those easy-to-process categories as being the most important and overlook the unique information about a person. For example, if a young child sees an astrophysicist who is Black, skin color trumps the advanced degree as an attention-grabber. Since they can't cognitively hold onto two pieces of information (race and profession) simultaneously, they pick the cognitively easier category to remember and distort or forget other information that doesn't "fit" the stereotype that they hold of people in that category.[14] So, before age eight, almost all children hold biases simply because biases are the easiest way to think about people.

Toward the end of elementary school, around age ten, children's biases begin to diverge from one another.[15] At this age, they start incorporating more outside information into their understanding of social groups. This is when the experiences and societal messages they have been absorbing start to show themselves. For example, children seem to be sensitive to the status of groups early on, and if they can, they latch onto societal messages that benefit them. As a result, children in higher-status, dominant groups hold more biases than children in lower status, minoritized groups. For children who belong to a minority or marginalized group or a group associated with lower status in a society, their biases typically decline at this age until they look pretty unbiased. In action, that means that, on average, White kids in the United States are the ones holding the strongest racial biases,[16] and boys drive gender biases more than girls.[17]

Children latch onto status messages even when assigned to a fake group. I've seen this in research that I have personally worked on: we randomly assigned elementary school children to novel groups based on if they had gotten a red T-shirt or a blue T-shirt to wear in summer school.[18] When posters on the classroom walls showed red group members were higher in status (they were the past class president and had won previous field days and spelling bees), the kids in red shirts zeroed in on this information and developed biases favoring the red group. The children in the blue group, however, remained unbiased. Even though teachers never pointed out the posters, children noticed these status cues, and those cues shaped and drove their biases—just like they do in real-life race and gender groups.

But even the children who belong to those real-life higher-status groups—the ones who are more motivated to hold onto biases—will show less bias if they interact with people from other groups.[19] The process of exposure to diverse others leads to greater comfort with others, which leads to fewer biases. This bias-reducing effect of diversity even occurs when that exposure was just based on school diversity. That meta-analysis on racial bias worldwide that I mentioned earlier showed that, around age ten, racial bias looked less intense among White kids if at least 5 percent of the students at their school were Black or Latino. Similar effects result from exposure to other types of diversity—taking more mixed-gender (rather than gender-segregated) classes leads to fewer gender biases,[20] knowing LGBTQ+ people leads to fewer LGBTQ+ biases,[21] and knowing people of different religions[22] leads to fewer religious biases. Knowing diverse people helps children be more comfortable with and accepting of diversity.

Living in a world that lacks diversity not only contributes to greater biases in children, but also changes how we literally see others. As humans, we adapt to what we see and hear, following a perceptual "use it or lose it" rule: if an ability is not being used, it disappears. Because we are exposed to segregated worlds from infancy and primarily see same-race faces, we lose the ability to differentiate other-race faces as our brains discard it as an unnecessary skill. It is a phenomenon called the *other-race effect*.[23] It is why, although all racial groups are equally diverse in their facial features, it is not uncommon to hear someone say, "They all look alike to me!" about people of a different race. Individual out-group members look more *homogenous* or similar than in-group members who look like unique humans to us because of a process called *perceptual narrowing*. We are not born with this perceptual glitch: at three months old, infants can be taught the differences between individuals who belong to their own race as well as individuals within another race. But by nine months, infants have lost that ability. They now do what adults do, recognizing same-race individuals much better than other-race individuals. For example, a nine-month-old White baby can be shown pictures of White men, and later recognize which are the familiar faces from a larger array of White faces, but can't do the same with Black men.

But this is not inevitable. It's simply a result of living in a segregated world and seeing mostly same-race faces. In a study where infants were taught the individual names of other-race faces (their mothers would point to the face and say, "This is Linda," for example), those babies retained the ability to see people as individuals.[24] Studies also show that this other-race effect was reduced, or even reversed, when children attended more integrated (rather than segregated) schools[25] or when children were adopted into other-race families.[26] This shows that children just need to see diversity more often in order to counteract the kind of early perceptual processes that eventually lead to things like people picking the wrong person out of a lineup and ruining someone's life.*

Taken together, all of this suggests that biases develop for a few reasons.[27] First, we have biological tendencies to like humans who are familiar. Second, we are born into a society that exaggerates differences between groups: gender is repeatedly labeled, color-coded, and used to sort people, and we have limited exposure to racially diverse others because we live in segregated homes and communities. These social cues tell children to pay close attention to gender and race as meaningful categories of people. Third, we are inundated with messages conveying some groups are more valued than others. Combined with the biases embedded in our institutions, policies, and laws that center, and even elevate, some voices more than others, it's no wonder that children develop biases.

THE BIAS ON THE SURFACE

The overt biases we see—the open expressions of disdain toward others because of their race, ethnicity, gender, religion, sexual orientation, or country of origin—are simply the tip of the iceberg. People commonly assume that children learn biases when their parents make racial slurs or sit them down at the kitchen table and point out who to hate and who to love—that if someone isn't using racial slurs or displaying a swastika, then they are not racist—and thus, neither are their children. But that view of

---

* This is why eyewitness identification, particularly when a White witness is asked to pick out a Black suspect, is largely inaccurate. For a heartbreaking example of this injustice from both sides of the glass, read *Picking Cotton* by Jennifer Thompson-Cannino, Ronald Cotton, and Erin Torneo.

bias is only focusing on *explicit* biases and ignores the deeply entrenched *implicit* biases.

There is no doubt that overt biases do exist in childhood. The Southern Poverty Law Center, the nonprofit legal advocacy organization based in Montgomery, Alabama, that tracks hate and bias incidents in the United States, gave almost three thousand K–12 educators a questionnaire in the fall of 2018. Of the 2,700 teachers who responded, two-thirds of them had witnessed hate and bias incidents (most of them more than once) at their elementary, middle, and high schools in the first few months of the school year. Of those hate and bias incidents, 33 percent were based on race, with Black kids being called "ape," nooses at school in a locker, the use of the "N-word" at "near constant" levels. One-fourth of the incidents were anti-LGBTQ+, with one teacher saying, "Using gay as an insult is done on a DAILY basis. Students use the word 'f**got' as if it were no big deal." Almost one in five incidents were anti-immigrant, captured by a story of elementary school students circling children of color and chanting, "Build the wall. Build the wall." Other incidents were anti-Semitic, with teachers reporting swastikas scratched into bathroom tiles, painted in parking lots, and written in the yearbooks of Jewish students; and others were anti-Muslim, as one ten-year-old Muslim girl found a note in her cubby telling her, "You're a terrorist. I will kill you."

Overt biases are only getting worse as the political climate becomes more nationalistic, racialized, and misogynistic. According to the FBI's 2017 data on hate crimes (which most people acknowledge is a conservative estimate), hate crimes in K–12 schools rose by 25 percent from 2016 to 2017. The big event of 2016, of course, was the election of President Donald Trump. The FBI report from 2020 found that hate crimes in the United States were at their highest point ever in 2019, and only slowed down in 2020 because of COVID and social distancing.

But as bad as these incidents and statistics are, the biases that are subtler are where much of the damage happens. Most people (the same ones who point out that they treat everyone equally whether they are "black, white, green, or purple") believe that all people are created equally. They believe in the American dream, that everyone is worthy of success if they work hard enough. They assume *they* are not biased. It's gotten to the point that researchers rarely ask explicitly about biases anymore because so few people think they have them. But when people are asked in subtler ways, it's apparent that almost all of us are biased—we just don't know it or admit it to ourselves or others.[28]

AND THE BIAS THAT IS MORE SUBTLE

Implicit biases operate outside our conscious awareness and are a function of the very fast processing our brains use to survive in a world that moves fast and has too much information to slowly and methodologically contemplate.[29] As humans, we see something and instantly have to decide safe or not safe, good or bad, whether that something is a lion or a person. It would involve a lot of cognitive effort to stop and process detailed information about every individual we encounter, so to save effort, we take shortcuts. One shortcut the brain relies on is recognizing patterns between social groups and certain traits and behaviors.* Unfortunately, because society is replete with biases, the patterns we detect and learn are biased ones.

Those biased patterns can be specific. For example, if a child consistently sees men in leadership positions (which happens every time they see a president on TV), their brains recognize that pattern and form strong links between the concepts "men" and "leaders." Then, when asked to think about good leaders, the image of a man is the one that automatically gets activated. But those patterns can also be very general—just about who is good or bad. If White people are consistently shown in a positive light, children automatically link "White people" and "good."

Implicit biases come out in subtle behaviors and instant assumptions, so someone with an implicit bias favoring White people may smile more at White people, lean in more closely when talking to White people, and give White people the benefit of the doubt more often. But beyond that, implicit biases also influence the way the brain represents perceptual information about social groups. The greater the implicit racial bias, the bigger the distinction in the neural representation of Black and White faces[30]—and not at the low-level brain regions that focus on physical cues, where faces that

---

* Although it is impossible to know the true origin of this tendency, many argue that this evolved as a safety mechanism. For example, if I see a lion charging at me, I need to quickly think, "Lion . . . dangerous . . . run away." It would have been bad for my health to slowly process whether it looked angry, whether it was big, whether it seemed hungry. Quick decisions kept you alive. This strategy, while perhaps adaptive in this sense, is flawed when dealing with other human beings in the real world.

are lighter in color would of course be processed differently than faces that are darker. This occurs at the higher-level face-processing region involved in the encoding of more abstract information. In the areas of the brain that process abstract ideas, there are bigger differences in how Black and White faces are processed when people hold implicit biases. Individuals with fewer biases process faces from different races more similarly to one another, just like a series of similar individuals.[31] In other words, implicit biases are literally shaping how we see other people.

Implicit biases, because they occur at the unconscious level, don't necessarily match a person's explicit beliefs. People can truly believe that all people are equal, *and* simultaneously hold implicit biases favoring their own group. Indeed, that is the case for most people,[32] and many people are legitimately upset when they learn they hold these automatic biases because they run counter to their felt beliefs.

Children also hold implicit biases about race and gender, which are in place by early elementary school. But unlike the decline in explicit biases that happens around age ten, implicit biases don't go down with age. Once the neural links that detect those patterns are in place, implicit biases are extremely difficult to change and require effort on all our parts to override.

IGNORING BIAS IN CHILDHOOD IS NOT WORKING

People don't want to be biased or appear biased to others, so they often avoid talking about bias.[33] Parents and teachers act like children are color-blind, and if they discuss race in any way, their kids will suddenly notice race for the first time, as though racial differences miraculously will be revealed after one conversation about race like a cataract surgeon removing a cloudy lens. As one White parent stated in an email to me, "We are all God's children. Why get them in the habit of categorizing by race? They will pick up more from how they see me treat others than anything I say to them."

Most White parents never talk about race with their children, taking a color-blind approach to parenting. Even when parents are expressly asked to have conversations about race, they shy away from them. When researchers enrolled parents in a research project in which one of the assignments was to talk about race-related issues with their children, they ended up having to change how they analyzed the results because only 10 percent of the parents reported having meaningful conversations with their children.[34] Two parents actually dropped out of the study altogether once they found out that it involved discussions of race.

Not surprisingly, children learn this message. By age ten, White children have learned the message that talking about race is taboo. When researchers asked White children to play a game like Guess Who?, where to be successful you have to physically describe people and race is a useful descriptor, they found that eight- and nine-year-old children would win over ten- and eleven-year-old children.[35] The older kids refused to mention race, even when it was the most efficient way to describe a person. These types of findings show that White parents and their White children, the ones most likely to hold racial biases, are collectively quiet about race, which allows those implicit biases to stay intact.

Parents of color don't have the luxury of color-blind parenting. They live in a world where they need to prepare their children to handle other people's biases. For example, after Trayvon Martin was murdered, many Black moms gave their children specific safety advice to protect themselves.[36] One mom told her son, "As a last resort, if you're close to home, run to the house as quickly as possible and run in a zig-zag fashion in case he decides to shoot at you." Other conversations that parents of color have focus less on the negatives, like coping with prejudice and avoiding bias, and more on the positives, like having pride in their racial or ethnic group and finding creative forms of cultural expression.[37] Similar patterns emerge with parents of girls, who largely shelve conversations about the patriarchy in favor of a focus on "Girl Power."

WHERE DO THESE BIASES COME FROM?

For years, researchers have tried to figure out exactly how children are learning biases, often assuming that if they give both parents and their children questionnaires about their racial or gender attitudes, they will see a connection. That doesn't usually reveal much. In one study where almost 70 percent of White parents said they had a Black friend, 40 percent of those parents' children said they were unsure of whether or not their parents even liked Black people—and there's no real way to know who was the more accurate reporter of the parents' attitudes. In 2013, researchers conducted a meta-analysis by combining the results of 131 different studies that have been conducted over the past sixty years that looked for connections between parents' and children's prejudices, capturing over forty-five thousand parent-child pairs.[38] They found that there is *some* overlap, mostly for biases about immigration, sexual orientation, or social class, but relatively little overlap between children's and parents' race and gender prejudices. That probably wouldn't be the case if parents were having thoughtful conversations with children about their beliefs. Indeed, research shows that parents and children's implicit racial attitudes become less biased and more synchronized after thoughtful conversations about race (and this is true even when parents are really uncomfortable or anxious about the conversation).[39]

But in the absence of real conversations about bias, children are left to pick up clues where they can. Children are usually much more observant than parents realize, absorbing things that parents may not even realize they were displaying. Research has shown children are learning some biases from parents' subtle nonverbal cues, paying attention to whether a parent leans toward or away from someone of a different race, and how much the parent smiles at the person.[40] Children whose parents looked hesitant or uncomfortable around people from different races had stronger biases than children whose parents seemed relaxed and happy. In other words, children often learn stereotypes and biases from what is *not* said. And because parents and teachers rarely have conversations with children about biases, children are free to unquestioningly absorb the prejudices around them. They learn stereotypes and biases from media, from toys, from teachers, from overheard conversations between parents' friends, from kids at school, and from the older brother's friend who comes to hang out.

They even pick up biases from politicians and political campaigns. For example, in 2008, the campaign for Proposition 8 in California, an initiative attempting to ban same-sex marriage in the state, spent $39 million on media ads arguing that the state should "protect traditional marriage" and not let "public schools teach our kids that gay marriage is okay."[41] That same year, homophobic bullying in California schools shot up (a 30 percent increase in a single year).[42] To be explicitly clear, other types of bullying did not increase, only bullying targeting kids who might be gay. It is no stretch to say that everything children are exposed to has the potential to shape their biases—and that in the absence of any conversations to combat, nuance, or challenge that exposure, those outside forces become much more influential.

FEELING THE EFFECTS OF BIAS

The children who are targeted by all of this bias—the ones who experience race, immigration, gender, or LGBTQ+-based discrimination—feel the effects deeply and in myriad ways. Hundreds of studies have shown that being the target of discrimination results in kids having worse grades, less motivation to stay in school, higher dropout rates, lower self-esteem, greater rates of depression, less satisfaction with life, more worry, greater feelings of hopelessness, more thoughts of suicide, more delinquency, more drug use, and more aggression.[43] Although we often think of childhood as a period when children are protected from society's failings, meta-analyses have shown that the harm that discrimination does to one's psychological well-being is even greater for children than adults. Across all types of discrimination, meta-analyses have clearly shown that registering that you're being discriminated against on the basis of ethnicity, gender, and sexual orientation has negative psychological outcomes.[44*]

Bias doesn't just affect the thoughts, feelings, and grades of the kids it lands on; it also affects their physical health. When anyone faces a stressor, blood pressure and heart rate increase.[45] Cortisol, the stress hormone, shoots up under duress.[46] When this stress response stays high, the parts of the body that keep you regulated, including the endocrine, cardiovascular, metabolic, and immune systems, get worn down no matter how old you are. There are links between discrimination and systolic blood pressure in Black children by elementary school,[47] and adolescents who experienced discrimination show higher rates of overall cortisol.[48] People who face a lifetime of bias, because it is a chronic stressor, are at increased

---

* Discrimination harms children and teens whether they are aware of it happening or not. For example, a Black girl may be placed in a lower-level math class than she is actually qualified for. She may be unaware that discrimination drove that decision, assuming instead that her math skills are poor. On the other hand, she may detect that bias was at play and recognize she was treated unfairly. Although both situations harm her, they are psychologically different experiences that lead to different psychological and educational outcomes. Most of the research on the effects of discrimination on youth refers to it as *perceptions* of discrimination, because it is nearly impossible to measure "objective" discrimination (we can't pop ourselves into the brain of the math teacher to see her true motives). Also, in our experimental studies, we show that individuals *under*estimate how often discrimination happens. So, measuring how often people perceive or register discrimination is considered a conservative estimate of how much discrimination they actually faced.

risk for diseases such as heart disease, diabetes, cancer, and stroke (this has been documented in Black Americans and lesbian, gay, and bisexual individuals[49]).

So, where does all of this leave us? First, we have to move past assumptions that well-meaning adults don't unintentionally pass along biases to children and that children are exempt from biases simply because they are young. Second, we have to accept that bias is pervasive and harmful, and reducing bias is everyone's responsibility.

To do that, we must change our individual, deeply held implicit and explicit biases. We must work to reduce biases believed by the individual children in our lives, but we must also address bias at the structural level. We must recognize how schools, community organizations, media images, and policies perpetuate biases—and then we must act to change them. We must work to change both at the same time. To begin our push for all of that change, we need to understand how those biases became so entrenched, understand why the biases from long ago are still relevant and wreaking havoc today, and understand exactly how that plays out in the lives of children. Only then will we be able to figure out what we need to do next.

PART I

THE BIASES EMBEDDED IN CHILDREN'S INSTITUTIONS

When Bias Was Legal and What Changed It

2 When the Courts First Listened to Social Scientists

How Racial Bias Shaped American Schools and the Fight to Change It

Had there been no May 17, 1954, I'm not sure there would have been a Little Rock. I'm not sure there would have been a Martin Luther King Jr., or Rosa Parks, had it not been for May 17, 1954. It created an environment for us to push, for us to pull. We live in a different country, a better country, because of what happened here in 1954. And we must never forget it. We must tell the story again, over and over and over.
—US Representative John Lewis at the forty-eighth anniversary of *Brown v. Board of Education* at Topeka's First United Methodist Church

To understand the issues of today, it is critical to understand the issues of yesterday. It is important to understand how long-standing structural biases affected the daily lives of children and caused a ripple of inequities to persist for generations. But it is also important to reflect on the occasions when biased laws were successfully changed, when committed people—usually in a courtroom—made compelling arguments at the right moment in time. So, to unravel today's biases, we begin by exploring how change has been won in the past.

The problems of today are not that different from the first half of the last century. The arguments raised in the 1940s and 1950s are the same ones we hear today in those same hallowed courtrooms:

- What does it mean to treat children truly equally?
- If discrimination is not intentional, should schools be held accountable?
- Should we, and can we, change biased laws if the majority of people support those laws?

These questions were at the crux of court decisions to ban racial segregation in public schools in the 1950s, which then set standards that were echoed in court decisions to ban sexual harassment of girls and homophobic harassment of LGBTQ+ teens in public schools in the 1990s, and again brought back in court decisions to ban schools from denying transgender teens the right to use the correct bathroom in 2020. Here, we begin with the cases that first asked these questions: the cases that racially segregated, and then desegregated, schoolchildren.

HOW RACIAL BIAS TOWARD SCHOOL CHILDREN WAS MADE LEGAL

In 1849, when a Black child in Boston, Sarah Roberts, had to walk miles to her Black school, passing a much closer White school, her parents sued the city of Boston. Her attorneys argued that "the separation of schools, so far from being the benefit of both races, is an injury to both. It tends to create a feeling of degradation in the blacks, and prejudice and uncharitableness [sic] in the whites."[1] But the Boston justices were unmoved by this argument and ruled that the segregated Boston public schools were substantively equal to one another and integration would only serve to increase racial prejudice. The judges went one step further and claimed, "This prejudice, if it exists, is not created by law, and probably cannot be changed by law." In short, the courts threw up their hands, claiming both that laws should reflect people's current beliefs and the opposite was impossible—that there was no way that people's current beliefs were themselves a reflection of the law.

This local Boston case from 1849 gained importance when it was brought up in 1896 in the US Supreme Court case of *Plessy v. Ferguson*. That case revolved around whether Homer Plessy, a Creole man with seven White great-grandparents and one Black one, should be convicted of violating the Separate Car Act of 1890. The Separate Car Act of 1890 stated railroads in Louisiana should provide equal but separate accommodations for White passengers and passengers for color, and passengers were not allowed to enter cars not assigned to them. Plessy, working with a citizen committee of civil rights–focused, upper-class Afro-Creoles in New Orleans, intentionally sat in a White railway car to challenge the law. After he was arrested and convicted, he appealed his conviction, but the Louisiana courts upheld it, citing that *Roberts v. City of Boston* case from fifty years before. The attorneys prosecuting Plessy argued that if schools could segregate by race, so too could railway cars.*

Homer Plessy's attorneys appealed that Louisiana decision to the Supreme Court, relying on a new argument that the Boston attorneys didn't have as an option: that segregation was a violation of the Fourteenth Amendment, which had only been adopted in 1868, *after* the Boston school case. The Fourteenth Amendment guarantees "equal protection of the laws" for all US citizens. Specifically, it asserts that "no State shall make or enforce any law which shall abridge the privileges or immunities of citizens of the United States, nor shall any State deprive any person of life, liberty, or property, without due process of law, nor deny to any person within its jurisdiction the equal protection of the law."

Although the Fourteenth Amendment would, in time, be used success-fully in many modern court cases (as we'll see in the next few chapters), it failed in 1896. Consistent with the lower Louisiana district and state courts, the Supreme Court ruled against Homer Plessy in a 7–1 decision. The lone dissent was submitted by Justice John Marshall Harlan, who wrote, "In the eye of the law, there is in this country no superior, dominant, ruling class of citizens. There is no caste here."[2] He argued that the "arbitrary separation of citizens on the basis of race" was inconsistent with the equality promised by the Constitution. But the equal-rights argument didn't win the day in 1896.

---

* What the Plessy judges failed to mention was that the Black parents of Boston protested the legal segregation of schools so much that, in 1855, Massachusetts became the first state in the United States to pass laws banning racial segregation.

Instead of being swayed by an equal-rights argument, Justice Henry B. Brown, who wrote the majority opinion, stated that the Fourteenth Amendment "could not have been intended to abolish distinctions based upon color, or to enforce social, as opposed to political, equality, or a commingling of the two races." In other words, seven justices shrugged off any responsibility to enforce or even encourage social equality. To justify that decision, the court relied on precedent: Between 1849 and 1890, plenty of people had sued to racially integrate schools,[3] and lawsuits in eight different states all upheld segregation as legal.* The Supreme Court essentially upheld bias by saying bias had always been upheld, so it always should be. Furthermore, because the *Plessy* decision came from the Supreme Court, rather than state courts, it firmly established that *any* public institution, from railway cars to public schools, could be separated by race as long as there were "equal" accommodations. Thus "separate but equal" became the official law of the land.

WHAT "SEPARATE BUT EQUAL" REALLY MEANT FOR KIDS

By the mid-to-late 1920s, "separate" schools were the norm throughout the country, but nothing approximating "equal" was anything close to reality. Schools—and the running of schools—cost money. Yet among the seventeen states where racial segregation of children was required, the most "equal" school districts had White students getting three times more funding than Black students. In some states, it was far worse: in South Carolina, a White student's education cost the state fifty-three dollars, compared to a Black student's five-dollar education.[4]

The funding disparities led to very real differences in children's education: schools for Black children, where children of all grades and abilities were often in one room, were typically in session two fewer months a year

---

* There were a couple of exceptions. Most notably, in 1884, Mamie Tape's parents sued their San Francisco, California, school district when their Chinese daughter was banned from attending the nearby White school. Although the Tape family won in court, the California legislature quickly passed new laws to mandate separate schools for "Mongolians." So even though there was an individual victory, the case was not a class action suit nor made it to the Supreme Court. Therefore, no widespread changes took hold.

than White schools. In the 1936–1937 school year, for example, the average term for Black schools was only seven months, while that of White schools was nine months.[5] Black children were forced to meet in buildings that were falling apart, using outdated textbooks cast off from the White schools. Black teachers, who couldn't get hired at White schools, were paid substantially less than White teachers yet had to fill many more roles because the school was so understaffed.

All of those problems could only happen if there even was a school. For Black students in southern states, most were forced to stop their education after elementary school. In 1933, there were only sixteen Black high schools accredited for four-year study in Florida, Louisiana, Mississippi, and South Carolina combined.[6] Even where there was a high school option, the school rarely taught science, foreign languages, music, or art.

In 1941, Dr. Charles Johnson, on behalf of the American Council on Education, talked to Black parents and students in Jim Crow schools in the south. Johnson, a sociologist by training, was the director of social science at Fisk University, the prestigious historically Black university in Nashville. His report, *Growing Up in the Black Belt: Negro Youth in the Rural South*, describes a classic school, Dine Hollow, as "a dilapidated building, once whitewashed, standing on a rocky field unfit for cultivation." This single school taught all of the Black children in the community. Once inside, the researchers noticed "the broken benches are crowded to three times their normal capacity. Only a few battered books are in sight and we look in vain for maps or charts." Because four grade levels of students were in one room, the teacher had to manage each group working on a different task. The researchers recorded that the first two grades worked on an assignment to "write your name ten times. Draw an dog, an cat, an rat, an boot [sic]." The older children were asked, "What word would rhyme with hung? How can you pluralize the word 'jelly'?"*

Despite these poor school conditions, one of the most common complaints by these resilient students was that it was so difficult to even get to school. Beulah King, a fourteen-year-old girl in the sixth grade, told Johnson's team of researchers, "Now if they ain't got money enough to

---

* The challenges to teachers were also profound. Johnson wrote about how the teachers struggled to work within this system, telling the story of a teacher who "came forward with her face wrapped up in a white cloth. 'I am suffering from neuralgia.' We have no substitute teachers here, and when one of us gets sick we just have to keep right on."

buy a bus for both white and colored children to ride in I don't see why they couldn't let some of the colored children have some of the seats in there [the white bus], and ride. It just don't seem fair to me for them to let the white children ride and make us walk. 'Cose it ain't so bad when the weather is good, but I just get so mad I want to cry when it's rainy and cold. The little ones at home can't go at all when the weather is bad."[7] Fifteen-year-old Maggie Red "just loves to go to school . . . but had to walk twelve miles every day to make it happen." She noted, "If I just had some way of getting to school when it rains I'd be so much further along in school than I am now."[8] Even though the schools were falling apart and the curriculum was below their abilities, the students would still go to great lengths just to get there.

The legacy of this biased system lives on today. The funding differences between schools attended by Black students and by White students exist today and is an entrenched structural bias we will circle back to in chapter 7. But the tenacity and persistence of the children and parents fighting to change these systems and thrive in spite of them has also never gone away.

TRYING TO CHANGE RACIAL BIAS, FROM ONE SCHOOL AT A TIME TO THE SUPREME COURT

By the mid-1940s, after four decades of "separate but equal" schooling, the lawsuits to integrate schools started to add up. One of those lawsuits began in 1945 when Felicitas and Gonzalo Mendez wanted their three kids to attend Westminster Elementary School in Orange County, California, but the school wouldn't allow them to. The Mendezes, along with four other families, filed a joint class action suit against Orange County in federal court, in a case referred to as *Mendez v. Westminster*. They argued that separate schools violated the equal protection promised under the Fourteenth Amendment. The school district counterargued that segregation was necessary because of the difficulties of bilingual education. They also, of course, relied on the *Plessy* precedent. But for Judge Paul McCormick, the equal-rights argument was compelling, and he ruled in favor of the parents, saying, "A paramount requisite in the American system of public education is social equality." The case was even upheld in federal appeals court, becoming the first federal case ordering schools to desegregate. It prompted state-level legislative changes.* In 1947, only two months after the court case was settled, the popular California governor, Earl Warren, who was opposed to segregation and had befriended Mr. Mendez during his gubernatorial campaign, pushed through legislation that repealed all of the school segregation statutes in California's laws.[9]

Because the *Mendez* case was in the federal court system, it garnered a lot of national attention, most notably from the legal team for the National Association for the Advancement of Colored People (NAACP), which was gearing up to fight racial segregation in American schools writ large. The NAACP's grand plan, crafted by the Harvard-educated former head of the Howard Law School Charles Hamilton Houston, was built on legal realism: the idea that laws can be "tools for social engineering" and that "in order for courts to make good law, they had to be aware of the social consequences of their rulings."[10]

Thurgood Marshall, Robert Carter, and Spottswood Robinson were leading the fight as attorneys for the NAACP's Legal Defense Fund. The Legal Defense Fund's strategy was based on the understanding that they had neither the time nor the resources to target every school district. Instead, they needed to make a constitutional argument to eliminate segregation in one fell swoop—which they would do by taking on test cases at the state level and pushing them to the Supreme Court.[11] The first case they took on was in Clarendon County, South Carolina, in 1949. South Carolina laws required that all schools be racially segregated. Harry Briggs, along with nineteen other parents, was suing Clarendon County School Board because the school district refused to fund buses for Black students and spent a quarter on the Black students for every dollar spent on the White students (even though Black students made up 70 percent of the district).[12] In *Briggs v. Elliott*, the NAACP attorney, Robert Carter, decided to bring in social scientists to serve as expert witnesses.

The NAACP had begun using social science research to varying degrees of success in earlier cases. While the NAACP was not directly involved in the *Mendez* case in California, they did submit an amicus brief, written by Carter, arguing that segregation in and of itself was a form of inequality. In *Mendez*, their brief heavily relied on social science research

---

* Sixty-five years later, in 2010, President Barack Obama awarded Sylvia Mendez a Medal of Freedom for her role, as an eight-year-old student, in helping end school segregation; two schools in Los Angeles are named for her parents.

from, among others, sociologist Ambrose Caliver, who had collected data from seventeen states and the District of Columbia. This research suggested that "best single index to the quality of education" was how much money was spent on each student. Caliver found that the average amount of money spent on White students in nine Southern states was 212 percent greater than the average money spent on Black students.[13] Drawing from that, the NAACP amicus brief argued that school districts with finite resources could not afford to keep up two high-quality school systems; therefore, whenever a district required segregation, the same pattern of discrimination would emerge. The brief also cited sociological research from Charles Johnson, arguing that segregation would negatively affect the personality development of Black youth. Although the *Mendez* case only banned segregation by national origin in the state of California, it was an important victory because it taught the NAACP about the value of social science in shaping the court's decision.

Now with this new case in South Carolina, the higher-ups of the NAACP told Robert Carter and Thurgood Marshall to "develop the social science portion of the argument with as little delay as possible,"[14] because they needed evidence to show that racial segregation caused psychological damage to Black children. All of the previous research presented in court regarding segregation had been based on sociology or economics (like how much money was being spent on each child),[15] but now they saw the import of something more direct that gave voice to the children themselves.

They weren't the only ones to see the value in social science research. After the horrors of the Holocaust were exposed following World War II and the world struggled to understand how biases could lead to such atrocities, there was an international push within governments and among researchers to better understand the causes and consequences of discrimination and prejudice.[16] The US administration was interested in how discrimination at home might be harming American children. In response to that interest, someone named Kenneth Clark wrote a report for the White House Conference on Children and Youth. Clark's report described the latest research on how discrimination and prejudice directly affected the personality development of children—and that report brought him to the attention of the NAACP. Clark, who was also the first Black graduate student to receive a PhD in psychology from Columbia and a brand-new assistant professor of psychology at New York City College, was exactly who the NAACP needed.

Clark quickly became the Legal Defense Fund's primary expert witness, testifying in South Carolina in *Briggs v. Elliott* in 1951. He also helped recruit other social scientists from around the country to testify.* Based on their social science testimony, the attorneys in the *Briggs* case argued that segregated schools psychologically harmed children. One judge on the three-judge panel, Judge Waring, agreed, noting that "segregation is *per se* inequality." The other two judges, though, deferred to *Plessy* once again. The NAACP attorneys, not satisfied with losing, appealed *Briggs* to the Supreme Court.

Around the same time, in February 1951, the NAACP plan branched out to Kansas. Robert Carter and Jack Greenberg, another key NAACP attorney, represented a dad named Oliver Brown and thirteen other parents† in a case called *Brown v. Board of Education of Topeka, KS*. Although Kansas wasn't the Jim Crow Deep South (so segregation was allowed but not mandated), the Topeka School District only offered four elementary schools for all Black students, which resulted in many having to take long bus rides to attend their assigned school. With Greenberg, Carter argued, as he had in South Carolina, that segregation harmed Black children and failed to provide them with equal protection under the law. As with the *Briggs* case, the testimony of social scientists was the bedrock of the NAACP's case for *Brown*. Although the three-judge panel was largely sympathetic, the court decided that the Topeka schools were not engaging in "willful, intentional or substantial discrimination." Citing *Plessy* once again, the court made a critical legal distinction, saying that if schools are not discriminating *on purpose*, then it really isn't discrimination.‡ Ultimately, the courts were declaring that there is no legal recourse for unintentional discrimination.

Although the judges sided with the Topeka school district, the presiding judge, Walter A. Huxman, took a pivotal step that changed the course of the case: he included nine "Findings of Fact" at the end of his opinion. The second-to-last "fact" said that, according to science, segregation

---

* They included Professor David Krech, a social psychology professor at the University of California, Helen Trager, a lecturer at Vassar College, and Robert Redfield, an anthropologist who had served as the Director for the American Council on Race Relations.

† By many accounts, although plenty of parents were involved in the Kansas lawsuit, Oliver Brown was selected as the name on the case because he was a man (the complicated intersections of sexism and racism).

‡ This distinction will reappear in later cases of bias in schools.

indeed had a detrimental psychological effect on Black children. Having this fact in words and as part of the official decision of the case was critical because though the NAACP lost *Brown* in 1951, they were good at filing appeals.[17] Once it was officially part of the record, they could use this now-established fact as part of their argument in their appeal to the Supreme Court.

Just a few weeks before the *Briggs* case was about to be heard in court, the NAACP legal team was called to Virginia by the president of the Virginia chapter of the NAACP,* Francis Griffin. Griffin, who also happened to be the local minister and president of the Moton High School Parent-Teacher Association, had been called to Moton High by some students who were seeking his advice.[18] The leader of the group was an eleventh-grader named Barbara Johns, who was determined to make her Farmville, Virginia, school better. Moton High was the only high school for Black students in Prince Edward County, Virginia, in 1951. Four hundred and fifty students were educated in a dilapidated, tar paper–covered building built for 180 students. The high school had no gym or cafeteria, no infirmary or teachers' restroom, and many classes were held in old school buses.

Barbara, along with a "strike committee" of several fellow students, had a plan they dubbed "the Manhattan Project."† The strike committee lured their principal off campus by reporting that there were disruptive students downtown. While the principal was away, the committee gathered all the other students in a common area and asked the teachers to leave. Barbara and her committee convinced the other students to go on strike, to boycott the school because of the inadequate conditions. The protests and boycotts that followed continued for two weeks—and while the students and parents were protesting, the students reached out to Griffin, who put them in contact with the NAACP attorneys he knew, Spottswood Robinson and Oliver Hill. The NAACP was reticent about accepting the case (they knew they would lose), but they were motivated by the students. Hill later said, "We were going to tell the kids about the *Briggs* suit, which was about to begin

---

* The NAACP had a history of extensive legal activity in Virginia. They had filed more lawsuits tackling racial inequality in Virginia than in any other state. By 1941, the Virginia chapter of the NAACP was the largest state chapter in the United States.

† An excellent book for young readers details this case. Written by Teri Kanefield, it is *The Girl from the Tar Paper School: Barbara Rose Johns and the Advent of the Civil Rights Movement.*

in Charleston in a few weeks, and how crucial that would prove, but a strike in Prince Edward was something else again. Only these kids turned out to be so well organized and their morale was so high, we just didn't have the heart to tell 'em to break it up."[19] They accepted the case and argued on behalf of more than a hundred students and parents in the case of *Davis v. County School Board of Prince Edward County, Virginia.**

In this 1951 case, social scientists again got involved—this time on both sides of the argument. Professor Henry Garrett testified for the school board. Garrett was the head of the psychology department at Columbia, former president of the American Psychological Association, and a segregationist from Virginia. He argued that segregated schools were necessary because of the innate differences between Black and White children, with Black children being inherently inferior to White children.

His testimony was rebutted by the NAACP's expert witness in the case: Garrett's former doctoral student, Mamie Clark, the second Black graduate student to receive a PhD in psychology at Columbia and the wife of Kenneth Clark (she's important, so we're coming back to her in chapter 6).

Around the same time in 1951, in Washington, DC, twelve-year-old Spottswood Bolling and ten other students tried to enroll in a brand-new White junior high school. Their Black school, like almost all Black schools in the country, faced inadequate funding, overcrowded buildings, and insufficient educational options. One problem with the case that would come to be known as *Bolling v. Sharpe* was that it took place in DC. In all of the other cases in the NAACP's campaign, the attorneys had argued that segregated schools violated the Fourteenth Amendment, which mandated that "no state" could deny citizens equal protection under the law. But Washington, DC, is not a state. As such, Washingtonians are not given the same protections as state residents. The attorneys had to rely on the Fifth Amendment and arguments about due process. But it didn't change anything: in both Virginia and DC, the courts said that *Plessy* was the law of the land. Another two losses. Another two appeals.

Finally, in 1952, in Delaware, two separate class action cases were filed on behalf of twelve Black students.[20] These cases bear the names of two of those students, Shirley Bulah and Ethel Belton. In a suburb

---

* Barbara's parents feared for her safety and sent her to live with an uncle in Montgomery, Alabama. The named plaintiff was another student, Dorothy Davis.

of Wilmington, Delaware, Ethel Belton had to travel two hours every day, more than ten miles each way, past the White school Claymont High School (and past two other White schools), to get to the all-Black Howard High School, which was also the only college-prep high school for Black students in the entire state of Delaware. Meanwhile, in a rural community just outside Wilmington, Shirley Bulah had to watch a school bus of White children pass her house every day on their way to the nearby all-White school, while her mother had to drive her to the one-room all-Black school. When her mother complained, she was told that school buses were provided for the White children only.

The Bulahs and Beltons, along with other parents, all reached out to Louis Redding, the first Black attorney in the state of Delaware. For both cases, he suggested the parents petition their neighborhood schools to attend; when their requests were denied, Redding, along with NAACP attorney Jack Greenberg, filed two lawsuits against the state board of education, in the cases *Bulah v. Gebhart* and *Belton v. Gebhart.** Because both cases originated in New Castle County, Delaware, the cases were consolidated and heard before the Delaware Court of Chancery. In this consolidated case, the court said that the Black schools were indeed inferior and students should be allowed to go to the White schools. Of all the school segregation cases the NAACP was tackling, only the Delaware case saw a victory for plaintiffs. However, the courts stopped short of banning segregation per se. The case only affected the twelve students named in the case who were allowed to attend the White school. The courts in Delaware passed any bold decisions off to the US Supreme Court.

In 1952, the US Supreme Court agreed to finally decide about school segregation. The *Brown* and *Briggs* cases had reached the top court first; the others, *Davis*, *Bolling*, and *Belton* (*Bulah*), soon followed. These five cases—from Kansas, South Carolina, Virginia, Washington, DC, and Delaware—were bundled together as *Brown v. Board of Education of Topeka, KS*. Any decision made at the top court would extend beyond the specific districts addressed in the cases and would reverberate throughout the country. It had the potential to overturn *Plessy* and force the country to reckon with separate schools that were anything but equal.

---

* The defendant in the cases was the Delaware State Board of Education, and the individual board members were named defendants. Francis B. Gebhart was the first school board member named.

PEOPLE IN POWER OPEN UP TO CHANGE

The NAACP attorneys were facing major challenges in their push for sweeping structural change. The Fourteenth Amendment did not explicitly ban racial segregation, so there was no clear-cut legal violation to highlight. They also didn't have legal precedent on their side: of the forty-four challenges to school segregation heard in state appellate courts and lower federal courts between 1865 and 1935, all of them ruled for segregation. Prior to *Brown*, only one federal judge, in the *Mendez* case in California in 1947, rejected segregation. So, what the NAACP attorneys needed was, first, a group of justices generally open to the idea of desegregation and, second, a compelling argument, one that could override the legal challenges to desegregation.

In the 1950s, many of the justices were open to considering the possibility of desegregation, but they struggled with whether courts should—or even could—make decisions that go against accepted norms and popular opinions. There were arguments that the Supreme Court must be willing to lead the charge in change. For example, Robert Redfield, a lawyer turned anthropologist who was one of the social scientists recruited by Kenneth Clark to testify in the desegregation cases, stated that the "law itself is education . . . they help men to make up their minds in accordance with a major trend or ideal of their society."[21] He was arguing that laws sometimes need to change first and people's attitudes and beliefs will follow.

But for many justices, the law could only go where public opinion led the way. One of the justices, Stanley Reed, who was largely supportive of segregation, argued that the courts should not interfere until the "body of people think [segregation] is unconstitutional."[22] But by 1954, attitudes about segregation *were* shifting. Slightly more than half of the United States approved of desegregating schools,* which was an important change for some of the justices. Justice Felix Frankfurter said he would not have voted against segregation prior to the 1950s, because "public opinions had not then crystallized against it." But with changing times, in a country less than a decade past World War II and facing a burgeoning civil rights movement at home, the court was more receptive to the idea of racial equality than it had been fifty years before. The court also had a brand-new chief justice: the former governor who had recently banned segregation

---

* That percentage differed by education level, with 73 percent of college graduates in favor of desegregation, whereas only 45 percent of high school dropouts approved of it.

in California following the Mendez case, Earl Warren.* The *Brown* case would be his first major case on the Supreme Court.[23]

A STATEMENT FROM SCIENCE

In 1954, in the courtroom of the Supreme Court, the NAACP had to be creative because their legal case was not well supported by precedent. The NAACP attorneys placed a lot of their hope on the science of segregation and, for the Supreme Court case, took an extra step in highlighting research about the damage segregation caused to Black children. Kenneth Clark, who had been involved since *Briggs*, helped recruit thirty-two social scientists—psychologists, psychiatrists, sociologists, anthropologists—who signed off on and submitted a single brief titled "The Effects of Segregation and the Consequences of Desegregation: A Social Science Statement."[24] It was signed by the most prestigious social scientists of the day.[†]

In the brief, the social scientists wrote, "The segregation of Negroes and of other groups in the United States takes place in a social milieu in which race, prejudice, and discrimination exist." They argued that segregation

---

* The *Brown* case had first made its way to the Supreme Court when Chief Justice Vinson headed the bench. He, however, suddenly and unexpectedly died before much progress had been made. Meanwhile, Earl Warren had been an extremely popular governor and was poised to run for president. Eisenhower had made him a deal that if he did not run for President, he would appoint him to the next available position on the Supreme Court. When Chief Justice Vinson died, Earl Warren reminded Eisenhower of their deal, noting that the next available position was open, even though it was the chief justice position. (See *Mendez v. Westminster: A Living History* by Frederick Aguirre et al.)

† Of the thirty-two scientists to sign the statement, some included Floyd and Gordon Allport, Isidor Chein, Robert Redfield, David Krech, Gardner Murphy, and Otto Klineberg. Only four were women, and Mamie Clark, who testified against her segregationist doctoral advisor in the *Davis v. County School Board of Prince Edward County, Virginia*, was one of them. The other women were Charlotte Babcock, MD, a professor of psychiatry, who, at the time, practiced psychoanalysis in Chicago and later moved to the University of Pittsburgh; Viola Wertheim Bernard, MD, a New York City–based psychiatrist whose work focused on adoption; and Else Frenkel-Brunswik, PhD, a psychology professor at Berkeley. Frenkel-Brunswik lived only four years after the Brown case. Following the suicide of her husband, and because of "resentment around aspects of her career related to her gender," she committed suicide on March 31, 1958, by an overdose of barbital. (See profile of Else Frenkel-Bruswik by Lisa Held on *Psychology's Feminist Voices.*)

of schools is a form of discrimination, and when racial minority children detect the differences in treatment, they feel "humiliated," "inferior," and develop "self-hatred." From there, children will find ways to cope with this humiliation. For some children, this may take the form of "overt aggression" directed toward the dominant group or "delinquent behavior." In the brief, the scientists highlighted the irony inherent in the fact that discrimination leads to aggression and delinquency, as those are some of the very behaviors that are used as a justification by Whites to continue prejudice and segregation. Other things that are also used as justification for segregation are also a result of such segregation, as the report highlighted when describing how segregation impacts White children: "When comparing themselves to members of the minority group, they [White students] are not required to evaluate themselves in terms of the more basic standards of actual personal ability and achievement." In other words, racial privilege gives White students an inaccurate and unearned sense of confidence, which, in turn, perpetuates the idea that there was somehow a need for segregation because of supposed inherent differences in ability.

The scientists also asserted that some racial minority children in segregated schools would cope with the discrimination by ultimately disengaging from school. They wrote that there may be a "lowering of pupil morale and a depression of the educational aspiration level." All of this is worsened—and becomes especially pernicious—because *policies* that are prejudiced carry extra weight compared to face-to-face interactions with a prejudiced person. As they noted, "The child who, for example, is compelled to attend a segregated school may be able to cope with ordinary expressions of prejudice by regarding the prejudiced person as evil or misguided; but he cannot readily cope with symbols of authority, the full force of the authority of the State— the school or the school board, in this instance—in the same manner."

It is a heavy burden to be seven years old and have to cope with a kid down the street shouting racist slurs at you as you walk down the sidewalk.

It is a different burden altogether to be told (regardless of how implicitly) that the state of South Carolina (or Virginia, Kansas, or Delaware) considers you too inferior to go to school with White kids.

The statement worked. In May of 1954, the US Supreme Court unanimously banned the segregation of school children on the basis of race. Chief Justice Earl Warren read the decision aloud, "We come then to the question presented: Does segregation of children in public schools solely on the basis of race, even though physical facilities and other 'tangible' factors may be equal, deprive the children of the minority group of equal educational opportunities? We believe that it does." He continued, "To separate [Black children] from others of similar age and qualifications solely because of their race generates a feeling of inferiority as to their status in the community that may affect their hearts and minds in a way unlikely ever to be undone." In the history of the United States, very few people in power had ever considered the hearts and minds of Black children. This decision marked a huge step toward valuing the lives and well-being of Black children.

The impact of the social science statement is felt all over the court's decision: Chief Justice Warren wrote in his opinion, "Whatever may have been the extent of psychological knowledge at the time of *Plessy v. Ferguson*, this [*Brown*] finding is amply supported by modern authority. [Footnote 11]. Any language in *Plessy v. Ferguson* contrary to this finding is rejected." Footnote 11 cited the studies taken from the "Social Science Statement" and the social scientists who wrote it were the "modern authority" that Warren's opinion recognized. In other words, the justices had taken that statement seriously, read the evidence cited, and absorbed the details in order to make their decision.

Although many political, economic, and cultural issues led to that pivotal court decision in 1954, evidence of how bias harmed children was clearly influential, marking a watershed moment in our history when social science informed decisions to reduce structural racial biases against children. The lead *Brown* attorney, Thurgood Marshall, who would eventually wear the robes of a Supreme Court justice when he became the first person of color to integrate the Supreme Court, said years later, "You do what you think is right and let the law catch up." The law was finally, just barely, starting to catch up with what was right.

3 All of America's Children

How Immigration Laws Have Shaped the
Lives of Latino American Children

> *Every great dream begins with a dreamer.*
> —Harriet Tubman

Being the "land of immigrants" is an important, defining characteristic of America. Indeed, there are more immigrants in the United States than in any other country in the world.[1] But America has a long and charged history with integrating immigrants into the "melting pot." Italian, Irish, and Polish immigrants, those with light skin, although once heavily stigmatized, have been more accepted into the American identity. Other immigrants, particularly those with dark skin, have been less welcome. This is clearly evident for the largest immigrant group in the United States, those

individuals from nearby Mexico and Central America.* For Latino American†
children specifically, there have been historic and modern challenges for access
to equal education, rooted in society prioritizing the legality of immigration
over the well-being of immigrant children. At the core of the biases facing
Latino immigrant youth is the persistent question of who is allowed to be
part of the collective in-group and who must remain on the outside (I will
return to biases facing other children of immigrants in chapter 8).

BRUTALITY, CRIMINALS, AND DEPORTATIONS

The United States has a violent history with its residents of Mexican descent.
In 1848, the Treaty of Guadalupe Hidalgo ended the Mexican-American
War (which began when the United States decided to annex Texas), and in
exchange for $15 million, the United States took from Mexico all of what
is now California, Nevada, Utah, most of what is now Arizona, and parts of
what are now Colorado, New Mexico, and Wyoming. Absorbing this large
swath of land, combined with Texas, meant the United States got a slew of
new American citizens. As a Mexican American colleague of mine used to
say about his family, "We didn't move to America; America moved to us."
As the twentieth century approached, the population of Mexican American
citizens grew. As the population grew, so too did anti-Latino sentiments
and violence.[2] According to historians, approximately five thousand people
of Mexican descent were killed or vanished in the United States between
1910 and 1920, including children.[3]

Then, in the 1920s, severe limitations on the ways brown bodies could
enter and live in the United States exacerbated anti-immigrant attitudes.

---

* According to the Migration Policy Institute, in 2019, 44 percent of all immigrants in
the United States reported having Hispanic or Latino origins. I am using the umbrella
term *immigrant* to refer to someone who was born in another country than where they
live now (unless I specify otherwise, this can also include refugees and asylum-seekers).
Also, at times, I designate a first-generation immigrant as someone who moved during
their lifetime, a second-generation immigrant as someone whose parents moved, and a
third-generation immigrant as someone whose grandparents moved.

† Throughout this chapter, I will switch between referring to individuals as Latino
American, Latino, Mexican, and Mexican American. I am balancing, albeit
imperfectly, the goals of being precise when appropriate (for example, when a policy
specifically affected people from Mexico) and being inclusive when possible (because
the biases facing people of Mexican descent are also applied to Latinos more broadly).

For example, the Immigration Act of 1924 set quotas and bans for who was allowed entry. The act favored immigration from Northern and Western European countries, limited immigration from Southern, Central, and Eastern Europe, and completely banned immigrants from Asia (except the American colony of the Philippines).⁴* By legally allowing White European immigrants and banning immigrants of color, the act racialized immigration and turned biases originally based on nationality into biases based on newly defined ethnic categories.†

Although Mexican immigrants were not "subject to numerical quotas or restrictions on naturalization" by the Immigration Act of 1924, they "were profoundly affected by restrictive measures enacted in the 1920s, among them the deportation policy, the creation of the Border Patrol, and the criminalization of unlawful entry."⁵ One of those restrictive measures was when, in 1929, South Carolina Senator Coleman Blease (a White segregationist) proposed Section 1325 as part of Title 8 of the US Code. When Section 1325 was passed, unauthorized entry into the United States became a misdemeanor.‡ The goal was to limit Latino immigration, since Mexico had not been given quotas or bans in the Immigration Act of 1924.⁶ Then, when the Great Depression of 1929 led to overwhelming job loss, many White people needed someone to blame, and so began the now-common refrain that Mexicans were stealing American jobs.

With a scapegoat identified, the government began massive deportations between 1929 and 1936, euphemistically called "repatriations." Close to two million people of Mexican descent were forcibly removed from the United States, 60 percent of them American citizens, some even US Army veterans. Some White employers would drive their Latino employees to the border and force them out of the car. Thousands of Latinos were rounded up from parks, neighborhoods, and workplaces in Los Angeles, and loaded

---

* This quota system was in effect until it was overturned by the 1965 Immigration Act, also known as the Hart-Celler Act, signed by President Johnson.

† As an example, prior to this period, people from China and Japan had been excluded from immigration to the United States. The courts of the period, however, extended this ban to Koreans, Thais, Vietnamese, Indonesians, and people from other Asian countries, who had represented discrete national and ethnic groups, all because they were "non-white." Thus, the immigration bans served to create a category of "Asians" that were collectively considered "ineligible for citizenship" (Ngai, 1999).

‡ The US Code also defines "any person not a citizen or national of the United States" as an "alien." As of 2021, President Biden is attempting to change that to "noncitizen."

onto leased trains bound for Central Mexico (far enough south so they couldn't easily walk back to the United States).[7] Then, in 1955, there was another round of mass deportations, these labeled—not so euphemistically—"Operation Wetback."[8] According to government records, the United States deported 1.3 million people who looked vaguely Latino, including, yet again, American citizens and those who had entered legally through a farm work program. For Latino immigrants, these massive rounds of deportations would create a climate of fear and a belief in the need to live in the shadows that continues today.

THE FOCUS ON BEING "ILLEGAL"

In addition to fear of deportations, the other modern holdover from the immigration policies of the 1920s is the criminalization of immigration, especially focused on Latino immigrants. Because it is still an enforced part of the US Code, and has many ramifications for children past and present, it is important to be very clear on what Section 1325 (and the related Section 1326) means. The current misrepresentation of these laws, which were created because of biases in the 1920s, contributes to the continuation of biases against immigrants.

The truth is, there are actually three offenses related to immigration:

- The first, and perhaps most misunderstood, is "unlawful presence in the United States," or simply being in the United States without proper authorization. This is actually a *civil* violation, and means that the Department of Homeland Security (created in 2002 and charged with immigration enforcement) can issue a fine and begin deportation proceedings.[9] No criminal offense is involved in being in the country without authorization.
- The second is "illegal entry," or Section 1325, which makes crossing the border without going through border patrol a misdemeanor. There is a penalty (usually deportation and a fine), but it is the same level of violation as a parking ticket and does not rise to the level of crime often implied in the national conversation of "illegals."
- The third offense is "illegal re-entry," or Section 1326, in which someone reenters the country without authorization after they have already been deported or denied entry. Violating Section 1326 is the

only time unauthorized immigration is a felony offense,* and can lead to a maximum sentence of two years in prison.[10]

Many anti-immigrant biases are centered on the rhetoric of unauthorized immigrants doing something legally wrong, couched behind the importance of "following the rules." By linking concepts of immigration and illegality, people began to assume immigrants, and people who "look" like immigrants, were lawbreakers.[11] And people can justify, in a law-abiding society, disliking lawbreakers—but the way that that dislike has manifested is biased. After all, as a society, we don't show the same level of animus to people with parking violations as we do to unauthorized immigrants—despite those being the same level of offense, legally—and we often overestimate how many immigrants are here without authorization. By the best estimates, less than one-quarter of immigrants are in the country without authorization,[12] and immigrants from Mexico make up less than half of unauthorized immigrants.

So the animus is not only far outsized given the offense, but also applied too broadly. This suggests that anti-immigrant biases—especially anti-Mexican or anti-Latino bias—are predicated on *more* than violating a rule. Those biases stem from ideas of who is allowed to be a part of America and who will always be an outsider. If you are an "illegal alien," you can never be a real American. It is a distinction based on race and ethnicity that was codified and perpetuated when the Immigration Act of 1924 and Section 1325 were passed.

These issues—over who was an "illegal alien," who was an American, and even what rights people had no matter what their immigration status—reemerged in the 1970s in public school systems. For Latino American children who were trying to enroll in American schools, the question of who was entitled to a public education was about to be answered in court.

DECIDING WHO CAN GO TO SCHOOL

Children have long been at the center of the debates about immigration policy, and as with the legal battle to end racial segregation, the public

---

* According to the US Sentencing Commission, in 2019, one-third of all defendants in US District Courts are tried for immigration-related charges.

school system is often a key battleground. In 1975, the Texas Legislature approved a bill that let school districts deny enrollment into public schools and withhold state education funds from children "not legally admitted" to the United States.[13] Not long after, the school district in Tyler, Texas, created a policy that required students to pay tuition if they could not provide documentation about their legal immigration standing. The Tyler school district was trying to charge the children of undocumented farmhands (who came from Mexico to work in the east Texas town) $1,000 tuition for a public education that other children were getting for free, effectively preventing them from being able to attend the school.

Quickly after the new policy was put in place, attorneys for the Mexican American Legal Defense and Educational Fund (MALDEF) filed a class action suit against James Plyler, the superintendent of Tyler Independent School District, on behalf of four families with elementary school children, the lead child labeled John Doe for the case. The district court, which first heard the case, *Plyler v. Doe,** in 1977 ruled that the new law violated the equal protection clause of the Fourteenth Amendment, and the appeals court upheld that ruling. But the school district appealed again, and the case made its way to the Supreme Court in 1982.

The court ruled in a five-to-four vote that the Texas law indeed violated the equal protection clause, which asserts that "no state shall deprive any person of life, liberty, or property, without due process of law; nor deny to any person within its jurisdiction the equal protection of the laws." According to the majority opinion, that equal protection applies to *any person* within the country, regardless of their citizenship status.[14] Justice William Brennan wrote the majority opinion, and Justices Thurgood Marshall, Harry Blackmun, and Lewis Powell each wrote their own concurring opinions. The majority opinion stated that "education has a fundamental role in maintaining the fabric of our society." The justices also made the point that punishing children for the actions of their parents served no greater good, noting "legislation directing the onus of a parent's misconduct against his children does not comport with fundamental conceptions of justice." They highlighted how denying children an equal education would perpetuate a caste system, and that these undocumented children, "[a]lready disadvantaged as a result of poverty, lack of English-speaking ability, and undeniable racial

---

* The case was originally listed as *Doe v. Plyler*, but became *Plyler v. Doe* in the appeals process.

prejudices, ... will become permanently locked into the lowest socio-economic class." Blackmun, in particular, wrote, "Children denied an education are placed at a permanent and insurmountable competitive disadvantage, for an uneducated child is denied even the opportunity to achieve." Essentially, they declared that denying equal opportunities for education on the basis of legal documentation punishes children for the actions of their parents, limits their potential for lifelong success, and ultimately harms all of society by exacerbating socioeconomic inequalities.

The dissenting opinion, written by Justice Warren Burger, did not argue that immigrant children should be denied an equal education. The dissent actually began, "Were it our business to set the Nation's social policy, I would agree without hesitation that it is senseless for an enlightened society to deprive any children—including illegal aliens—of an elementary education." However, Burger argued that the courts should not be in the business of setting new social policy, stating, "the Constitution does not constitute us as 'Platonic Guardians,' nor does it vest in this Court the authority to strike down laws because they do not meet our standards of desirable social policy, 'wisdom,' or 'common sense.'" In a challenge very similar to what the attorneys fighting for *Brown* faced, Burger argued that the Fourteenth Amendment was not relevant because it did not *specify* protections for undocumented immigrants. Both in arguments against *Brown* on its way to the Supreme Court and in *Plyler v. Doe* when it reached the court, the idea was that because the law didn't specifically ban certain conduct, that biased conduct was allowed. The lesson from this is that equal protection laws that do not enumerate specific protections leave themselves open to conservative approaches to the law, which, by definition, maintain the status quo and the entrenched structural biases.*

---

* There is an important distinction to make when thinking about laws (although the full details of these distinctions go beyond the scope of this book). Laws come from three sources: state and federal constitutions (such as the Fourteenth Amendment), statutes and agency regulations (such as Sections that are part of the US Code), and judicial decisions (such as US Supreme Court decision in *Plyler*). When thinking about equal protection laws, statutory protections are much easier to adapt to enumerate specific protected groups, as they are determined by the legislative branch and often change with each new congressional election. This means as we begin to recognize new groups who may need specific protections, Congress can go back and make changes to be more specific and/or inclusive. Changing constitutional laws (via amendments) involves ratification by the states, requires a purposefully onerous approval process, and happens rarely (only twenty-seven times in the history of the

Although the *Plyler* decision was handed down in 1982, communities still periodically try to discriminate against immigrant children. For example, in 1994,[15] California passed Proposition 187, which banned undocumented children from public schools and required schools to report those children to authorities within forty-five days. Prop 187 was overturned as a violation of *Plyler,* but the fact that it was still attempted shows the pernicious nature of bias. Then, in 2006, a school district in Elmwood Park, Illinois, denied—although later allowed—entry to a student who had overstayed a tourist visa.

But one of the harshest attempts to limit immigrant children from receiving an equal education came from Alabama in 2011, when the Alabama Legislature passed a wide-ranging anti-immigrant measure: HB 56.* Section 28 of that bill required schools to determine and report the immigration status of their students.[16] The bill's sponsor, Rep. Micky Hammon (R), described the bill as being motivated by the costs of "educat[ing] the children of illegal immigrants," and the result of the bill was preventing immigrant children from attending school. According to data from the Department of Justice, the day after HB 56 went into effect, more than two thousand Latino students were notably absent from their Alabama schools, and the Latino student absence rate tripled in the period after.[17] In the first six months HB 56 was on the books, 13.4 percent of Alabama's Latino student population withdrew from school.

The US Department of Justice wrote to Alabama's Department of Education to convey the damage Alabama's policy was having on children. The DOJ spoke of interviews they had conducted with students and

---

United States). Many argue that it is good for constitutional laws to be broad and general to keep the scope of protection wide. Judicial decisions, which interpret the other types of laws, *become* the law once decided. When the constitutional protections are broad, conservative justices can make a conservative, status quo interpretation of that law; in contrast, liberal or progressive justices can make a liberal, more inclusive interpretation of that law.

* HB 56, called the Beason-Hammon Alabama Taxpayer and Citizen Protection Act, is a wide-ranging bill to target immigrants statewide. Among other provisions, it required police to determine someone's legal status if they have "reasonable suspicion" that a person is an immigrant; prohibited undocumented immigrants from receiving any public benefits and banned them from colleges or universities; nullified all contracts with undocumented immigrants; and prohibited landlords from renting to undocumented immigrants.

teachers, reporting that "many students conveyed that HB 56 made them feel unwelcome in schools they had attended for years. Hispanic children reported increased anxiety and diminished concentration in school, deteriorating grades, and increased hostility, bullying, and intimidation." Students weren't even the only ones impacted, as "teachers and administrators also describe their efforts to respond to calls from fearful parents and console and provide guidance to students whose family members or friends had departed or disappeared."

The DOJ reminded the Alabama Department of Education about the *Plyler* ruling—and of Titles IV and VI of the Civil Rights Act of 1964. Title IV prohibits discrimination "against students in the public schools on the basis of race, sex, religion, color, or national origin," and Title VI bars "school districts and state departments of education from adopting practices that have the effect of discriminating on the basis of race, color, or national origin." Furthermore, the DOJ noted, because of the "pivotal role of education in American society," public schools may not "chill or discourage students" from attending public school "based on their or their parents' national origin or actual or perceived immigration status." In short, public schools cannot ban certain students from attending, *and* they cannot require students to provide the type of information that would make them too scared to attend. Eventually, Alabama's measure was blocked by a federal appellate court because it also violated the equal protection clause of the Fourteenth Amendment,[18] but the damage was already done to countless children and their families and communities.

This draconian bill highlights how institutionalizing biases ultimately harms everyone. While the original motivation for this bill was to save taxpayer money by not paying for the education of undocumented immigrant children, the bill served to drive away much of the Latino labor force of the state, who were a critical part of the agricultural economy. An economist estimated that HB 56 would actually cost Alabama (already one of the poorest states in the country) up to $10.8 billion, up to 140,000 jobs, $264.5 million in state tax revenue, and $93 million in local tax revenue. In other words, the bill, which was disguised as an attempt to save money, was really just an extremely expensive way to discriminate and stigmatize members of the community based on national origin and ethnicity.

DREAMERS AND DACA AND THE CURRENT
BATTLES FOR IMMIGRANT CHILDREN

Beyond the debates over whether all children—regardless of their paper-work—should have equal access to public education, immigrant children are also at the center of the fight about who should be deported. This is a continuation of arguments about which children can be American. The DREAM Act, an acronym for Development, Relief, and Education for Alien Minors Act, was first introduced to the Senate in 2001, and has since been unsuccessful in attempts to get it passed through Congress ten different times.[19] At its core, the DREAM Act would have allowed individuals who immigrated when they were children to the United States without documentation to apply for citizenship, as long as they had completed school and broken no laws. Although the DREAM Act has yet to became law, the acronym has certainly been effective: children of undocumented immigrants who have grown up in the United States are now commonly referred to as "Dreamers."

The most recent debates have focused on the executive order signed by President Barack Obama in 2012, when, frustrated with congressional stalemates, he created DACA, or Deferred Action for Childhood Arrivals. DACA allows undocumented immigrants who came to the United States when they were children, who attend school or work, and who have committed no felonies to have a two-year break from worrying about possible deportation. Every two years, they get to renew their DACA status, and according to the Migration Policy Institute estimates, more than one million children of immigrants have enrolled in DACA at some point. President Trump, who had famously spewed anti-immigrant sentiments, removed DACA protections in 2018. With that policy shift, all DACA recipients were left without protection from deportation. According to Migration Policy Institute, "thousands of young people had come to rely on the program, emerging from the shadows to enroll in degree programs, embark on careers, start businesses, buy homes and even marry and have 200,000 children of their own who are US citizens, not to mention . . . pay $60 billion in taxes each year" were suddenly left high and dry. However, the lower courts intervened, blocking President Trump's policy reversal.

In the summer of 2020, the Supreme Court voted five to four to uphold DACA, although Chief Justice John Roberts's majority opinion focused on the improper procedure President Trump used to rescind DACA, rather than the anti-immigrant sentiment behind the order. Then, hours after President Biden was inaugurated on January 20, 2021, he signed an executive order "Preserving and Fortifying Deferred Action for Childhood Arrivals (DACA)." In our current political climate, the children of immigrants are caught in a tug-of-war featuring temporary fixes followed by policy reversals.

This tug-of-war leaves chaos in its wake. As the country continues to grapple with immigrants and immigration, there needs to be a more stable immigration policy that protects children from the constant fear of deportation (we'll go more into the consequences for children of constantly fearing deportation in chapter 8) and ensures equal access to the same education other American children have. Policies cannot be simply about balancing budgets on the backs of children or focusing on paperwork more than humanity. Because children are politically voiceless, adults committed to removing biases have to continually remind policymakers that real children, children who are just like their own, are harmed when policies are centered on excluding others and enforcing inequalities.

4 Boys and Girls Weren't Segregated, but the School Day Wasn't Equal

The Battle for Title IX and Protection from Sexual Harassment

We have to build things that we want to see accomplished, in life and in our country, based on our personal experiences . . . to make sure that others do not have to suffer the same discrimination.
—US Representative Patsy Takemoto Mink (D-HI), the first woman of color elected to Congress and the coauthor of Title IX

Many of the lessons from early legal battles to reduce racial and ethnic bias in schools informed the battle to reduce gender biases in schools. While the push for gender equality in schools took a different path than the one for racial equality, moving first through the halls of Congress with the passage of Title IX, like *Brown* and *Plyler*, it was ultimately hashed out and refined in the US Supreme Court.

EQUAL OPPORTUNITIES IN EDUCATION

In 1920, the Nineteenth Amendment, which guaranteed White women's right to vote, was officially adopted, but fifty years later, women still were not treated equally. In 1963, Betty Friedan published *The Feminine Mystique* and put into words the silent feeling of oppression women felt but were rarely able to rage against. Three years later, in 1966, the National Organization for Women (NOW) was founded, and in August 1970, led by Betty Friedan, NOW organized a Women's Strike for Equality.[1] This strike, and this second wave of women's activism in general, centered around fighting for equal pay in jobs, access to abortion and childcare, and equal opportunities in education. After all, even after fifty years of being able to vote, women were employed at only half the rate of men (earning only sixty-two cents for every dollar men made*) and earned one-fourth fewer college degrees.[2] More than fifty thousand feminists marched along the streets of New York City, and thousands more marched around the country. Although their other demands (such as access to affordable childcare†) were less successful, the demand for equal education was about to get some help from the US Congress.

In February of 1972, Senator Birch Bayh (D) from Indiana introduced to the US Senate ten amendments—referred to as the Education Amendments—that modified the Higher Education Act of 1965, the Vocational Education Act of 1963, the General Education Provisions Act, and the Elementary and Secondary Education Act of 1965. He offered up a 147-page document that covered a wide range of educational issues, from how to improve youth camp safety to how colleges could seek emergency aid. The most famous amendment, the one that would have the greatest impact on gender equality in schools, was listed on page 139, labeled "Title IX: Prohibition of Sex Discrimination." That amendment had been

---

* Between 1970 and 1975, there were few differences in earning between Black women and White women; both, however, earned more than Latina women. By 1980, and through today, White women, on average, earned more than Black and Latina women, but less than Asian women.

† In addition to access to 24/7 affordable childcare, women were also demanding free access to abortion upon request. While *Roe v. Wade* legalized abortion three years later, it has remained highly politicized, contentious, and restricted. Similarly, affordable childcare has yet to happen.

primarily written by Representatives Edith Green (D) from Ohio and Patsy Mink (D) from Hawaii* because, as Green later described, she grew irritated by school districts offering extracurricular programs for boys but not girls, ostensibly because boys needed extra opportunities as they were to be the "breadwinners of their families."[3] Representative Patsy Mink, who was the first woman of color elected to the US House of Representatives and the first Asian American elected to Congress, took over much of the writing. The amendment stated, "No person in the United States shall, on the basis of sex, be excluded from participation in, be denied the benefits of, or be subjected to discrimination under any education program or activity receiving federal financial assistance."[4] It required public school districts, colleges and universities, for-profit schools, career and technical education programs, and libraries and museums to offer equal opportunities regardless of gender and required they be protected from gender-based discrimination.[†]

With Mink and Green working together, along with Bayh's Senate sponsorship, Title IX of the Education Amendments quickly passed both chambers of Congress and was signed into law in June of 1972 by President Nixon. Although making it through the Congress and into law had seemed easy enough, the battles over what constitutes gender discrimination at school (versus what is normal teen behavior) were just beginning.

---

* Edith Green had already proposed the Equal Pay Act in 1955 to ensure equal pay for equal work (although that wouldn't be signed into law until eight years later), and authored two significant bills that changed the face of secondary education: the Higher Education Facilities Act (1963) and the Higher Education Act (1965), which authorized federal financial assistance to low-income college students. Patsy Takemoto Mink was a third-generation Japanese American. Like Green, she quickly became known as someone motivated by both education reform and gender equality. As a member of the Committee on Education and Labor, she had worked on the Early Childhood Education Act and the Elementary and Secondary Education Act of 1965. Pioneering a path later walked by Anita Hill and Christine Blasey Ford, Mink was also the first person to testify in opposition to a Supreme Court nominee, George Carswell, because of his history of gender discrimination. After her death in 2002, the official name of Title IX was changed in her honor to the Patsy T. Mink Equal Opportunity in Education Act. She was also posthumously awarded the Presidential Medal of Freedom.

† There were some important exclusions to this protection. Music, choir, sex education classes, and sports involving bodily contact were exempt from Title IX, as were religious institutions "if the law would violate their religious tenets." Admissions policies at private undergraduate institutions were also exempt.

BRINGING SEXUAL HARASSMENT INTO THE PUBLIC CONVERSATION

Although Title IX is often thought about as the mandate for girls to have equal funding for sports, it really requires that no student can be "subjected to discrimination" "on the basis of sex." The underlying premise is that boys and girls should have comparable experiences at school. But by the early 1990s, it was increasingly clear that girls' experiences at school were definitely not the same as boys—and gender biases played a role. The fact that girls faced daily and distressing sexual harassment throughout the school day was about to enter public conversation, sparked by a related conversation about workplace harassment that gained national attention in October 1991 when attorney Anita Hill testified to Congress about her experiences with her former boss, Judge Clarence Thomas. He had been nominated to the Supreme Court, and she spoke during his confirmation hearing about the egregious sexual harassment she had endured while working for him. The details were salacious enough to fully capture the nation's attention, and the term *sexual harassment* entered the public lexicon.

From there, attention soon turned to girls' experiences in schools. In March of 1992, an article in the *New York Times* was headlined, "Schools Are Newest Arenas for Sex-Harassment Issues," and detailed interviews with high school girls about boys lifting their skirts or "poking private parts with pencils."[5] In September of that year, *Seventeen* magazine's cover promised to tell its 2.1 million readers about "No joke, Jeans that fit" and "The AIDS cover-up: What they don't want you to know." In green font, just above the headline promising "TV's greatest looking guys," the cover read, "Sexual Harassment at School: Are you a victim?" That edition of the magazine included a survey for teens to talk about their experiences. More than four thousand girls mailed in a response.

At the same time the public was talking about it, researchers were paying more attention to sexual harassment in schools. The American Association of University Women (AAUW), a nonprofit organization that had researched gender discrimination in schools for fifty years, issued a report in 1992 about how "schools shortchange girls."[6] They documented that gender bias of teachers led to decreases in girls' self-esteem. They also documented that one of the biggest ways that girls are discriminated against in schools is by facing a daily barrage of sexual harassment. Based on those early findings, they funded a survey of more than 1,600 public school students in middle schools and high schools nationwide to explore sexual harassment in schools more thoroughly.

While that was in the works, in May of 1993, *Seventeen* magazine published their survey results: 89 percent of girls reported experiencing some sort of sexual harassment at school. More than one in three girls said they were sexually harassed every day. Then, one month later, the AAUW published their massive report, aptly titled "Hostile Hallways."* A key takeaway from the AAUW survey was how common sexual harassment was in teens' lives and how distressing it was for girls. Overall, 85 percent of girls and 76 percent of boys reported that they had been sexually harassed, with one in three girls and one in five boys reporting being harassed "often" at school.[7]

The nature of what boys and girls experienced was quite different, though. For boys, they were most often harassed in a locker room or a restroom by other boys. For girls, sexual harassment usually came from boys right out in the open, in the public spaces in a school, like classrooms and hallways. The specific type of harassment also differed: one-half of girls were on the receiving end of sexual comments, jokes, and gestures, whereas one-third of boys were. About 40 percent of girls had been touched, pinched, or grabbed in a sexual way, while 17 percent of boys had been. Given that sexual harassment of girls often involved physical harassment by boys (who, since this occurs after puberty, are typically bigger and stronger than girls are), it is not surprising that 70 percent of girls felt upset after experiencing sexual harassment and frequently reported being scared afterward. For girls, sexual harassment often brought up fears of sexual assault and rape. Boys' experiences were slightly different. Boys were three times more likely to be called gay in a negative way than girls were. Only about one-fourth of boys reported being upset about sexual harassment, often saying they took it as a joke.[8] The cultural norms in which boys use homophobic slurs in their daily interactions with one another causes its own damage, even if many boys weren't overtly upset about it (we'll come back to this specific harassment in detail in chapters 9 and 10, where we see that homophobic sexual harassment is especially upsetting to gay boys and reinforces toxic masculinity to straight boys).

---

* The public was interested: details of the report were covered by *The Today Show, Good Morning America, NBC Nightly News, CBS Evening News, CNN, Nightline*, and the ultimate cultural touchstone of the era, *The Oprah Winfrey Show*—all of this showing how fully this conversation had entered the collective cultural consciousness.

One last important takeaway comes from the fact that although the survey also asked students if their school had an explicit policy about sexual harassment, only one-fourth of students knew of any such policy. That likely stemmed from the fact that while 1972's Title IX banned discrimination on the basis of sex in schools, it didn't specifically call out sexual harassment as a form of discrimination. So, in 1993, schools were largely ignoring the sexual harassment happening on their watch.

TAKING TEEN SEXUAL HARASSMENT TO COURT

While the public was learning about the pervasiveness of sexual harassment in schools, students and their parents were beginning to take schools to court to hold them liable for the sexual harassment occurring in their buildings. By the early 1990s, more and more sexual harassment cases were making their way to the courts. The first Supreme Court case on sexual harassment (*Meritor Savings Bank, FSB v. Vinson* in 1986[9]) focused on adults in the workplace and established that the sexual harassment of an employee created a "hostile work environment" and was a form of gender discrimination protected under Title VII of the Civil Rights Act.

That workplace standard began to be applied to students in schools in the 1992 Supreme Court case of *Franklin v. Gwinnett County Public Schools*, where student Christine Franklin had been repeatedly sexually harassed and raped by her teacher, but the school had ignored her complaints. She sued the school for damages, and the Supreme Court ruled that because of Title IX, a school could be held liable for monetary damages if they knowingly allowed sexual harassment to occur.[10] The court ruled unanimously that if sexual harassment could create a hostile *work* environment, it could also create a hostile *school* environment. The *Franklin* case was important for ruling that sexual harassment at school was a form of gender discrimination protected under Title IX, but it was limited in how useful it would be to the majority of students because *Franklin* was focused on the sexual harassment of a student by a teacher—and most sexual harassment that was occurring in schools was from one student to another student. As would become evident, the courts had a much more difficult time coming to a consensus about student-to-student sexual harassment.

The first case of peer sexual harassment appeared in 1993 at the District Court of Northern California in *Doe v. Petaluma City School District*.[11] Jane

Doe had been verbally sexually harassed by fellow students for more than two years. Her attorneys from the National Organization of Women Legal Defense and Education Fund (NOWLDF) used an approach similar to the NAACP legal team from in the *Brown* cases: using research to help shine a light on the how sexual harassment harmed girls. The lead litigator on peer sexual harassment for NOWLDF said, "[I]t's really critical that you have the data to support whatever legal arguments you're going to make . . . I think [social science research is] persuasive [to courts], especially from an anecdotal point of view. One of the most helpful things about the *Seventeen* survey was just sort of putting the girls' own words in front of the court."[12] In other words, they sought to use girls' quotes in their briefs to remind the courts of the realities of girls' experiences.

Jane Doe's attorneys successfully argued that a school could be liable for damages under Title IX if the other students created a hostile school environment *and* the school did nothing to stop it. The lower courts, over a series of decisions, adopted the standard that schools were responsible for the experiences of their students if they "knew or should have known" what was going on, finding that "hostile environment sexual harassment is a type of intentional discrimination." As the court ruled, because Jane Doe was "driven to quit an education program because of the severity of the sexual harassment she is forced to endure," she was "surely denied the benefits of" an equal education. However, since it hadn't made its way to the highest court in the land and had only stayed within a district court, the decision couldn't have a nationwide impact.

After all, for every court ruling like *Doe* that held a school responsible for peer sexual harassment, another court ruling would say such harassment was normal teen behavior and shouldn't be litigated.[13] For example, in *Bruneau v. South Kortright Central School District* in 1998, the judge wrote, "Sixth grade students experience that mysterious in-between time of life where they are too old for Barbie dolls and toy soldiers, but too young for high heels and drivers' licenses. Even adults are unsure how to interpret pre-teen behavior." That same year, in *Doe v. University of Illinois*, a judge wrote, "[Eliminating peer sexual harassment] would be an impossible task, for schools are full of all sorts of kids, and every school has its share of buffoons, yokels, and dunderheads of all stripes . . . Schools are also full of kids with raging hormones who may be crude and insensitive when dealing with students of the opposite sex." The argument was that preventing sexual harassment among teens was impossible, as sexual harassment is just a normal part of school life, and therefore the courts should not even try to intervene. Because of disagreement over the fundamental question of whether teen sexual harassment is problematic or kids being kids, these types of cases bounced around twenty-four different district courts with no patterns to their rulings.

The issue of whether schools were responsible for preventing peer sexual harassment as a form of gender discrimination under Title IX finally made it to the Supreme Court in 1999 in the case of *Davis v. Monroe County Board of Education.*[14] The case started almost seven years before it reached the Supreme Court, when LaShonda Davis, a fifth grader at Hubbard Elementary School in Monroe County, Georgia, was repeatedly sexually harassed over a five-month period in 1992–1993 by a classmate identified as GF. GF tried to fondle LaShonda and shouted offensive language at her. He tried to touch her breasts and genital area, telling her, "I want to get in bed with you" and "I want to feel your boobs," and he "placed a door stop in his pants" and chased her.

LaShonda told her mother.

LaShonda told her teachers.

She told her mother again.

She told her teachers again.

Her mother called the teacher and the principal.

Her mother demanded that the school do something, anything, to protect her daughter.

But nothing was ever done.

It took the school three months before they even let her to move to a desk farther away from GF. Her grades started to slip, and in April 1993, her dad found a suicide note LaShonda had written. She told her mom she "didn't know how much longer she could keep [GF] off her." Since LaShonda wasn't his only target, a group of girls tried to meet with the principal, but they were dismissed without a meeting. Finally, in 1994, her mother sued Monroe County Board of Education on behalf of her daughter, arguing that school officials knew of the harassment but failed to take any meaningful action to prevent it from continuing. At first, the case was dismissed, then went through a series of appeals. Finally, on January 12, 1999, the case of *Davis v. Monroe County Board of Education* was argued before the Supreme Court.

Once in the Supreme Court, a sharply divided 5–4 decision emerged,* falling along liberal-conservative ideological lines.[15] Writing for the majority, Justice Sandra Day O'Connor acknowledged that sexual harassment in schools can be ambiguous. She noted, "It is thus understandable that, in the school setting, students often engage in insults, banter, teasing, shoving, pushing, and gender-specific conduct that is upsetting to the students subjected to it."[16] She argued, though, that school boards *are* liable when officials are "deliberately indifferent to sexual harassment, of which they have actual knowledge." She also clarified that "in the context of student-on-student harassment, damages are available only where the behavior is so severe, pervasive, and objectively offensive that it denies its victims the equal access to education that Title IX is designed to protect." These very high standards continue to be critical criteria today: in order for the school to be liable, the sexual harassment must be severe, pervasive, and objectively offensive, *and* the school has to have had knowledge of the harassment but do nothing to redress it. Although it was important to have clearly defined criteria to judge when schools are liable, this opinion makes it very difficult to hold schools liable because, given our deeply divided body politic, it is nearly impossible to find agreement on what is "objectively" offensive. As we see time and again, what is offensive to some can be labeled as "locker-room banter" by others.†

That divide was clear in Justice Anthony Kennedy's harshly worded dissent. Although he had multiple concerns with the decision, including the role of federalism and unchecked liability, he frequently pointed out that this is normal youth behavior that should not rise to this level of concern or oversight. He claimed that these types of complaints are "not new." He pushed back against comparisons to hostile work environments, saying those standards "are not easily translated to peer relationships in schools, where teenage romantic relationships and dating are a part of everyday life ... [where] a teenager's romantic overtures to a classmate (even when persistent and unwelcome) are an inescapable part of adolescence."[17] He even

---

* Voting for Davis were Justices Sandra Day O'Connor, John Paul Stevens, David H. Souter, Ruth Bader Ginsburg, and Stephen G. Breyer. Those dissenting were Justices Anthony Kennedy, Antonin Scalia, Clarence Thomas, and Chief Justice William H. Rehnquist.

† This lack of cultural agreement was evident, for example, in conversations in 2016 about whether then-candidate Trump's on-air descriptions of sexual assault are offensive or "locker-room banter."

normalized, and trivialized, the negative effects of harassment on educational outcomes, arguing that "almost all adolescents experience these problems at one time or another as they mature." The crux of his dissent was that because it is common, it is acceptable.

These types of arguments—that preventing biased behavior is "impossible" and thus shouldn't be attempted—echo those of the racial segregation case heard by the Boston judges in 1849, where the judges declared that "prejudice, if it exists, is not created by law, and probably cannot be changed by law." This perspective presumes that if a behavior or an attitude is common, then it must be an inevitable part of our nature; and if it is part of our nature, then it must not be too harmful nor easily changed. But this passive approach, this maintaining of the status quo, is how biased laws are kept in place. Just because something is common does not mean it is not toxic and should not be changed. Luckily, with the *Davis* case, enough of the Supreme Court recognized that commonplace does not equal acceptable, and sexual harassment among teens—at least as long as it was severe, pervasive, and objectively offensive—was officially banned.

HASHING OUT THE DETAILS OF ENFORCEMENT

Although the *Davis* case officially ruled that Title IX protections include protection against peer sexual harassment at school, predictably, enforcing these policies proved to be quite challenging. The legal protections themselves were clearly necessary, but not sufficient. After *Davis*, the Department of Education (DOE), the agency responsible for enforcing Title IX, distributed vague guidelines to school districts about preventing sexual harassment. But it wasn't until 2011, under President Obama, that the DOE made specific recommendations to schools about being proactive in preventing sexual harassment.* The DOE expected schools to "encourage students to report sexual harassment early, before such conduct becomes severe or pervasive." They urged schools to offer prevention programs that are "sustained (not one-shot educational programs), comprehensive, and address the root individual, relational and societal causes of sexual assault." They also reminded schools there was a legal mandate that "if a school knows or

---

* The recommendations came in the form of a "Dear Colleagues" letter. This did not carry legal weight or ramifications and only served as guidelines for schools to follow.

reasonably should know about student-on-student harassment that creates a hostile environment, Title IX requires the school to take immediate action to eliminate the harassment, prevent its recurrence, and address its effects." The ultimate goal of the 2011 recommendations was to change not only the frequency of sexual harassment, but the social attitudes that accepted and allowed for the harassment.[18] The regulations were mere guidelines, however, and did not have the full weight of the law behind them.

The fact that they were suggestions became significant when Betsy DeVos became the new secretary of education in 2016 under President Trump. She immediately withdrew the Obama-era recommendations. Then, in August 2020, the administration pushed through the first major legally binding rules regarding Title IX since 1975, and the only one focused specifically on sexual harassment.[19] The core change of this new rule was centered around the belief that victims of sexual harassment had been given too many protections compared to the accused,[20] ushering in several changes limiting protections for victims of sexual harassment. DeVos's office argued that Title IX "does not represent a 'zero tolerance' policy banning sexual harassment as such," but should only limit harassment that is "severe" and "pervasive." They also limited what might be considered sexual harassment, with the stated goal of protecting "free speech." They claimed they wanted to ensure that Title IX "does not punish verbal conduct in a manner that chills and restricts speech and academic freedom, and that recipients [of federal money] are not held responsible for controlling every stray, offensive remark that passes between members of the recipient's community."[21]

These changes implied that students' right to free speech (even if that speech is offensive and discriminatory) should trump students' protection from sexual harassment. Again leaning toward protecting the accused, schools are now "required to start all sexual harassment investigations with the presumption that no sexual harassment occurred."[22] Furthermore, proving sexual harassment did occur no longer requires just a "preponderance of evidence" (which means believing there is a greater than 50 percent chance that the harassment occurred), but the more stringent threshold of "clear and convincing evidence." The other big changes of 2020 were that schools can now hold live disciplinary hearings that allow the student who was targeted by sexual harassment to be cross-examined by the accused. On top of those changes, all of the Obama-era suggestions to be proactive and to focus on preventing sexual harassment have been completely removed. With a new administration in 2021, more changes are no doubt in the future.

There is clearly a challenge inherent in the enforcement process: schools must ensure that the procedures are fair for all students, while not discouraging students who are victimized from coming forward. Policymakers have long grappled with this fine line, but the 2020 interpretation has taken the approach common in criminal court cases, where people are presumed innocent and the burden of proof is extremely high. The assumption powering these changes is that many sexual harassment claims are false and overstated. It is an assumption that ignores the research on sexual harassment among teens: girls who have been harassed are often scared, they often blame themselves, and they are too afraid or embarrassed to tell anyone. If anything, sexual harassment claims are understated—and underreported. In addition, how does a student *prove* sexual harassment happened? Teenagers don't walk the hallways of school with body cameras, recording every interaction. The likely results of these new policies are that schools will more easily ignore sexual harassment until it happens, and when it does happen, the victims will have so many hurdles to jump through they will be discouraged from telling anyone. And as we'll discuss in further detail in chapter 9, the psychological, social, and academic consequences of experiencing sexual harassment at school without any support are profound.

As with the cases fighting for racial desegregation and for all children's—no matter what their immigration status—inclusion in schools, it took both cultural and political changes to lead to an increase in the laws and policies that limit gender discrimination in schools. Just as racial prejudice was written off as inevitable and outside the reach of the law, sexual harassment was also often written off as normal teen behavior and not within the purview of the courts. There is a pattern to the biases that face children and the way we unravel those biases: there is a constant push and pull between public attitudes about what is acceptable and policy decisions. While it is true that part of what led to changes in recognizing sexual harassment as a form of gender bias was the growing public awareness of the problem facing girls, and students and parents repeatedly pushing schools, by way of the courts, to protect students, changes in policies can also lead to individuals developing fewer biases to begin with. For example, if schools were required to be more proactive in educating about and preventing sexual harassment (as they were under the Obama-era recommendations), teens' attitudes about what is acceptable would become less biased. That push and pull comes up again in the biases aimed at LGBTQ+ students.

5 Civil Rights Are Not Just Black and White

The Legal Battles to Protect Gay and Trans Teens in Schools

All young people, regardless of sexual orientation or identity, deserve a safe and supportive environment in which to achieve their full potential.
—Harvey Milk, gay-rights activist and the first openly gay elected official in the state of California

Even as children of color and girls were starting to make some legal strides toward greater equality, institutional biases against LGBTQ+ children and teens were still deeply entrenched. Students were bullied at school because of sexual orientation and gender identity, but such rampant harassment went ignored by teachers. The gender identity of trans youth went unacknowledged and disrespected by their schools. While building off of the protections promised by the Fourteenth Amendment and Title IX, some progress toward reducing these biases has recently been made, courts are still grappling with how schools can respect all children.

WHEN BEING GAY WAS A "DISEASE" AND VIOLENCE WAS COMMON

In the 1970s and '80s, the very existence of LGBTQ+ individuals was criminalized and pathologized, with diagnoses and laws epitomizing institutional bias. For example, all major mental health organizations considered being "homosexual" a mental disorder, one that was labeled a "sociopathic personality disorder" by the American Psychiatric Association.* Any individual who had a disparity between their sex identified at birth and their felt gender identity was assigned the mental disorder "transsexualism."[1] Restrictions on same-sex sexual behavior were still on the books ("antisodomy" laws were upheld in the 1986 Supreme Court case *Bowers v. Hardwick*), and when LGBTQ+ characters were portrayed in the media, they were either a punchline or a cautionary tale (wherein they battled a disease, were dangerous or predatory to others, or contemplated suicide).[2]

When biases are that entrenched, violence is never far behind. In the mid-1980s, the US Department of Justice reported lesbian and gay individuals were the group most victimized by hate crimes in America.[3] In certain surveys, 92 percent of lesbian women and gay men reported hearing antigay verbal threats at some point in their lives, and 24 percent reported being physically assaulted.[4] Researchers noted "disapproval of homosexuality has so permeated society that violence against lesbian and gay people has become a norm."[5] Such homophobia and other related biases facing LGBTQ+ individuals paralleled racism and sexism.[6]

While this culture of extreme stigma was damaging for all LGBTQ+ individuals, LGBTQ+ teens faced the added challenges that come from the confluence of puberty, peers, and parents.[7] With puberty and the associated surge of hormones, sexuality becomes not only a major topic of conversation in high school hallways and locker rooms but also an important identity for many teens. But having a sexuality that was not the accepted norm was especially tough for LGBTQ+ teenagers, who, like all teens, just wanted to fit in. As researchers wrote in 1987, peers "will make fun of and reject the lesbian or gay youth. If the young homosexual cannot conform to the group's identity and mores, then that youngster is isolated. Rejection by one's peer group is difficult to handle, and most young people lack the coping skills to handle it. The rejection can be devastating."

---

* The World Health Organization kept homosexuality listed as a disease until 1990.

Beyond rejection, harassment and violence were also common in schools: one-fifth of the lesbian girls and nearly half of the gay boys said they were harassed, threatened with violence, or physically assaulted in high school or junior high because they were perceived to be lesbian or gay.[8] A report by the Vermont Department of Health during that period revealed that LGBTQ+ students were seven times more likely than cis-straight students to have been injured or threatened with a weapon.[9] Given this school-based violence, it is not surprising that LGBTQ+ students were five times more likely than their cis-straight peers to miss school because they were worried for their safety.

Meanwhile, home was not much better than school, as many of these teens also faced violence and rejection from their parents, the same people they depended on for food and shelter. A survey from 1987 found that one out of four gay and lesbian youth were forced to leave home because of conflicts with their parents about their sexual orientation.[10] It's no wonder that LGBTQ+ students were also three times more likely to attempt suicide[11]—after all, for many LGBTQ+ youth, neither school nor home was safe. But while parents are responsible for what happens at home, because the government funds and regulates public schools, the government is responsible for what happens there—and they were doing a poor job protecting their LGBTQ+ students.

THE RESPONSIBILITY OF SCHOOLS TO PROTECT ALL STUDENTS

Although schools are meant to be safe places for all students to focus on learning, LGBTQ+ students often find schools to be one of the most perilous places they go, the setting where they are most likely to be bullied and harassed.[12] Throughout the 1990s, that threat of violence at schools was exacerbated by the fact that very few school districts had any policies prohibiting discrimination on the basis of sexual orientation or gender identity. In 1998, among the country's forty-two largest school districts, half of them did not have a single policy protecting the rights of LGBTQ+ students.[13] Individual teachers in schools were not much help either, as they often made negative comments to the LGBTQ+ students or stood by silently when students were being harassed by their peers.[14] According to the *Yale*

Law and Policy Review's summer 1986 edition, teachers "harass, misinform, and unfairly punish gay students; almost always, they refuse to protect gay youth from peer violence. In many schools, the discriminatory atmosphere forces gay students to concentrate on survival rather than education and destroys gay teenagers' self-esteem during a crucial developmental period."[15] Schools were toxic environments filled with biased individuals who were supported by biased structures—and like the other biases we've looked at in this book, dismantling those structures required that several brave students take the battle to court.

The most influential case in changing how schools protect their LGBTQ+ students started with Jamie Nabozny, a middle school student in Ashland, Wisconsin.[16] In 1988, when Jamie was in the seventh grade, he came out as gay. Immediately after doing so, he began facing daily harassment from kids at school. According to court documents,[17] the harassers regularly called him homophobic slurs, accosted him in the bathroom, tripped him in the hallway, and shoved him against the wall. Jamie repeatedly reported the harassment to the school principal, Mary Podlesny.

Then, one day, when a teacher stepped out of the science classroom, three boys threw Jamie to the ground, straddled him, and pretended to rape him in front of the rest of the class.[18] According to sworn affidavits, when Principal Podlesny was told about this, she said that "boys will be boys." She told Jamie, "If you're going to be so openly gay, you have to expect this kind of treatment." Right after that meeting, he ran home, and the next day he was "forced to speak with a counselor, not because he was subjected to a mock rape in a classroom, but because he left the school without obtaining the proper permission." The boys who harassed him were never disciplined for what they did and such harassment continued through middle school, with each account reported to, but ignored by, Principal Podlesny. Before eighth grade was over, Jamie attempted suicide for the first time.

The harassment followed him to high school. At one point, a harasser purposefully urinated on Jamie in the bathroom, but when he reported the incident to the principal's office, no one was punished.[19] Later, Jamie was physically attacked in the school library, but when Jamie reported the physical assault to the assistant principal Thomas Blauert, he "laughed and told Nabozny that Nabozny deserved such treatment because he is gay." Weeks later, Jamie collapsed from internal bleeding caused by the assault and required surgery. Jamie's parents begged Blauert to take action to protect Jamie, but "each time nothing was done." By the end of eleventh grade, Jamie had attempted suicide several more times, dropped out of school, and moved to a new city.

In 1993, although he had already left the school and was living out of state, Jamie decided to sue his old school district to help ensure that other gay students were more protected than he was.[20] His first attorney wanted to downplay that this case focused on LGBTQ+-biased harassment, thinking it would hurt their chances if this was portrayed as a "gay-rights lawsuit" in the media. The case was dismissed in court, but Jamie decided to get a new attorney and appeal. About the same time, Lambda Legal, the oldest gay-rights organization in the United States, was starting to rethink their legal strategies to protect gay-rights.[21] While they had successfully argued for many LGBTQ+ rights in general, by the mid-1990s, they wanted to broaden their focus to include protections for youth.* They took on Jamie's case as their first, deciding the case might work well because it was so severe and the school officials were so negligent.[22]

In 1996, the US Court of Appeals heard the case of *Nabozny v. Podlesny*,† with the Lambda Legal attorneys arguing that school officials had violated Jamie's rights to equal protection guaranteed in the Fourteenth Amendment. This case was characterized by the intersection of state laws, old federal laws, and new precedents. Basically, there were multiple things at play. First, there was a 1988 Wisconsin statute explicitly banning school discrimination on the basis of both gender *and* sexual orientation.‡ Although Title IX protected all students in public schools in the United States from gender discrimination, Wisconsin was one of the first states to prohibit

---

* During their first twenty years as an organization (from their founding in 1973 to 1993), Lambda Legal tried almost two hundred cases focused on LGBTQ+ rights. Only two of the two hundred involved youth. In the next decade, they would handle twelve cases focused on LGBTQ+ harassment in schools, one of which was *Nabozny v. Podlesny*.

† The named defendants were the principals at Jamie's middle school and high school, Mary Podlesney and William Davis, and the vice principal, Thomas Blauert.

‡ The statute, Section 118.13(1), regulated general school operations, provides that: "No person may be denied . . . participation in, be denied the benefits of or be discriminated against in any curricular, extracurricular, pupil services, recreational or other program or activity because of the person's sex, race, religion, national origin, ancestry, creed, pregnancy, marital or parental status, sexual orientation or physical, mental, emotional or learning disability."

schools from discriminating against students on the basis of sexual orientation (a protection not offered at that time to public school students at the national level).

Second, according to Section 1983 (referred to as the Ku Klux Klan Act), a federal law dating back to the aftermath of the Civil War, government officials are required to provide individuals protection from violence and harassment. In Jamie's case, the attorneys argued that public school officials violated the century-old federal law *because* they had failed to protect him from the harassment as defined by the more recent state law. Third, based on some 1980s legal precedents, in order to hold the school liable, the attorneys had to "show that the defendants [i.e., the school] acted either intentionally or with deliberate indifference," "showing nefarious discriminatory purpose." So, at the trial, the attorneys argued Jamie was bullied in a way that would not have been tolerated if he had been a girl or if he had been straight, and they presented evidence of how the school had repeatedly protected girls from much milder harassment (such as being called a "slut") and described how the principals treated Jamie as though he "was asking for" the harassment because he was gay.

The attorneys made sure to show that even though the school had antibias policies on the books, the principals (the ones who were named defendants) were "deliberately indifferent" to his harassment. Jamie's attorney, Patricia Logue, argued, "We're talking about four years of abuse, daily abuse, clearly escalating in severity with the ages of the abusers. The abuse occurred on their [the principals'] school grounds and on their watch. They had the power to stop it." While the principals did not kick Jamie in the library, they actively ignored the reports of abuse coming from Jamie and his parents—and to a kid being harassed, that is virtually the same thing. After deliberating for only four hours, the jury returned a unanimous verdict, stating that the school officials had intentionally discriminated against Jamie because he was gay and were liable for close to $1 million in damages.

This marked the first judicial opinion in the United States stating that a public school could be held financially liable for not stopping homophobic harassment. As Jamie's attorney said in the days after the trial, "Countless gay kids paid a high price for abuse. Now the tables have turned and it is prejudice that is costly." The success of this case, particularly its financial consequences, opened up the recourse other bullied LGBTQ+ kids could seek. This case set a powerful precedent that other students could rely on in court, making it more likely future lawsuits would be successful.

Indeed, in the decade after the case was decided, school districts paid approximately $4 million dollars to LGBTQ+ kids in either lawsuits or settlements because of the bullying those children were subjected to at school and the schools' lack of protection.[23] Additionally, beyond the financial impact of those individual cases, many schools, often at the behest of their insurance companies, put new antiharassment procedures and training in place to avoid costly lawsuits all together. Jamie later said, "I don't care why people do the right thing; they just need to do the right thing. And if it means they're afraid of losing their house or their life savings, then hey, they'll protect kids and that's what needs to happen." This is the real (often flawed) world: in the absence of officials believing in and committing to equality for all students, financial liability for our institutions is often the most effective way to reduce the biases embedded. Money talks, even when compassion doesn't.

Despite the intricacies of constitutional law, statutory law, and the implications of the language like "deliberate indifference," it is critical to remember the impact on the kid being harassed. As Jamie said, "Sometimes I thought I somehow deserved what was happening to me. In middle school and high school, I started wondering what was so wrong with me." Despite the ultimate success of this case and cases like it, the toll of this type of harassment is profound on the person at the center of the case and isn't erased by a large financial payout.

THE CURRENT BATTLES FOR LGBTQ+ KIDS IN SCHOOL

Despite the success of the *Nabozny* case in 1996, there are still legal battles being waged to reduce biases facing LGBTQ+ youth. One battle concerns what can be taught in the classroom. As of 2020, six states (Alabama, Louisiana, Mississippi, Oklahoma, South Carolina, and Texas) have "no promo homo" laws on their books—laws explicitly prohibiting the positive portrayal of LGB people in the curriculum by banning the "promotion of homosexuality."[24] In Alabama, for example, "Classes must emphasize, in a factual manner and from a public health perspective, that homosexuality is not a lifestyle acceptable to the general public and that homosexual conduct is a criminal offense under the laws of the state."[25] In South Carolina, health education "may not include a discussion of alternate sexual lifestyles from heterosexual relationships including, but not limited to, homosexual relationships except in the context of instruction concerning sexually transmitted diseases."[26] In other words, being gay needs to be either invisible or pointed to as a cautionary example of crime and disease.

Schools that have "no promo homo" laws not only erase LGBTQ+ individuals from the classroom, they are also less likely to have Gay-Straight Alliances (GSA, sometimes called Gender and Sexuality Alliances). GSAs are student-led, teacher-sponsored, school-based clubs for LGBTQ+ students and their straight allies. They are support groups to help students connect to one another, to feel less alone in a culture full of LGBTQ+ bias. They may host a book club or have LGBTQ+ movie night. They may volunteer together at a food bank or shelter. They may have a drag queen story hour or attend a pride march together. They may raise money for LGBTQ+ books for the library. Or they just may sit around and talk about their experiences. They can be safe havens and places of joy. They are also demonstrably beneficial to the health and well-being of students.

Schools with GSAs are perceived by both students and staff as less hostile and more supportive for LGBTQ+ students than schools without GSAs.[27] LGBTQ+ students who attend schools with GSAs report less homophobic harassment, feel a greater sense of school belonging, earn higher grades, use drugs less, and report fewer suicide attempts than students at schools without GSAs.[28] The differences are significant: LGBTQ+ students at schools without a GSA were *three* times more likely to use cocaine than their more supported peers. Research shows that the sheer presence of GSAs at a school may actually be more influential in LGBTQ+ youth's positive outcomes than their membership in the GSA.[29] It seems to benefit LGBTQ+ teens to have a GSA at their school, regardless of whether they actually go to the meetings or not. Having a GSA signals what is valued, what is tolerated, and reflects that the school should be a safe and inclusive space for all students. LGBTQ+ teens often feel culturally invisible at school. Most students report that their sexual education classes only discuss relationships between boys and girls. Outside of health or sex ed classes, across the school curricula, only a small minority of students (16 percent) report that they were taught positive representations about LGBTQ+ people, history, or events in their schools. And half of LGTBQ+ students cannot even find information about LGBTQ+-related issues in their school library or access it on school computers.[30] Having a GSA changes that feeling of invisibility.

In general, positive LGBTQ+ representation in school curricula is important for all kids—straight or not—to see, as positive representation establishes what is valued and accepted. When schools do provide LGBTQ+- inclusive curriculum, studies show LGBTQ+ students experience less harassment at school and they feel safer at school.[31] Students also report that their teachers are more supportive. Supportive teachers help students feel like they belong, giving them someone for students to talk to when they face homophobia. With supportive teachers, suicide rates go down. Beyond that, when teachers are trained to intervene to stop harassment, LGTBQ+ students feel safer at school.

Beyond the battles to increase positive representation in schools and drop "no promo homo" laws from the books, to help reduce biases facing LGBTQ+ youth, current fights are also aimed at having enumerated policies on the books explicitly naming and banning LGBTQ+-based harassment. All fifty states have antibullying and harassment laws, but only twenty-one have comprehensive, specified policies. South Dakota and Missouri have actually banned school districts from having an enumerated policy.

It may seem redundant for a school to call out harassment on the basis of sexual orientation and gender identity as specific types of banned behavior, if bullying and harassment are generally banned already, but studies have shown that teachers feel more comfortable intervening to stop harassment when explicit policies are in place protecting LGBT students.[32] One-fourth of teachers intervened "most of the time or always" when there was an enumerated policy at their school, versus only 14 percent of teachers when there was no enumerated policy (and only 8 percent when there was no antibullying policy at all). And when these policies are clearly laid out and teachers are trained in what to do, students feel safer, hear fewer homophobic epithets, are bullied less, and are less likely to attempt suicide.[33]

These explicit antidiscrimination policies that enumerate LGBTQ+ status as a protected category also help reduce bias among the straight students at the school. Researchers Stacey Horn and Laura Szalacha found that straight students believed that excluding and teasing a lesbian or gay peer was less acceptable, more hurtful, and more unfair when they attended schools with enumerated school policies, compared to students at schools without enumerated school policies—and it was the enumerated policies of Wisconsin that determined the success of the *Nabozny* case, showing that, even when such policies don't prevent harassment for every student, they enable it to be punished. And although they don't erase this biased treatment completely, they make it a little less likely that youth will be harassed because of their sexual orientation or gender identity, and that is movement in the right direction.

Although posting and enforcing a simple policy—"Harassment and bullying because of someone's sexual orientation, gender identity, or gender expression will not be tolerated"—is an easy structural change that individual schools can make, it is also important that long-running efforts to extend this protection to kids nationwide succeed. The Safe Schools Improvement Act, an amendment to the Elementary and Secondary Education Act of 1965 (the same act that was amended with Title IX), would have required these enumerated protections nationwide, much like Title IX is required nationwide. If passed, it would have required that schools "establish policies that prevent and prohibit . . . bullying and harassment that is sufficiently severe, persistent, or pervasive . . . based on a student's actual or perceived race, color, national origin, sex, disability, sexual orientation, gender identity, or religion." In other words, it would enumerate protections for all kids. But the act has been introduced for more than ten years (the latest unsuccessful effort was in 2020) and has yet to make it out of committee. The pushback against the act is the hackneyed argument that it prevents "kids from being kids." Critics argue that it will restrict the natural banter between kids. I assert that now is the time to change what it means to be a kid: we must find a definition of childhood that does not include tolerating bias and harassment.

BEING TRANS AT SCHOOL

Transgender youth, in addition to dealing with the kinds of LGBTQ+-biased harassment at the center of the *Nabozny* case, face other unique challenges at school because of how schools determine and enforce gender identity. Typically, school records are based on information from the birth certificate that parents have to bring with them when they register their child for kindergarten. The birth certificate lists the child's name (which is usually gender-specific) and indicates "boy" or "girl" based on the doctor's assessment of the newborn's external genitalia. As kindergarteners, trans kids usually know their gender identity but they often haven't socially transitioned yet (they may still be going by the name and gender reflected on their birth certificate). When they do transition and want to use the gender that aligns with their felt gender identity and a matching name, schools sometimes dig in and refuse to make the change.[34] This results in things such as, in 2019, one-fourth of trans kids not being allowed to use their chosen name or pronouns at school.[35]

It is difficult to think of anything more personal than one's name. Neuroscience research has even found that our brains respond differently when we hear our own name than when we hear other names. We can hear our own name being whispered in a noisy cocktail party. It rings out because it represents who we are—and the parts of the brain that are related to how we think about and describe ourselves are activated when we hear our name.[36] That is just as true for trans youth as well. Letting trans youth use their chosen name and pronouns is extremely important for their mental health. For example, when trans youth can use their preferred name, especially at home, school, work, and with friends, they are less depressed and have fewer suicidal thoughts and attempts.[37] For every extra context where they get to use their chosen name, there is a 56 percent decrease in suicidal behavior.[38]

In addition to getting the right to go by their chosen name, another challenge for trans youth at schools relates to the bathroom that they are allowed to use. Some trans youth are forced to use the bathroom of the sex they were assigned at birth, regardless of their gender identity. This policy is a bizarre invasion of privacy, where one hidden body part overrides every other publicly presented—and personally identified—sense of self. It's a policy that, in practice, conveys that genitalia are private for everyone except transgender kids. As one trans girl who transitioned in middle school explained, "Being a trans girl is already making me different from everybody else, and now I'm not even allowed to use the same bathroom as the girls, so people weren't seeing me as a girl."[39] Because of the shame and awkwardness of being forced to use a special restroom or one that does not align with their gender, more than 40 percent of transgender students fast, refuse to drink anything, or find other ways not to use the restroom.[40] As a result of not using the restroom when needed, trans youth regularly suffer from urinary tract and kidney infections.[41]

In 2017, state legislation and national attention were focused on this question of which bathroom trans students should be allowed to use when North Carolina passed HB2,[42] the "bathroom bill." The bill forbade trans youth from using the bathroom that matched their gender identity.* And though North Carolina was occupying most of the news coverage in 2017, these types of bathroom bills had been gaining traction between 2013 to 2016, during which time at least twenty-four states considered legislation that would only give students access to bathrooms and locker rooms that matched their sex assigned at birth.[43] All of the bills failed to pass, except for the one in North Carolina. This legislative focus on trans students' bathroom access began to wane by 2019, when only one state (Indiana) introduced a bathroom bill that went nowhere. And by December 2020, even North Carolina ended up repealing HB2. A large part of that reversal came because of financial pressures from businesses like PayPal and Amazon, who pulled their business out of the state following the passage of the discriminatory law. But policymakers were also likely following a trans student's court case that was slowly making its way through the legal system.

THE LEGAL BATTLE ABOUT GENDER IDENTITY AT SCHOOL

While half of the states in the United States were discussing the adoption of their own bathroom bills, a legal battle that would nullify those biased pieces of legislation was working its way through the courts. In 2014, Gavin Grimm, a high school sophomore, and his mother informed his high school in Gloucester County, Virginia, that he would be changing his previously female name to Gavin and should be identified as a boy, thus socially transitioning. The school was fine with it. For seven weeks, Grimm used the boys' restrooms at Gloucester County High School without a complaint. The teachers were okay with it; the students were okay with it.

Two months of peace ended when the superintendent, principal, and school board members started receiving complaining emails and phone calls, not only from adults within Gloucester County "who caught wind

---

* Although communities would justify these bathroom bills by parading out the myth of men dressing as women to nefariously enter the women's restrooms and assault them, there are no reported cases of this happening. Rather, these claims tap into the fear-mongering that has reliably been used throughout history to make people afraid of anyone different. Claims that women need protecting, in this case from men dressing as women, echo the claims that justified the murder of Black men in the Jim Crow South to protect the (sexual) safety of White women.

of the arrangement" but also adults in "neighboring communities and even other states."[44] Instead of focusing on Gavin's well-being, the school centered those voices from outside of the school, caved to the complaints, and told Gavin he could no longer use the boys' restroom. But because he was a boy (and clearly presented that way), it would have been uncomfortable for him, and raised more complaints from bigoted busybodies, to use the girls' restroom. Eventually, the school had Gavin use a converted single-stall restroom or the restroom in the nurses' office.[45] The restrooms were on the opposite end of the large school building from his classes, and Gavin would either be late to class or have to wait until the end of the day to go to the restroom. During after-school activities, the only restrooms he could use were locked, and he would have to ask a friend to drive him to a public restroom or his mom would have to come pick him up early. His mother kept medicine stocked at home because he had so many urinary tract infections. Then, in 2015, he, with help from the ACLU, sued the Gloucester County School Board. In the case of *Grimm v. Gloucester County School Board*, they argued that Gavin's inability to use the restroom that matched his gender identity violated his Fourteenth Amendment right to equal protection and violated Title IX guarantees.

The case was working its way through the lower courts to the Supreme Court until President Obama's administration issued guidelines indicating that Title IX regulations meant that transgender youth should be treated in accordance with their gender identity. That made the policy clear, so the Supreme Court declined to hear the case as there was nothing to argue. But when President Trump was elected in 2016, his administration quickly rescinded the Department of Education's previous guidance regarding transgender students' rights under Title IX. With that guidance removed and the legalities again under question, Gavin's case went to the Fourth Circuit Court of Appeals to be reconsidered.

Through all of this, Gavin was trying to work with the school to use the boys' restroom. He had been issued a new driver's license and a new birth certificate that he forwarded to the school board, but the school board declined to update his school records. When Gavin spoke in front of the Gloucester County School Board Meeting during this years' long court battle, he pleaded with them, saying, "All I want to do is be a normal child and use the restroom in peace." He argued that he just wanted basic human rights, "I didn't choose this. This is just who I am . . . This could be your child. I deserve the rights of every other human being. I am just a human. I am just a boy."[46]

In August of 2020, after a five-year legal battle, and after Gavin had already graduated high school, the three-judge Court of Appeals ruled 2–1 in favor of Gavin.[47] Judge Henry Floyd, writing the majority opinion, relied heavily on social science and medical research in his decision. He repeatedly cited the amicus briefs from scientific organizations,* noting, "Seventeen of our foremost medical, mental health, and public health organizations agree that being transgender 'implies no impairment in judgment, stability, reliability, or general social or vocational capabilities.'"[48] He argued that the school board ignored important scientific findings that showed the importance of gender affirmation for the health of children. Judge Floyd extensively cited the research findings showing that "transgender people face major mental health disparities: they are up to three times more likely to report or be diagnosed with a mental health disorder as the general population . . . and nearly nine times more likely to attempt suicide than the general population . . . And harassment at school is correlated with mental health outcomes for transgender students." Social science thus clearly played a significant role in Judge Floyd's final conclusion: "At the heart of this appeal is whether equal protection and Title IX can protect transgender students from school bathroom policies that prohibit them from affirming their gender. We join a growing consensus of courts in holding that the answer is resoundingly yes."

Judge James Wynn wrote a concurring opinion wherein he drew sharp comparisons between transgender student rights and the rights of students of color in the *Brown* era, showing that both systems produce "a vicious and ineradicable stigma. The result is to deeply and indelibly scar the most vulnerable among us—children who simply wish to be treated as equals at one of the most fraught developmental moments in their lives—by labeling them as unfit for equal participation in our society." Wynn further highlighted the fact that the school's policy was "not hypothetical," but one that caused real pain to a real boy, and, because it involved basic necessities, the "pain is overwhelming, unceasing, and existential."[49] Wynn's point is an important one: the biases embedded in our policies have real consequences in the lives of real children.

---

* The court case had received amicus briefs from seventeen top medical, public health, and mental health organizations, including the American Academy of Pediatrics, American Academy of Child and Adolescent Psychiatry, American Medical Association, and American Psychiatric Association.

TRANS STUDENTS ARE ATHLETES TOO

The struggles for LGBTQ+ students' rights are ongoing, and for the next few years, many of the legal battles will focus on transgender student athletes. The question at hand is which team will students be allowed to play for. By early 2021, nineteen states had interscholastic athletic associations with policies that are supportive of trans students in K-12 schools, but thirteen states have no standard policies, and eighteen states (largely in the South and Midwest) have discriminatory policies. Some states even require students show medical proof of having sex reassignment surgery before they are allowed to register for sports in accordance with their gender identity. The argument now is that it is unfair to girls to have "boys" competing on their teams.*

In 2020, the case before the courts was *Soule et al. v. Connecticut Association of Schools*. The lawsuit started when three female student athletes on the track team, Selina Soule, Chelsea Mitchell, and Alanna Smith, started losing track meets they were used to winning. The lawsuit claims that the three girls had been winning until two transgender students joined the track team, naming Terry Miller and Andraya Yearwood as the usurpers of their success. The lawsuit claims that the Connecticut Transgender Participation Policy "has enabled biological male athletes to displace them (along with other girls in competitive track and field events) from earned victories, honors, and opportunities for championship competition, as well as proper public recognition of their performances."[50] The claim at the heart of their lawsuit is that an inclusive participation policy violates Title IX, because girls supposedly no longer have a protected opportunity to compete with one another. Their argument is basically that because the plaintiffs don't win everything anymore, the girls who are beating them shouldn't count as girls. The argument is also steeped in the biased view that (cisgender) girls need protection.[51] They state, "Unfortunately for Plaintiffs and other girls in Connecticut, those dreams and goals—those opportunities for participation, recruitment, and scholarships—are now being directly and negatively impacted by a new policy that is permitting boys who are male in every biological respect to compete in girls' athletic competitions if they claim a female gender identity." Throughout the lawsuit, the attorneys refer to the transgender girls as boys, using he/him pronouns. This misgendering was

---

* Again, the trope of "protecting" (White) girls has become the rationale for bias.

so pervasive and offensive that the court, in April 2020, demanded that the attorneys stop referring to the students as males, but as transgender females.

The ACLU became involved on behalf of the defendants. They counter-argued that the claim that Title IX protections should not apply to a subset of girls (namely, transgender girls) would ultimately hurt all students and "compromise the work of ending the long legacy of sex discrimination in sports." Additionally, they showed that language of the complaint, which deliberately misgenders transgender youth and demands that high school athletics be "organized by chromosomes," is an "assault on the basic dignity and humanity of transgender people and a threat to the privacy and equality of all students."*

Beyond the argument to respect humanity, it is also worth clarifying that trans athletes rarely have the physical advantages many may assume. Assuming they necessarily have physical advantage reflects a lack of under-standing of testosterone (which varies widely across people regardless of sex chromosomes) and athletic performance (which does not consistently correlate with testosterone).[52] Further, according to the director of the Tucker Center for Research on Girls and Women in Sport, in this court case, "Both girls are on hormone suppression, which negates any competitive advantage due to testosterone, but most people are unaware of this fact. There are many factors that go into athletic performance—for example, to name a few, physical training, conditioning, dedication, motivation, quality of coaching, nutrition, and psychological skills that get erased when the sole focus is on gender identity and hormones."[53] If compassion for teen athletes isn't compelling, people should at least be moved by the scientific inaccuracy of the controversy.

Terry Miller, a student athlete who has been forced to the center of the controversy by the discrimination the suit subjects her to, said,

> "I have faced discrimination in every aspect of my life and I no longer want to remain silent. I am a girl and I am a runner. I participate in athletics just like my peers to excel, find community, and meaning in my life. It is both unfair and painful that my victories have to be

---

* As of 2021, the case is working its way through the courts. Although by February of 2021, with a new administration in position, the Department of Justice was reversing their position on the case to make their policy consistent with the Executive Order 13988 on *Preventing and Combating Discrimination on the Basis of Gender Identity or Sexual Orientation.*

attacked and my hard work ignored . . . The more we are told that we don't belong and should be ashamed of who we are, the fewer opportunities we have to participate in sports at all . . . I will continue to fight for all trans people to compete and participate consistent with who we are. There is a long history of excluding Black girls from sports and policing our bodies. I am a runner and I will keep running and keep fighting for my existence, my community, and my rights."

Andraya Yearwood, the other student athlete explicitly discriminated against in the suit, added, "I hope that the next generation of trans youth doesn't have to fight the fights that I have. I hope they can be celebrated when they succeed not demonized." The girls' statements are reminiscent of Gavin Grimm's plea to the Gloucester County School Board: he didn't want special treatment; he just wanted to be treated like a normal boy. That request is so simple it is heartbreaking.

By April 2021, this specific case was dismissed because Miller and Yearwood had graduated, could no longer compete in track meets, and the decision was then moot. But this issue is not going away so quickly. In 2021, thirty-three states have seen 117 anti-trans bills introduced into their state legislations, with most of those bills focused on trans youth—fifty-eight bills are focused on bathrooms/locker rooms and student athletes and twenty-nine bills attempt to ban gender-affirming health care (such as puberty blockers) for trans youth.[54] At the same time, while states are seeing record numbers of anti-trans bills, the Equality Act (HR 5), which "prohibits discrimination on the basis of sex, gender identity, and sexual orientation" in public institutions including public education, is successfully making its way through the United States Congress.[55]

Ultimately, the onus for change is on all of us. The politicians we elect, the laws we pass, the voices we choose to elevate—they all shape the lives of children for good or bad. Those laws can either exclude and other children, making them feel unsafe and unwelcome at school and harming their mental and physical health, or they can convey to children that they are valued, worthy of respect, and full of potential. The choice is ours.

Across all of these court cases, legal challenges, and policy changes, marginalized children and teens are trying to live in a world free of bias, trying to go to the best school possible without being harassed or shamed. Regardless of race or ethnicity, immigration status, gender, sexual orientation, or gender identity, children deserve to be treated equally—by individuals and by institutions.

One of the reasons prejudice and biases are so persistent in our society is because they are knotted around these institutional policies and laws. The way to move past institutional and individual biases (both of which feed into and are fed by the other), as we've seen time and again in the success of social science research to change structural biases, is to understand the harm that prejudices cause. And science not only has the potential to change laws and policies—it can also help us understand how to eradicate (or, at least, lessen) the biases that individuals hold and how to protect the children targeted by bias. That science is the focus of the next part of the book.

PART II

BIAS IN CHILDREN'S EVERYDAY LIVES

What Science Has Taught Us About Children and Bias, from the Early Days to Today

6 First Forays into the Social Science of Bias

Scientists Started by Asking Children About Race

Thoughtful, moral, rational social scientists must be the contemporary custodians of such enduring human values as justice.
—Dr. Kenneth Clark, key expert in the NAACP school segregation cases, husband of Mamie Phipps Clark

Unraveling the multiple threads of bias—the structural and the individual—will require multiple approaches. Some people fight biases by boycotting schools, some by marching, and some by speaking up at their city council meetings. Some people fight bias in the courts and persist through appeal after appeal, using constitutional arguments to make our laws more inclusive and socially just. Some social scientists, like me, fight bias by conducting studies and talking to children and their families, using good science and providing clear evidence, and hoping that policymakers and the public are listening. All of these approaches, from engaging in boycotts to writing scientific journal articles, are necessary because the problem that we're facing is that complex.

While in the first part of the book we dealt with biased policies and institutions and the people who fought for change, in the second part of the book, we'll be focusing on the evolving science of bias—and what we have learned about how children develop biases and how they are affected by others' biases. Along the way, I'll also share the stories of some of the scientists who do this work, women from marginalized groups who contributed to our understanding of bias in children even while battling the very biases they studied. But first, let's start with those initial studies about children and racial bias, because they laid an important foundation for what we know now.

SCIENCE AT THE RIGHT TIME

Research—because it's conducted by researchers who are a product of their time and place—is a reflection of the cultural zeitgeist of the day. We see the same pattern time and again: as a marginalized group gains cultural visibility, more people acknowledge the prejudice that a group faces, then more researchers study the effects of that prejudice, and then court cases emerge where that research is cited and structural biases hopefully begin to be dismantled. Recently, transgender individuals have gained greater visibility and recognition thanks in large part to trans actors and celebrities like Elliot Page and Laverne Cox. Following one beat behind, research on the development of trans kids and gender-nonconforming kids has seen a major boost over the past five years. This research is currently being used in ongoing legal battles for the protection of trans kids in schools. Before that, it was Anita Hill in the news, then conversations about sexual harassment, and then the research followed. But in the early days of research with children, Nazism, worldwide anti-Semitism, Jim Crow laws, and lynchings were widespread. As a result, the earliest work tried to address the impact of *racial* prejudice on children.

"The Effects of Segregation and the Consequences of Desegregation: A Social Science Statement," submitted to the Supreme Court in 1954 in the *Brown v. Board of Education* case, relied on the best science of the day—and was the first time that social science research was successfully cited in a Supreme Court case.[1*] That social science statement referred to

---

* The Brandeis brief from 1908 introduced the concept of using social science data, and a 1908 case on race segregation, *Berea v. Kentucky*, would introduce

studies showing "from the earliest school years children are . . . aware of the status differences among different groups in the society."[2] The single greatest impact on that social science statement came from a series of studies later known as the doll studies, mostly conducted by Mamie Clark, the same person who testified in the 1951 *Davis* case we went over in chapter 2. But to even be able to conduct such research required a major shift in thinking about race.

FROM "RACE PSYCHOLOGY" TO RACIAL PREJUDICE

In the 1920s, two decades before the doll studies, most social scientists who studied "race psychology" (who were primarily White men[3]) were creatively "documenting" racial differences, focusing their efforts on whatever test showed White people to be biologically superior to everyone else. The most common approach was to administer an IQ test, usually the Stanford-Binet intelligence test, to a group of White and Black children (or Mexican immigrant or Native American children) and compare their scores. This always conveniently favored White children,[4] in ways that were typically ignored at the time. For example, no one seemed to care that such IQ tests usually focused on English vocabulary words and Mexican American children were often being tested in their second language.[5]* A rare dissenting voice of the time was Horace Mann Bond (the first Black president of Lincoln University), who argued, "To compare the crowded millions of New York's East Side with the children of some professorial family on Morningside Heights [on the campus of Columbia University] indeed involves a great contradiction; and to claim that the results of the tests given to such diverse groups, drawn from such varying strata of the social complex, are in any wise accurate, is to expose a fatuous sense of

------

pseudoscientific "anthropometrics" arguing White and Black people had different size skulls (Acker, 1990; Jackson, 2001). Justices, however, had never cited this research in their opinions. The *Brown* case, however, is widely considered to be the first time social science evidence was cited in a Supreme Court opinion, brief, or lower court opinion.

* It would be another fifty years before researchers would study all of the cognitive advantages of being bilingual.

unfairness and lack of appreciation of the great environmental factors of modern urban life."[6] Still, despite the illogicality and illegitimacy of such tests, by using studies expressly designed to show White children were more intelligent than all other racial and ethnic groups, it was easy to justify the segregation of schools as simply following the natural order of things.

But by the 1930s, several changes throughout the world led to changes in research methods and topics.[7] The Great Depression in the United States turned many researchers' focus to how poverty, rather than biology, harms children's development. In both Europe and America, Nazis were becoming increasingly powerful, and researchers were growing worried about the cultural threat.[8] At the same time, the field of social psychology (with its focus on the impact of groups and situations) was developing, with an influx of Jewish and Black research psychologists pointing out the flaws in the existing race psychology, which had been solely focused on pinpointing nebulous racial differences. Instead, the new researchers, who had personal experience with others' biases, began to focus on racial prejudice.[9]*

By 1939, even the world's most prolific researcher on race psychology, Thomas Garth, realized that contemporary evidence was plagued by researchers' own race biases and stated that "racial differences are skin deep only and are due entirely to environment and opportunity, not heredity."[10] This seismic shift, however, left researchers with a conundrum: If research shows that people from racial and ethnic-minority groups are not genetically inferior, then why are the lives of individuals from different racial groups so different? The answer, researchers started to believe, might lie in prejudice. At the time, people believed that prejudice came from childhood frustrations that were repressed and then spewed out in adulthood.[11] Although social psychology was rapidly growing, researchers were not yet doing much research *with* children, and many psychologists of the era relied on Freudian theories about negative thoughts being repressed in childhood. Although those theories would quickly fizzle out because they were never supported by empirical research, the new focus on children did stick. So, researchers turned to childhood to find the source of, and answer to, prejudice. And thus, the study of bias in children began.

---

* Much of this early work is highlighted in the 1954 landmark book by Gordon Allport, *The Nature of Prejudice*.

THE EARLIEST STUDIES ON CHILDREN'S BIASES

In 1936, people knew very little about prejudice in children. Ruth Horowitz and her husband Eugene Horowitz, research psychologists funded by the Social Science Research Council, were among the first to explore children's attitudes toward "race, sex, age, and (perhaps) economic status."[12] To uncover—or at least try to shed light on—*why* children showed racial biases, they traveled from New York City to rural Maury County, Tennessee. Ruth and Eugene visited farming communities—staying with poor White families in the middle of winter in houses best described as shacks, with no heaters and no indoor plumbing—where all the White children attended one school, with only four teachers, spanning first through tenth grades.* The Horowitzes showed pictures to the White children of White girls and boys and "colored" girls and boys† and asked them to: "Show me all those that—

- you'd like to sit next to at school . . .
- to play with . . .
- look stupid . . .
- live in a dirty house . . .
- [you] would like to have as a cousin."

They also asked them a series of "Would you rather?" questions:

- "Would you rather play with a girl or a boy?"
- "Would you rather play with a White boy or a colored boy?"
- "Would you rather play with a rich boy or a poor boy?"

The biases that Ruth and Eugene found were clear. Without exception, children preferred their own sex and their own (White) race. They also found that "the race distinction, the dichotomy of Negroes and Whites, was of fundamental importance and represented a more important distinction than

---

* The Black children in the community went to one of four one-teacher-only segregated schools.

† They also included pictures of "Filipino" boys and an owl to "permit further comparisons . . . of responses to unfamiliar with familiar, as well as to serve as distractions and outlets for unfavorable responses without any necessary social repercussions in the community."

any of the other categories studied." As modern research would confirm,[13] children latch onto the social groups adults treat as the most important, and as was clear for White children in the 1930s in rural Tennessee, racial distinctions dominated.

The Horowitzes were primarily interested in *how* children developed biases, so they asked the children to explain if anyone had told them who they should, or should not, play with. The youngest of the school children would quote their parents as saying, for example, "Mother doesn't want me to play with colored children. [They] might have pneumonia." A third-grade boy said, "One time I slipped off and played with some colored people, back [behind] our house, when [my mother] told me not to, and I got a whipping." A fourth-grade girl said, "[My mother says] not to play with colored boys, tells me they might get after me and carry me away."

Yet when the Horowitzes asked the parents about how they might be influencing their children's racial attitudes, they rejected the idea that they might contribute to their children's biases. One mother said, completely without irony, that her son "never played with any Negro children. I have to chase them out of the back yard, they keep coming around, but I never had to tell him not to play with the [n-word]." As the Horowitzes concluded, "There was a general acknowledgement of practices such as chasing Negros away and preventing play . . . but no appreciation of these as possible factors in determining children's attitudes." Even when the children would provide direct quotes from their parents about racial boundaries, the parent wouldn't recall making any comments that they felt could have impacted their children's biases about race.

This disconnect between children's and parents' impressions of each other's racial attitudes was an important discovery in 1936. However, it didn't answer the question of whether parents actually did not remember making comments about race or whether they simply chose to not disclose such comments (at least to the Yankees from New York). Although Ruth and Eugene weren't able to answer that question, it is one that future researchers continue to investigate, even today.*

Ruth and Eugene's findings, published in 1938, were important for early understandings of how and why children develop racial biases. However,

---

* Such as the major meta-analyses conducted in 2013, which captured forty-five thousand parent-child pairs and found few overlaps between the stated prejudices of parents and their children.

like most research into racial prejudice at the time, it focused on how White children developed racism toward Black children, not how Black children were affected by White children's racism. Once they were back in New York, Ruth decided to change that. She also wanted to understand how children were being affected by racism before they became too self-conscious to honestly talk about race.

ASKING YOUNG CHILDREN ABOUT THEMSELVES AND OTHERS

There is always a fundamental challenge when conducting research with young children: how can we learn what children know and how they think before they can fully articulate their thoughts? Imagine you want to know whether preschoolers understand social class. You could ask, "Tell me about social class." That would get you nowhere. You could simplify it and ask, "What does it mean to be rich? What does it mean to be poor?" That would get you some responses in elementary school, but probably no earlier than that. Indeed, you could easily conclude that a three-year-old child has no knowledge of social class at all. But imagine if, instead, you showed children pictures of rich people and poor people and asked them to sort the pictures into piles that go together. Although they can't describe their rationale or what exact clues they are relying on, even three-year-old children can categorize pictures on the basis of social class.* But in the 1930s, researchers didn't do this. Although developmental science was growing as a field by that point, there weren't yet clear techniques for systematically studying young children's ideas about complex topics.

In 1939, Ruth Horowitz pioneered the technique that would allow generations of researchers to do just that. It was called the "projective test,"[14] and provided a way to ask very young children—children who were too young to be self-conscious about taboo topics like race, but unfortunately also too young to have many verbal skills—about their attitudes about both their own race and that of others by using dolls and puppets. As part of her clinical practice, she developed a groundbreaking method to examine how both White *and* Black children identified their own race.[15]

---

* We know they can do this because Patricia Ramsey did this exact study in 1991.

In this study, she went to a public WPA* nursery school in New York where the kids ranged from two to four years old, seventeen of them White and seven of them Black. In what she called the "choice test," she showed each child a picture of a Black child and a White child. She said, "Show me which one is you. Which one is [you]?" Sixty-seven percent of the Black children picked a Black child in the picture when asked which picture was them; 40 percent of the White children picked a White child. Two White boys, brothers, when shown the picture of a Black child said, "That's How-ard"—who apparently was the Black child "in the nursery school who was a leader in the group." Every time those two saw a picture of a Black boy, they said, "There's a Howard," and Black girls were called "Howard's girl." Apparently, Howard, because he was a Black person they knew, was their generic representation of all Black children.

According to the study, "On the whole, the White boys[†] present a more confused picture than do the Negro boys."[16] Ruth noted, "Our Negro children seemed to have a more definite concept of their difference from one group and similarity with another than the White group." She noted that this can teach us about how children learn about their racial identification. "If the learning came only from observation," she said, "the White children should have profited equally. This difference between the groups seems to point to the inner workings of the minority group for cues." She was making the case that social stigma and prejudice forced Black kids to learn about their race earlier than White kids. In a society in which Black people have to be vigilant

---

* These were public preschools funded by the Works Progress Administration that was part of President Franklin Roosevelt's New Deal following the Great Depression. Only children from low-income families who were on "home relief" (a precursor to Aid to Families with Dependent Children) were eligible to attend. (Molly Quest Arboleda, *Educating Young Children in WPA Nursery Schools: Federally-Funded Early Childhood Education from 1933–1943* (London: Routledge, 2018). A. Cohen, "A Brief History of Federal Financing for Child Care in the United States," *The Future of Children* 6, no. 2 (1996): 26–40, doi:10.2307/1602417.)

† The girls' answers were scattered. Most of the pictures were of boys, so when they asked the girls to identify themselves, their answers were clearly confused. This exemplifies how entrenched biases can be: There were very few researchers who were women. So, as a field, researchers (even the few researchers who were women) weren't yet valuing girls' voices and experiences. Instead, everything was framed around looking at pictures of boys. It would take a larger influx of women into the field to start to shift the frame of reference. (Johnston and Johnson, "Searching for the second generation of American women psychologists," *History of Psychology* 11, no. 1 (2008): 40–72, doi:10.1037/1093-4510.11.1.40.)

about violent interactions with White people, it is adaptive for Black children to have more advanced concepts of race, as not being clear about race can have dire consequences. Modern research has confirmed this: White children, especially when they live in majority White communities, lag behind Black children in understanding their racial identity, often saying inaccurately, "I have no ethnicity, I'm just normal."[17] In my own research, White children, in contrast to children of color, struggle to define race and ethnicity and what it means to be White.* White kids have the privilege of not paying as much attention to race because they are not the target of racial discrimination and violence and because Whiteness is treated as the cultural norm.†

Although the projective test—children pointing to pictures of people or dolls in response to questions—was a technique that would eventually become a common strategy in studies with young children and would change the field of developmental science (I have used it dozens of times, in many of the studies described later in this book), it was first going to have a more immediate impact on another set of researchers. Because at the same time Ruth was publishing this research as her master's thesis at Columbia, Kenneth Clark, a recent psychology graduate of Howard University, arrived at Columbia, ready for his own doctoral work. He was newly married to Mamie Clark, who was beginning a master's program in psychology at Howard. Ruth's work was the inspiration for Mamie's thesis.[18]

In her 1939 thesis, Mamie Clark wrote that Ruth's research was important, but it simply had too few Black kids in the study (only seven) to be able to draw any solid conclusions.[19] So, to broaden the voices that were heard, Mamie individually interviewed 150 Black three-, four-, and five-year-olds from the WPA nursery schools, private nursery schools, and some kindergarten classes of segregated Washington, DC. She would arrive at the nursery schools around ten in the morning. According to her detailed case notes, she interviewed the kids between their storytelling time and art, and between their rest period and when they started washing up for lunch. For the first two mornings at any given school, she would stay all morning,

---

* When we ask White children, "What is your ethnicity?" we sometimes get humorous errors. We have had one White child label their ethnicity as "Kentuckian." One child said "archeologist." Some children have said "human."

† We can see this trend in businesses, as well, for example, in beauty stores where aisles are labeled "Ethnic Hair" and restaurant guides naming "Ethnic Food," which ignore that all people have an ethnicity.

playing with kids, helping the teachers, becoming a familiar and friendly face, and giving herself the opportunity to observe what the children were doing and who they were playing with. Once the kids were comfortable with her, using the techniques devised by Ruth, she gave them the choice test, with the kids pointing to the picture that looked like them. At the segregated schools in DC, slightly more than half of the Black children (more so the five-year-olds than the three-year-olds) picked the Black child as looking like them. About 40 percent picked the White child as being most similar.

Although these techniques were based on Ruth's work, Mamie went a step further than Ruth and focused on the differences *among* individual Black children, not just the group differences *between* Black and White children. First, she trained teachers in integrated nursery schools in several New York cities (White Plains, Mt. Vernon, and New Rochelle) on how to interview both the White and Black children there. Then she compared the 150 Black children she interviewed in segregated preschools in DC to the forty Black children interviewed in integrated preschools in New York. She found that the Black children from the segregated schools identified with the Black child in the picture more often than the children from the integrated schools did. She said that the northern, integrated Black children were more "confused" and "do not evidence the same identification in terms of skin color as compared with children in the segregated group." Then she analyzed children's answers based on whether the child had light-brown skin, medium-brown skin, or dark-brown skin.* She found that the boys with dark-brown skin were really consistent in picking the Black child as looking like them, and it was primarily the light-skinned boys who were picking the White child as "like them" the most often.

Taken together, these were important discoveries about how complicated it is for children to learn about race. One reason it is complicated is because Black as a race is arbitrary, not determined by actual skin tones, but some perception of "one drop" of African ancestry.† For the light-

---

* There is no description of how she determined skin color. In a Clark and Clark publication based on this study, they noted, "It seems necessary to state that the experimenter who actually worked with the children was medium-brown in skin color. This was fortunate in that it tended to neutralize the probable influence of an extremely light or dark investigator on the responses of the children." (K. B. Clark and M. K. Clark, "Skin color as a factor in racial identification of Negro preschool children," *The Journal of Social Psychology* 11, no. 1 (1940): 159–169.)

† This is a faulty premise from the start, given that in our evolutionary past, all humans

skinned children in Mamie's study, their "confusion" about their racial group may have reflected some of the social advantages that come with being light-skinned in the United States (similar to the confusion White children show), but also could have been a literal answer to the question of who they most resembled. Race only has the meaning that we ascribe to it culturally, and does not always map onto physical differences—that lack of direct connection to precise physical characteristics is complicated for children. Mamie's study also pointed to how important environment was for teaching children about the meaning of race. Segregation forced young Black children to have an increased awareness of their race because, by sorting the world along racial lines, it made racial distinctions salient and more culturally important—and that makes it easier for children to learn.

Once Mamie finished her master's thesis, she, along with Kenneth, followed up on this research by comparing the racial attitudes of Black preschool children in three towns in segregated Arkansas (including Hot Springs, her hometown) to the racial attitudes of preschool children in integrated Springfield, Massachusetts. They tweaked their methods slightly, using dolls instead of pictures. They showed 253 Black children, ranging in ages from three to seven, four dolls: two had pale skin with yellow hair, and two had brown skin with black hair. The Clarks asked the children to "give me the doll you want to play with," "give me the doll that is a nice doll," and "give me the doll that looks bad." Their hypothesis was that children should want to play with the dolls that look like them and should think the dolls that look like them are nice.

Instead, among their sample of Black children, 67 percent of the children said they wanted to play with the White dolls, 59 percent of the children said the White dolls were the nice dolls, 59 percent said the Black dolls look bad, and 60 percent said the White dolls are the "nice color." They concluded that Black children were showing a concerning preference for White people. It actually took several years before they published that research, as Kenneth said, "We left those data in our files for about two years before we published them [in 1947], because we were disturbed." They found it disturbing to "see the children in the test situation placed in this terrible conflict of having to identify with dolls to which they had previously ascribed negative characteristics."[20] What really hurt them, Kenneth reported, "were

originated from Africa. The heart of this distinction is what *Plessy* was about too, as he was only one-eighth Black. (*Mapping Human History* by Steve Olson.)

these literally defenseless human beings being required to incorporate into the developing sense of their own being their consciousness of rejection."[21]

After their publication, the doll studies, as they came to be known, made a splash even outside of academic journals. A picture of a Black child selecting a White doll, with a bespectacled Kenneth Clark standing in the background, was even featured in the July 1947 issue of *Ebony* magazine in a photo essay by famed photographer Gordon Parks. By the time the doll studies were cited in "A Social Science Statement" and in the *Brown* Supreme Court case, they were iconic. The dolls are now in the National Museum of African American History and Culture.

THE STAYING POWER OF THE DOLL STUDIES

Because the doll studies received so much attention, many researchers jumped in to conduct their own versions. In May of 1969, sociologists Joseph Hraba and Geoffrey Grant revisited them, the title of their paper, "Black Is Beautiful," foreshadowing their finding. They noted that, by 1969, the Clarks' observations had been replicated by other researchers across a variety of settings at least ten times—but there were encouraging signs that they wouldn't always produce the same results. Hraba and Grant's research took them to five integrated public schools in the very White community of Lincoln, Nebraska. They found that, even though a majority of their sample of Black kids had White friends (they had to, as Lincoln schools had fewer than 2 percent Black students), a majority of the kids preferred the Black doll, said the Black doll was nice, and so on—the exact inverse of the Clarks' study. In the 1990s, psychologists Myra Burnett and Kimberly Sisson from Spelman College revisited the doll studies yet again. Among their sample of Black children from Atlanta, most children showed no consistent pattern in their preferences. Only a minority of children preferred the White doll consistently, and as children got older, their positive associations with being Black strengthened. These more modern takes on the doll studies suggested that the stranglehold of racial stigma of the Jim Crow era was loosening a bit, and Black children were starting to internalize the 1960s positive black-consciousness movement, often called the "Black Is Beautiful" movement.[22]

In 2010, Anderson Cooper and CNN filmed a new version of the doll study, this time designed by Professor Margaret Beale Spencer, a highly respected professor of urban education at the University of Chicago. Under her direction, CNN redid the doll study with Black and White children from affluent and low-income schools around New York City and Atlanta. Just like with Ruth's study, and Mamie's study that followed, albeit with some tweaks that reflected more modern advances in research methods, these children were asked to "show" Spencer the nice child, the good-looking child, the bad child, the ugly child. Spencer and CNN found that Black children were no longer showing a preference for the White child in the image. They weren't showing strong preferences for Black children either. Rather, the Black children in this study looked pretty bias-free. The White children, however, were a different story. They showed strong biases favoring White kids—they rated the White child as the nicest and most attractive, and the Black child as the one who was bad and ugly.

All of this bias was captured by the CNN cameras. Some of it was shown to the children's parents and the CNN viewers. The White parents were horrified that their children looked so biased. As one White mom noted, though her tears, "She never asked me about skin color before." Like many parents, she had assumed that if her child was not talking about skin color or race, then she must have never noticed it. Her comment gets at what is ultimately one of the most important legacies of those early studies by Ruth Horowitz and Mamie Clark: even though children are not talking about race, they still notice and hold biases about race.

Those early studies, beyond contributing to major changes in school segregation through cases like *Brown*, also inspired the next generation of researchers to study children and bias. Although the methods would change, the samples of children would get bigger and more diverse, and the conclusions would get more nuanced, this early work led us to what we know now. *That* is what the rest of the book is about.

THE SCIENTISTS BEHIND THE SCIENCE

RUTH HOROWITZ AND MAMIE CLARK ————————

Researchers who study bias in children were often shaped by bias too—experiences of being discriminated against can be the inspiration for later scientific study. Ruth Horowitz and Mamie Clark are two examples of researchers who pioneered the study of bias in children, while facing the same types of biases.

Ruth Horowitz's life,* both personal and professional, was shaped by the anti-Semitism of the day. She was born in New York City in 1910 to Polish and Russian immigrant parents who spoke mostly Yiddish. When Ruth was only five years old, a successful Jewish businessman in Atlanta, Leo Frank, was lynched—a lynching that breathed life into rising anti-Semitism in the United States. Frank's murder coincided with increased activity of the Ku Klux Klan and, not coincidentally, led to the creation of the Anti-Defamation League.[23] But in New York, like many children of immigrants, Ruth was embarrassed by her immigrant parents. They were not the intellectual elite that Ruth aspired to be. According to her daughter, "She repudiated them"[24] and worked hard to lose any trace of an accent. Given the entrenched anti-Semitism in America before World War II, it is easy to understand why Ruth thought the best way to be successful was to distance herself from her Yiddish-speaking parents. Both smart and ambitious, Ruth worked hard in high school, earning a scholarship to Cornell University. Cornell was a perfect fit for what she wanted: a prestigious Ivy League school that was close enough to home to be attainable, but far enough away in Ithaca to get some distance from her immigrant parents. She powered through school, graduating when she was only twenty years old, earning a master's degree in psychology from Teachers' College of Columbia University only two years later. After earning her master's, she met and married Eugene "Gene" Horowitz, a social psychologist and another child of Jewish immigrants.

Ruth's daughter, Wendy, said that her mother's research was motivated by a lifetime of "always siding with the underdog, the down-trodden, the stigmatized."[25] And there was plenty of stigma to study at the time: The

---

* Very little research has been written about Ruth Horowitz, so the information here is based on family interviews, her own writings, and the documents kept in the family home.

same year Ruth published her pioneering research using projective tests to investigate racial identity, World War II began in Europe. Public opinion polls at the time found only 39 percent of Americans thought Jews should be treated like other people. The eugenics movement, which argued for the genetic inferiority (and forced sterilization) of Jewish people and people of color and was embraced by Hitler, actually began in California before migrating to Germany. European Jews were unsuccessfully seeking asylum in the United States and the United States was not interested in getting involved in the war.[26] Gene's older brother was a doctor and lost work because he was Jewish. So, while Ruth's interest in studying how Black children learned to identify their race was informed by her own experiences with bias, it was perhaps because of that bias that she seemed to lean away from her own Jewish background. The Horowitzes didn't celebrate Hanukkah, and two weeks after her second daughter was born, Ruth and Gene changed their last name from Horowitz to Hartley* to sound "less Jewish" and protect their growing family from growing anti-Semitism.

Born in 1917, Mamie Clark† forged a path that both parallels and diverges from Ruth's. Mamie was born in segregated Arkansas to educated and relatively affluent parents.[27] But even with a physician father and more opportunities than most other Black girls in Arkansas, Mamie found that "in 1934 [the year she was headed to college], a southern Negro aspiring to enter an academic college had relatively few choices."[28] When she was only sixteen, she enrolled in Howard University in Washington, DC. Her plan was to major in math and minor in physics. But her first year at Howard was not as smooth as she'd anticipated. She said, "I didn't know what I'd missed, so when I got to college, I enrolled in courses like physics and mathematics, literature, things like that. And then when I got in these classes, I realized that people were saying things I'd never heard of before."[29] Mamie was in a bind facing many bright Black students of that time, especially the ones coming from the segregated South: She was attending one of the most

---

* Gene's older brother had previously changed his name to Hartley too. (Throughout this book, I use the name they used at the time of the reference. For example, all of her research on projective tests and children's racial attitudes is published as Horowitz).

† Considerably more information is available about Mamie, so the information here is based on published interviews with her, profiles written about her, and a long oral history interview she provided Columbia University. In addition, her master's thesis and notes are in the library of Howard University, and her extensive writing, correspondence, and collaboration with Kenneth is housed in the Library of Congress.

prestigious historically Black universities in the country, but was coming from a segregated public school system in Arkansas that did not prepare her for the new environment.[30] She said, "the school [I attended in Arkansas] was poor, and later I realized how much we didn't learn."[31] So, Mamie took extra classes at Arkansas State University in the summer to catch up with her peers at Howard.[32]

Not long after she started at Howard, Mamie Phipps met the self-assured senior Kenneth Clark, who happened to be a psychology major. They spent the summer after her first year with her back in Arkansas taking summer classes and him working in New York, writing letters to each other almost every day.[33] According to Mamie's letters, she was not thriving in the math department, as the professors were indifferent at best and hostile at worst, to female math majors. Kenneth urged her to become a psychology major. From that beginning, their personal relationship and their shared studies were connected. She even began working in the psychology office to help pay for school. In 1936, when she found out she had received a tuition scholarship and didn't need to keep working in the office, Kenneth begged her to stay, "We . . . really need you in the Psychology Dept. Really—we'll both be terribly disappointed if you were to leave us now. We just couldn't take it. Who would correct our examination papers for us? Who would type our letters to the Dean for us? Whom could we talk to all day? Whom could I get to help me in Experimental Psychology?"[34] They married two months before she graduated magna cum laude in 1938.

The summer after she graduated, Mamie worked at the fulcrum of the legal battle to desegregate schools. She worked as a secretary in the law office of Houston and Houston—the law office of William LePre Houston and his son, Charles Houston, the architect of the NAACP strategy to desegregate schools. The NAACP had recently won the first legal challenge to desegregate schools in *Pearson v. Murray*. The battle to end segregation was beginning, and the NAACP attorneys were starting to build a strategy. Thurgood Marshall, having only graduated Howard Law School five years before, was in and out of the office.[35] She later recalled that this experience "was the most marvelous learning experience I have ever had—in the whole sense of urgency, you know, of breaking down the segregation."

Newly married, with her husband working on his PhD in psychology in New York, Mamie stopped working in the legal office and went back to Howard in the fall semester, enrolled in a master's program. When Kenneth told her about Ruth's work on the racial identification of children, Mamie was inspired.[36] She said, "I was very much taken with it. You know, it was just something that really gripped me. So I was fairly single track about this subject, of the development of consciousness of self, and the point at which children became aware of themselves and aware that they were black."[37] Her research built on Ruth's work, and she even thanked the Horowitzes in the acknowledgment of her master's thesis: "Dr. Eugene L. Horowitz, Columbia Univ, and Mrs. Ruth E. Horowitz for their many kindnesses and constructive criticism."

When she later attended Teacher's College at Columbia University for her doctorate, Mamie was the only Black student in the department. The only other Black student the department had ever had had been Kenneth, who had recently graduated. Her doctoral advisor was Henry Garrett, who was an expert in an advanced statistical test called *factor analysis*. Her historical interest in math guided her choice, and she picked an advisor based on what she could learn about statistics. But Garrett was also a segregationist and eugenicist who believed that Black people were genetically inferior to White people, and had (wrongly) assumed Mamie would get her degree and head South to teach in a segregated Black high school. But Mamie "wanted the challenge"[38] and fiercely decided to show him how smart a Black student was—which she did. The last time she would see Garrett would be 1952, when they were testifying on opposite sides of the segregation case of *Briggs v. Elliott*.[39]

On parallel tracks, both Ruth and Mamie had earned their PhDs from Columbia before WWII ended. They'd also each managed to have two children apiece while working on their dissertations. By the time each woman had a doctorate in hand, their husbands were both new professors down the street in the newly formed psychology department at the City College of New York. But at that early point in their research careers, the gender, racial, and religious biases of the time began to produce insurmountable obstacles. Although a quarter of women psychologists who earned PhDs in the period between women's suffrage in 1920 and the women's movement of the late 1960s never married, the other three-quarters did marry at some point. Of those women who married, more than half married other psychologists.[40] Ruth and Mamie were classic examples of that pattern: They married men who researched and cared about what they cared about, who valued their intellect and contributions. The problem was that most universities had antinepotism rules, so once the husband was hired, it was against university policy to hire the wife. So, the wives were relegated to affiliated positions, often labeled as research associates or instructors.

So, Ruth did what many women did, cobbling together positions teaching, conducting research, and providing psychological testing of children for a Jewish adoption agency. This jumping around was common for women, especially Jewish women, trying to find university positions.[41] When speaking about finding jobs in those years, another research psychologist, Mary Henle, said, "In addition to the scarcity of positions, anti-Semitism was prevalent and often explicit. Thus, if I did not get a job for which I applied, I could not know for sure whether I lacked the qualifications, or whether it was because I was a woman or Jewish."[42] Although Ruth managed to conduct some research here and there, she stayed frustrated for much of her career.[43]

Mamie learned a similar lesson to Ruth. "Although my husband had earlier secured a teaching position at the City College of New York, following my graduation it soon became apparent to me that a Black female with a Ph.D. in psychology was an unwanted anomaly in New York City in the early 1940s."[44] With her newly earned doctorate in hand, Mamie took a job as an analyst for the American Public Health Association, as the only Black person on staff, analyzing nursing records. That lasted a year, as it "was a ghastly experience," plus "it had nothing to do with children." By 1945, she was working for the private agency Riverdale Home for Children, to provide psychological testing for the homeless Black girls they served. After a year, she was fed up both with these jobs and with the inadequate mental health resources available to minority children. When she failed to get existing agencies to step up their services, she got a $936 loan from her father, rented a basement office in the Paul Dunbar Apartments in Harlem, and the Northside Testing and Consultation Center was born.[45] It was later renamed Northside Center for Child Development, and Mamie would be its director until her retirement in 1979. Northside, currently one of New York's oldest and most respected mental health agencies, serves more than four thousand children and their families.[46] Both Ruth and Mamie, although their research careers were cut short because of gender, racial, and religious biases, made contributions that would influence generations of researchers that came after them.

Like many of the biases discussed in this book, the discrimination they faced wasn't one person's fault; it was systemic and structural. Gene Horowitz was supportive, as "his entire life was about supporting Ruth."[47] Kenneth

Clark tried to make sure Mamie got credit, saying, "Mamie and I were into the racial preferences and identification of Negro student research . . . It was an extension of her master's thesis on racial identification of Negro students. That was the thing that came to be known as the 'Dolls Test' that the Supreme Court cited. The record should show that was Mamie's primary project that I crashed. I sort of piggybacked on it."[48] But Mamie never really got the credit due to her, and Ruth definitely was erased from the narrative. That is what bias continues to do: it makes achievements harder to reach and then renders those who made such achievements nearly invisible.

7 Racial Bias into the New Century

A Snapshot of Bias in Schools, Neighborhoods, and Social Media

> *Kenneth, there is only but so much lawyers can do.*
> *After we get the law clear, the hard job begins.*
> —Thurgood Marshall[1]

Researchers, building off the foundation of studies that informed *Brown*, have spent the past eighty years looking at the impacts of different levels of diversity in schools and how friendships and conflicts are born in those hallways. The idealists of the civil rights era might have imagined racially integrated schools, where all children had equal access to resources and developed friendships across racial lines. But more modern researchers have found that that is often not the case, and the racial makeup of the school drastically impacts the experience for students. Furthermore, in the new century, modern kids and teens aren't just interacting with diverse peers in their own school—they're online as well. The metaphorical schoolyard is worldwide and anonymized, but the biases are strikingly similar.

WITHOUT LEGAL OVERSIGHT, SCHOOLS RESEGREGATED

Although the *Brown* decision desegregated schools, the courts were purposefully vague about giving schools a timeline for when they needed to integrate, telling them to act with "all deliberate speed."* Many on the court worried that such a drastic shift in racial policy would be met with backlash, that southern schools "would never be a party to allowing white and negro to go to school together" and even worried that "our order may result in public schools being abolished."[2] Capitulating to southern Whites, the Justices didn't push integration too hard, wanting to "give them plenty of time" and "put off enforcement awhile." They were more concerned with the violence† and "prolonged social disorder" threatened by White people than the education of Black students.[3] Because the justices and the local politicians tasked with enforcing the new policy valued White voices more than voices of color, and refused to address questions of how and when to implement integration policies, there were few real changes to the biased status quo.

As a result of that vagueness, a decade passed before schools in all of the seventeen states that had mandated segregation made changes. In Summerton, South Carolina, integration didn't happen until 1965, more than ten years after *Brown*. In Topeka, Kansas, integration began in 1955, but the school district was sued again in 1979 because their schools were almost entirely resegregated. In Washington, DC, White families fled their now-integrated school districts, and by the 1970s, the DC school district was 90 percent Black students. In Prince Edward County, Virginia, the White community was so opposed to integration that all twenty-one public schools were completely shuttered from 1959 to 1964. All of the White children went to private schools, financed by segregationists from throughout the South—"people who sympathized with what [those in the White community] were attempting to do."[4] Black students were left to fend for themselves. Some left the county or even the state to attend schools near relatives—but most simply went without an education. In short, while *Brown*

---

* Even this vague timeframe wasn't handed down until the courts reconvened the following year in 1955 (in the continuation of the case called *Brown II*).

† A North Carolina poll at the time found that 193 of 199 local police chiefs predicted White violence in reaction to school integration (Klarman, 2004).

was intended to reduce school-based biases, the toothless lack of enforcing *Brown* led to far greater acts of bias.

It took President Lyndon Johnson signing the Civil Rights Act in 1964 for significant change to happen at the national level. The Civil Rights Act, which outlawed segregation in all public places, declared that schools would lose federal money and face lawsuits from the Justice Department if they didn't desegregate. The threat of losing money was a powerful motivator, and combined with the flurry of congressional acts and court cases that continued to push for and enforce the desegregation of public schools throughout the late 1960s and 1970s, major changes in many of the nation's school districts followed.* By 1970, schools in the South were the nation's most integrated.[5]

Unfortunately, though the Johnson administration (1963–1969) ushered in massive reforms to desegregate schools, court cases on desegregation in the 1970s† often ruled that schools did not have to desegregate unless racist intent could be proven, and decisions largely protected the suburbs from desegregation requirements.[6] With the Reagan administration (1981–1989), many of the earlier efforts to integrate were shelved, and by the 1980s, the desegregation efforts of the previous two decades were collapsing. President Reagan's first budget defunded the only remaining major federal program that focused on desegregation and race relations.[7]‡ In court cases, the Department of Justice began taking the side of school districts rather than students.[8] Not long after Reagan's vice president, George H. W. Bush, was elected president, and one administration seamlessly rolled into the next (1989–1993), the Supreme Court decided in *Board of Education of Oklahoma City Public Schools v. Dowell* (1991) that a school district no longer needed legal oversight of their school zoning to force integration as long

---

* In 1971, for example, the Charlotte-Mecklenberg (in North Carolina) school district was ordered by the Supreme Court to proactively integrate, rather than just avoid segregation, so they pioneered the practice of busing students across the district to even out the racial makeup of each school.

† The last major Supreme Court case expanding desegregation was the 1973 *Keyes v. School District Number 1*, Denver, when the court found that the Denver Public School system had engaged in de facto segregation of Black and Latino students for fifteen years and violated the Equal Protection Clause. The same year, however, the Supreme Court case *Milliken v. Bradley* ruled that school districts were not obligated to desegregate unless it had been proven that the lines were drawn with racist intent.

‡ According to Le (2010), "President Reagan has been accused of conducting a wholesale assault on civil rights, and school desegregation was no exception."

as they "reasonably" and in good faith tried to remedy past segregation to the extent that it was "practical."[9]* In other words, the courts were saying, "Do your best, without trying too hard, and we will leave you alone." Just like in the aftermath of *Brown* almost forty years before, the courts backed off and decided to let schools regulate themselves—despite ample evidence that such a system did not work.

As a result, in 1988, racial integration peaked.[10] That was the year Black and White students were most likely to walk the same hallways at school, have the same access to books, and be taught by the same teachers. But when courts changed tactics, schools did too. In a study that compared schools released from court orders to desegregate and schools not yet released from court oversight, it was clear that the segregation levels in dismissed districts grew steadily (relative to comparable schools in districts with oversight *and* relative to their own segregation levels prior to dismissal). This shift toward segregation was apparent within three years of no longer having legal oversight, and the schools continued to grow more segregated for at least ten years after.[11]

Even as the courts were ignoring schools' levels of integration, the population of students nationwide was growing more diverse. When *Brown* was decided, most students in the United States were either White or Black, with Black students representing about one-eighth of the student population (White students made up the bulk of other students, representing about 80 percent of public school students).[12] But based on the US Department of Education statistics, between 1965 and 2016, the number of Latino students in US public schools increased by eleven million, from 5 to 26 percent of the total student population (partially because of a major shift in immigration policy in 1965[13]); at the same time, the number of White students decreased by eleven million, from 79 percent to 48 percent of the student population (largely because of lower birth rates among White people[14]). During that same period of 1968 to 2016, the number of Black students increased by only one million, maintaining a steady 15 percent of the student population over time.[15] For Asian American students, the numbers have always been much smaller compared to other groups but are growing, as they represented only 0.5 percent of students in 1968 but 5.5 percent of students in 2017.[16]

---

* Based on this case, the legal term for a school to have eradicated segregation is called "unitary status." Schools that have reached unitary status are thought to no longer need government oversight.

Beyond that, since 2000, people have been allowed to choose "multiracial"* when filling out the US Census, and by 2017, more than two million US children were categorized as multiracial, which represents about 4 percent of all students.[17†] Although these numbers suggest that schools should be richly diverse because the nationwide population of students is richly diverse, in fact, most students are educated in a resegregated reality.

Since segregation has been steadily growing since legal oversight of school integration was stopped, between 1988—the peak of desegregation—and 2016, the percentage of schools that enroll almost all (90 to 100 percent) Black and Latino students has tripled from about 6 to 18 percent.[18] Latino students are the most segregated of all students (in other words, the group most likely to go to school with same-ethnicity peers), and Black students are more likely to attend schools with Latino students than with other Black students.[19] Asian students, representing a larger share of the school population than ever before, are also constantly faced with being a minority in their school, as they are more likely to attend a school with mostly White students than anyone else.[20] White students, though, because of the overall increase in the number of Latino and Asian students in public schools, have experienced a different trend: they are less likely to go to an almost all-White school than they would have been back in 1988, when more than one-third of schools nationwide were almost all White. By 2016, that number had dropped to 16 percent. This means there are more American public schools now that are almost entirely a mix of only Black and Latino students than are almost all White students. Granted, the average White student goes to a school that is still a majority White (about 70 percent White‡), but they attend school with more diverse classmates than ever before. For White students, although they are still attending schools with a majority of same-race peers, the

---

* Throughout the history of the US Census, mixed race categories (like mulatto, quadroon, and octoroon) have occasionally appeared, albeit briefly (*Shades of Citizenship. Race and the Census in Modern Politics.* Melissa Nobles).

† All of this, of course, varies by region of the country. In the West and Southwest, Latino students surpass White students as the single largest group of students. Also included in this is the 1 percent of students who are American Indian (Frankenberg et al., "Harming Our Common Future: America's Segregated Schools 65 Years After Brown").

‡ If schools were perfectly integrated, White students would attend schools that were 48 percent White, given that is their share of the student population.

changing demographics of schools means, more so than ever, they have to learn how coexist with diverse peers.

As would be expected from the history of race relations in the United States, there are of course regional differences in school integration. Because of a history of legal sanctions, the South is the *least* segregated region for Black students in the country (where they are more likely to go to school with White students than anywhere else). Black and Latino students are much more likely to be heavily segregated (in combination Black-Latino schools) in New York, Illinois, Michigan, and New Jersey—places where there is more residential segregation and a strong focus on school choice.[21] Even within regions, there are differences in segregation. Although the stereotypical suburb used to be a product of White flight, when White families left the centrally located schools that were newly integrating in search of "better" (but really Whiter) schools and neighborhoods, suburban rings around the cities are now predominantly non-White.[22] Suburban schools now are larger than before, filled with an increasingly diverse student population where many students are living in poverty, but where students are taught by primarily White teachers who often have little training in teaching a diverse group of students.[23]

One reason that schools, despite being unable to legally segregate, still have such high rates of de facto segregation is that that families still live in neighborhoods that are highly racially and economically segregated. When schools were no longer required to proactively integrate (for example, by busing students to neighboring schools or redrawing school boundaries with integration in mind), segregated neighborhoods fed into and created segregated schools. In school districts that focus on school choice, including districts with a high number of charter schools, many White parents chose to send their children to predominantly White schools.

Another reason that segregation has risen is because individual school districts were only banned from segregating their students *within* their district; there were no policies in place about segregating *between* districts, so that's where segregation has risen.[24] In other words, a loophole around district-level laws and policies is to simply create a new district. Now, in communities where school districts are smaller and more numerous, where individual districts encapsulate fewer neighborhoods, parents can more easily move to the school district they want. Instead of moving cities, parents only have to move streets. Instead of primarily White schools and primarily Black schools within a school district, there are now many cities where the White school district butts up against the Black school district. For example, in Los Angeles County alone, there are eighty independent school districts, carved out of pockets of what could have been the LA Unified School District. When I was a professor at UCLA and conducting research in schools in Los Angeles, we would have to recruit students from multiple school districts just to get a diverse sample. We would drive the ten miles from Santa Monica's district, where 50 percent of the students are White, 29 percent are Latino, but only 7 percent of students are Black, to Inglewood's district, where 39 percent of students are Black and 57 percent are Latino, but only 0.5 percent are White.

A lesson has emerged in the last half century: integration does not happen by accident or because of people's goodwill. When there is no explicit plan or legal oversight to enforce integration, schools drift back into segregation.[25] That is where we are now—and it is a lesson that we must learn when implementing future policies. Reducing the systemic biases of segregation requires explicit laws, enforced implementation with financial penalties for not complying, and continued oversight. In a society in which bias has existed within individuals and institutions for generations, biases are the default. Changing that default requires constant vigilance.

WHERE THERE IS RACIAL SEGREGATION, THERE IS ECONOMIC SEGREGATION

An important reason that we must limit the racial segregation of schools is because segregated schools—due to the deeply entrenched structural biases that link race and poverty*—are economically unequal. In 2017, half of the schools that were made up of 90 to 100 percent Black and Latino students were also 90 to 100 percent low-income students.† This is a huge problem when it comes to educational equality because most schools depend on local property taxes for their funding and revenue streams. Low-income

---

* The 2010 US Census reports that about one in eight White families live below the poverty line, in contrast to one in four Black families and one in three Latino families.

† This stands in sharp contrast to schools that educate mostly White or Asian students. Among the schools that are overwhelmingly White and Asian (with 0 to 10 percent Black or Latino students), only 4 percent of schools have 80 percent or more students living in poverty.

houses and apartments are clustered together, middle-class houses are clustered together, and richer houses are clustered together (often expressly to avoid the low-income and middle-class neighborhoods). But taxing million-dollar mansions to fund a school produces considerably more money for that school than taxing $100,000 shotgun houses or rented duplexes. So, when the school draws from a high poverty area, they have a comparably smaller tax revenue stream—leading to students who are lower-income attending poorer schools. As a result, in the 2015–2016 school year, predominantly non-White school districts received $23 billion less than predominantly White school districts, despite having the same number of students, purely because the students that those districts served were themselves poorer.[26] In the five hundred school districts of New Jersey, for instance, predominantly non-White school districts received $3,400 less per student than the predominantly White districts. Essentially, the racial disparities of the pre-*Brown* era (when the state of Alabama spent thirty-seven dollars on the average White student and seven dollars on the average Black student) have been adjusted for inflation.

Beyond official funding from tax revenue, schools serving primarily low-income students also receive fewer financial contributions from parents. Low-income parents are less able to donate to school fundraisers, which can easily tap parents for several hundred dollars per year across various campaigns (such as Jump Rope for Heart, Scholastic Book Fair, and BoosterThon, to name just the ones I donated to this year for my own elementary school child). This means that parents without discretionary money are less able to contribute to funding "extras" that public schools are always in need of, like computers, new books for the library, and new playground equipment. During my own research, I went to speak to a principal at a low-income, predominantly Black and Latino elementary school in Los Angeles. The principal was delayed for our meeting because the school didn't have enough copy paper for the students to do their class work or take tests. Instead, the principal, metaphorical hat in hand, had to call businesses and ask for help. As I waited outside his office for our meeting, the principal was on the phone with a national office-supply store asking for donations. At the same time, a school only two miles away, primarily White and firmly upper-middle class, was putting the finishing touches on its brand-new computer lab.

The educational inequalities associated with attending a school with inadequate funding are compounded by the effects of poverty at home. When there is less food available at home, children are more in need of the free breakfast and lunch offered at the school. Low-income families are more likely to have unstable housing options, and may have to move several times throughout the school year. A principal at a low-income Black and Latino school I work with now struggles to help her students succeed because one in five have no stable housing and move so often they can't keep books with them, making homework almost impossible to complete.[27] And when children do have trouble academically, low-income families struggle to supplement their education with expensive school supplies, tutoring, or extracurricular activities.

Altogether, because Black and Latino families are more likely to live in poverty than White families (due to centuries of structural and individual biases), when communities funnel Black and Latino students into segregated schools, they are ensuring that they are also attending underfunded and inadequate schools. Because those schools lead to fewer opportunities for students, it makes it extremely difficult to ever escape the poverty trap—and a biased system is recreated for the next generation.

THE SEGREGATION EFFECT

Modern segregation also exacerbates the other existing biases and inequalities that perpetually permeate schools. We see this "segregation effect" when we look at teachers. The training and experience of the teachers, and relatedly, how much teachers are paid, are lower at schools where Black and Latino students make up the majority of students.[28] For example, 10 percent of teachers in schools with a high percentage* of Black and Latino students are in their first year of teaching, compared to only 5 percent of teachers in schools with low Black or Latino student enrollment. Across the nation, as the percentage of Black students increases at a school, the percentage of teachers with full licensure decreases and percentage of new teachers increases.[29]

We also see the segregation effect when we look at the curricula. Segregated schools with a high number of Black or Latino students offer fewer advanced-placement and honors-level courses.[30] Only one-third of such schools offer calculus, whereas more than half of the schools with low Black

---

* Researchers typically use 90 percent of the student body as the threshold for what is considered highly segregated.

and Latino student enrollment do. Segregated Black and Latino schools are similarly less likely to offer physics, chemistry, and algebra II—trends which eerily parallel pre-*Brown*-era schools.

We also see the segregation effect when we look at the long-term impacts on children. Discipline is harsher and more punitive, and the rate of expulsion is harsher at schools with high Black and Latino enrollment.[31] Dropout rates are significantly higher in segregated and impoverished schools—nearly all of the two thousand "dropout factory" high schools are highly segregated by race and poverty. These differences don't disappear once students leave school. Black students who attended desegregated schools for at least five years earn 25 percent more than their counterparts from segregated settings. By middle age, the same group was also in much better physical health.[32] That's what happens when income is higher and educational opportunities are opened to students.

WHERE TEACHER BIASES COME IN

Biases can determine which schools children attend and the resources of that school, but biases also exist within schools that appear integrated because, even if a school is integrated in the hallways, individual classrooms rarely are. It begins in elementary school, where teachers frequently place students into small groups based on performance or reading levels[33] (71 percent of fourth-grade teachers sort students into reading groups by ability level[34]). By high school, this morphs into students being assigned to either the remedial English, general English, honors English, or advanced-placement English (80 to 85 percent of US high schools have ability grouping at the course level).[35] Students' high school pathways typically stem from middle school, when their teachers make recommendations for which courses the students should take. Teachers consider the students' grades, standardized test scores, and their own judgments. The problem: Every single one of those factors is susceptible to racial, ethnic, gender, and social-class biases.

Meta-analyses show that teachers hold their highest expectations for their Asian American students, followed by White students, then Black and Latino students.[36] Teachers asked more questions and provided more encouragement to their White students than their Black and Latino students, and sent their Black and Latino students to the office more often than their White students. Other studies have drilled down into that bias, showing it appears early and is driven by White teachers (Black and Latino teachers tend to assess their students equally across race and ethnicity).[37] Based on national data, by kindergarten, White teachers assess White students more positively than they assess Black and Latino students, even when researchers controlled for student behavior and their scores on standardized tests.[38] This same-race bias is there even when the assessment is seemingly objective, like when kindergarten teachers were asked to evaluate whether their student "produces rhyming words." All of this is concerning because, not only do teacher assessments drive academic placement, but also when researchers looked at students' test performance over time, they found that the teachers' assessments were a stronger predictor of later scores than students' own previous test scores. This is because when teachers have different expectations for students, they treat them in accordance with those expectations. Different expectations can cause teachers to provide higher-quality education to students from whom they expect more. Children often then internalize those expectations and perform accordingly.[39]

I have seen this happen repeatedly in my own research: when students detect discrimination at school, they begin to feel like they don't belong there.[40] That feeling of not belonging, in turn, leads to more negative attitudes about school, lower grades, and even dropping out. The opposite is true too: when students feel they are valued at school, they have more positive expectations for school, maintain stronger motivation to do well, stay in school longer, and earn better grades—even when controlling for how well students had previously performed in school.[41] It's a pattern that is repeated in populations as varied as third-, fourth-, and fifth-grade Latino children across an entire school district to Black college students at a predominantly White university.[42] In other words, teachers' biases aren't just about assigning some students lower grades than others; they are also about making students feel devalued and unwelcome.

Since 80 percent of US teachers are White, when teacher assessments are a key factor in deciding which classes students take, White students receive a consistent advantage.[43] As a result, not surprisingly, we see that academic tracks are highly racially segregated. Black and Latino students and students from immigrant families are more likely to be placed in lower academic tracks (such as special education and remedial class)[44] and less likely to be placed in gifted classes,[45] even when the students are matched on prior achievement scores, family background, and their own reports of how much effort they give in school. If Black students attend a segregated elementary school, the odds of being assigned to a college-bound academic track are even lower.[46]

This process of assigning Black and Latino students to lower academic tracks makes sure that students who start out marginalized stay marginalized. These lower academic tracks, instead of providing high-quality education to offer help to people who need it with the end goal of raising the academic success of those students in need, employ less qualified teachers who offer less challenging instruction using less effective teaching techniques.[47] Plus, if students don't have access to certain subjects, they get locked into that lower track and can never advance out of it. A self-fulfilling prophecy emerges: if a student wants to go to college, but was assigned to a lower track, they may not have the opportunity to take advanced classes; that lack of preparation, combined with lower-level instruction, will put them at a disadvantage on the ACT or SAT, making it harder to get into college (and making scholarships less likely, thus making college more expensive). So, the decision to sort the student into a lower academic track renders college less attainable, regardless of the student's motivation, effort, and abilities.

All of this shows that biases in the classroom affect Black and Latino students from the beginning of school, from poorer assessments by White teachers in kindergarten, which contributes to lower scores in fifth grade, which leads to biases in course placement in high school, which makes higher education less likely. And these educational inequalities translate to profound tangible economic inequalities, as people with college degrees earn (on average) $500 more per week than people with only a high school diploma,[48] which adds up to more than $1 million over a lifetime of working. Biases in education have a snowball effect, and can seem small when introduced early on, but accumulate and build up to be much larger later.

DIVERSE KIDS TOGETHER IN ONE SCHOOL

Segregated schools lead to greater and more entrenched inequalities, but *integrated* schools usually lead to better academic outcomes, lower prejudices, and more diverse friendships for children. However, the exact nature of the integration really matters, and it matters differently for different kids.

One important distinction is whether the focus is on students' academic opportunities or their social and emotional connections. Studies show that students at majority White schools, regardless of the student's race or ethnicity, show higher test scores, more academic engagement, and more focus on schoolwork than students at other schools.[49] These findings, though, are less about the actual race of the students and more about largely White schools having more funding, higher-quality and more-engaging education, and higher teacher expectations (because of all the biases described above).[50] But for all students, as the percentage of same-race peers increases, so too does their emotional attachment to school.[51] That's why, despite these higher performance metrics, when students of color attend largely White schools, the odds of them actually liking school go down.[52] There is often an academics/emotions trade-off for non-White students: they may get positive social connections *or* academic rigor (with a menu of college-track courses at well-funded schools), but they rarely get both.

Ideally, all students should have access to high-quality education (regardless of their race or the income level of their families) and have enough same-race peers and teachers at their school to feel a strong sense of belonging at school—but going to school with similar peers isn't enough. When the school is attended by just two racial or ethnic groups, an "Us vs. Them" dichotomy emerges.[53] Schools with complete integration of two racial or ethnic groups (a 50-50 mix) show the highest rates of racial segregation in friendships, where, for example, the Black kids are only friends with other Black kids and White kids are only friends with other White kids. In my own research with Latino elementary school children across nineteen different elementary schools—where the schools ranged from having only five or six Latino kids in all of third and fourth grade (out of hundreds) to having 60 percent Latino students—I found that the Latino students at schools where Latino students and White students were close to an even mix experienced *more* ethnic bias and discrimination from their peers than kids at other schools.[54] The 50–50 mix with only two groups seemed to exacerbate the "Us vs. Them" distinction and the White kids responded by being more biased.

However, once a school moves beyond two groups, they finally see the maximum benefits of heterogeneity—true diversity. For example, if there are four ethnic groups equally represented at the school, each ethnicity represents only one-fourth of the school. *Everyone* is in the minority. That diversity seems to bring security. In surveys of two thousand students at eleven public middle schools, researchers found that as schools, and classes within the schools, became more truly diverse (where multiple ethnicities were equally represented), students of color felt safer, less lonely, and had higher self-worth.[55]

Attending a diverse school can also help buffer students from the effects of day-to-day discrimination, as researchers found when looking at evidence that 97 percent of Black teens had at least one experience with discrimination over a single two-week period. For teens who attended either a mostly Black school or a mostly White school, they felt sad and depressed the day after they experienced discrimination.[56] But if they attended a school with no clear racial majority—where there was an equal "balance of power"—they didn't show an increase in sadness after experiencing discrimination. Rather, their diverse school provided a buffer that seemed to limit the negative emotions that can result from discrimination.

Not only do diverse schools help students of color feel safer and more connected to school, but they are also good for reducing children's racial prejudices.[57] There have been thousands of studies that have shown that having contact with people from different groups (dubbed "intergroup contact" by researchers) is the single best way to reduce prejudice. In 2006, researchers conducted a meta-analysis with 713 independent samples, taken from more than five hundred different studies, with people from thirty-eight different countries.[58] Time and again, contact with people from different racial or ethnic groups reduced prejudice—even when nothing else did. Not all intergroup contact is equal, though. Intergroup contact needs four things to effectively reduce bias:

1. Groups need to have equal status.
2. The group members all must share a common goal.
3. They all have to depend on one another to achieve that goal.
4. The contact must have institutional or authority figure support.

Think about a football team (I show my college classes *Remember the Titans* to highlight this effect):

1. Every player wears the same uniform (which reinforces a shared status and identity).
2. Every player has the same ultimate goal (to win the game).
3. Every player depends on their teammates to achieve that goal (even the best quarterback needs a good wide receiver to catch the ball).
4. And it is all sanctioned (sometimes aggressively) by the coach (an authority figure).

The end result is that individuals from different backgrounds bond and form their own in-group, rising above previous distinctions.

It works because, as humans, we like what is familiar (think about favorite comfort foods: they usually stem from childhood and feel very familiar). Exposure to peers from a different group breeds greater familiarity with that group, which, in turn, lowers uncertainty and anxiety. So, feeling more familiar and less anxious helps us like individuals more, which then gets generalized to liking the group more.

Diverse schools enable the potential for greater intergroup contact, which facilitates children and teens developing cross-race friendships.[59] There has to be an *opportunity* to make friends of a different race at school. One additional wrinkle, though, is that segregation imposed by the school bleeds into children's social interactions. As a result, cross-race friendships happen less in schools that academically track their students.[60] After all, it is hard to make friends with peers who never share the same class, especially when those classes vary in status and prestige. Still, diverse schools, and any cross-race friendships that develop, are overwhelmingly beneficial for lowering the prejudices of White students[61]—but cross-race friendships function in much more complex ways for ethnic-minority students.[62]

For cross-race friendships to be positive, those friendships need to be supportive for *both* members of the friendship. When a student of color experiences discrimination, they may want to talk to their friend about it. Unfortunately, researchers have shown that talking about an experience of discrimination with a White friend is not always helpful, and can even cause students of color distress, especially if the friend downplays the experience or suggests they are taking things too seriously.[63] Having to convince your friend that the discrimination was real and hurtful causes its own hurt. As a result, even though cross-race friendships are marked by less conflict and disagreements than same-race friendships, Black adolescents who only have White best friends show lower self-esteem and more depressive symptoms than those with only Black best friends.[64] At the same time, having diverse friendships can engender a greater sense of belonging for ethnic-minority students at predominantly White schools.[65] So, again, students of color are often forced to make trade-offs—though there is the potential to have the best of both worlds. In short, so long as the White friend appreciates and believes the lived experiences of racism—and isn't the only source of support—White friends can be good.

The growing diversity of American school children is a positive shift, as long as those diverse kids actually go to school together. When schools or classes are divided along racial or economic lines, students don't get the many benefits of interacting with people who differ from them: they don't get to learn new things they might not have otherwise had exposure to, they don't get to develop more advanced perspective-taking abilities and empathy, and they don't get to develop complex social identities that cut across racial lines.[66] For White children, they have fewer options for friends and are less likely to be successful in a diverse workplace in the future. For students of color, they are more likely to suffer from educational inequalities that accumulate over their lives. Diversity in schools can, should, and must benefit all children.

INTERRACIAL INTERACTIONS DON'T JUST HAPPEN IN SCHOOLS

Children and teens don't just have social interactions at school; the school-yard is now infinite. In 2020, more than 95 percent of teens had a smart-phone. According to Pew Research Center, in 2018, 45 percent of teens between thirteen and eighteen said they were online "almost constantly," and another 44 percent said they were online several times a day.[67] According to the same poll, most of this time is spent on social media, which despite their near-obsessive attention to their phones, teens feel mixed about—as about one-third of teens say they think social media is mostly positive, noting that it helps them connect with their friends and family.[68] But one in four feel that it can also be negative, with the largest percentage of those teens saying it brings bullying and gossiping—replicating the problems often found in hallways. In 2018, 85 percent of teens were on YouTube, and 72 percent were on Instagram. That had changed from just 2014, when the majority of teens were on Facebook—until Facebook was taken over by parents and grandparents. By the time you read this sentence, the most popular platform will probably be something completely different.* But while it is hard for researchers to stay on top of the positive and negative effects of social media because the landscape changes so quickly, no one doubts that the ubiquity

---

* In 2021, TikTok is popular, and Discord is growing in popularity among teens. But usually by the time adults can assess social media, teens have already moved to the next platform.

of social media is profoundly shaping youth—and it's almost certain that even the most secure Wi-Fi can't keep out bias.

Just as bias appears at schools, students also experience bias on social media, in text messages, and in online games. Researcher Brendesha Tynes asked teens about their online experiences with discrimination, and found that 71 percent of Black teens, 71 percent of White teens, and 67 percent of multiracial teens have witnessed same-race peers being victimized online at least once, and 29 percent of Black, 20 percent of White, and 42 percent of multiracial youth have experienced discrimination themselves online.[69] Even though it is online, the effects of this bias are very real. Teens who had experienced online racial discrimination were more depressed than those who hadn't.[70] Many were also more anxious—although the teens who felt really proud about their racial group and had a "strong sense of belonging" to their racial group were buffered from some of this anxiety.[71]

Online bias isn't always directed at any specific teens—sometimes it is viral. From all the way back to the 1991 beating of Rodney King, documented on a video clip that was replayed on a near-continuous loop on the new twenty-four-hour news channel, CNN, to every time a viral video clip of a police officer kneeling on the neck of George Floyd or Eric Garner, or shooting Walter Scott, is shared online, teens, because they are online "almost constantly," are seeing these modern-day lynchings "almost constantly." The effects of seeing these viral videos differs based on who is viewing it. They may be helpful for White people to help them understand the viciousness of racism—it makes it harder to deny and sweep it under the rug. Indeed, these video clips of George Floyd may have played a pivotal role in motivating White people to join the Black Lives Matter protests in the summer of 2020.[72] But when Black teens repeatedly watch the murder of someone from their own racial group, and then see it happen again a few months later, and then again a few months after that, the psyche is harmed. Indeed, the more often teens see these traumatic events online, the more depressed they are and the more post-traumatic stress disorder symptoms they show.[73] On the other hand, viral hashtags such as #BlackLivesMatter and #SayHerName allow communities of color to emotionally bond together, to feel a sense of solidarity, and to feel empowered.[74] Online experiences *are* real-life experiences, especially for youth, and the effects of online bias—and online solidarity—on their psychological well-being is also real.

For children of color, it has been a long fight for access to an equal education, but because courts and policymakers have not actively addressed racial disparities in education, equality in education has yet to be realized for a large proportion of youth. Biases in zoning and funding lead to schools that are separate and unequal. This is compounded by the individual experiences of bias that happen within the classroom and happen online in an increasingly connected virtual world. With this combination of structural and individual biases, the end result is an unequal education (whether measured by the number of years in school or the quality of that education) and unequal experience that continues to perpetuate racial and economic inequalities across generations.

THE SCIENTIST BEHIND THE SCIENCE

BRENDESHA TYNES ————————————————————

Brendesha Tynes,* a professor of education and psychology at the University of Southern California, recognized that as websites and social media platforms have proliferated, so too have opportunities for teens to experience bias. Her cutting-edge research teaches us about how race and racism play out in the lives of youth on social media, but her own journey to that scientific expertise was informed by her own race and others' racism.

Brendesha grew up in Detroit in the 1980s. She said, "Growing up in an all-Black city and going to predominantly Black schools helps you develop a sense of self, and a love for your Blackness that you can't get when you grow up in places where you might be the only Black person. Being in a Black city profoundly shaped who I am, the research that I do. My sense of creativity and innovation with my research is all because I had this foundation." When she went to high school, she was surrounded by high achieving students at predominantly Black Cass Technical High School. It was a college-prep high school that asked students not whether they were going to college, but where they were going and what they were majoring in.

Brendesha knew she was drawn to STEM and planned to major in computer science. To prepare, while she was still in high school, she took an advanced summer program at the University of Michigan. But walking across the Ann Arbor campus one day, a group of white teenage boys piled into a car shouted racial epithets at her, stopping her in her tracks. In that moment, she realized that that place was not going to be *her* place. So, despite her ambition, she settled on the smaller and less prestigious Michigan State. As she says, she quickly got "bored," knowing she had settled for less than she wanted. She left school not long after starting.

Disenchanted with academics, she entirely changed directions. She left Michigan and moved to New York to pursue modeling. An Armani runway show under her belt, she traveled to Paris, going where up-and-coming models go to expand their portfolio. At one of her auditions, she was told "we're not hiring Black models this season"—as though having Black models

---

* The information about Brendesha is based on my own interviews with her, published interviews, and her publications. In full disclosure, I have known Brendesha since she was a graduate student at UCLA and served on her dissertation committee.

was like wearing last season's pants. She decided then that her career "would no longer be up to other people's racism or opinions." Instead, she promised herself, "I would be known for and make a living off of my brain and not how I look."

Back in New York, she was accepted to Columbia University, where she dove into history, concentrating on African American studies, documenting in her senior thesis African Americans' perceptions of themselves based on 1930s WPA narratives—giving voice to the contemporaries of Kenneth and Mamie Clark. If her race was going to affect how others saw her, she thought, she would at least be an expert in it. But she was drawn to how children developed and she didn't want to only analyze archival records. So, she moved to Chicago and earned a master's degree in learning sciences at Northwestern. She knew she was getting closer to what she really wanted to do but wasn't quite there yet.

She realized, "Whatever I do, I want to make an impact on how Black children see themselves." She also understood—from both her research and her own life experiences—that it's impossible to study learning without attention to cultural influences. So she changed course again, but this time decided to make her own path. She moved to a doctoral program at UCLA and wove together her own training in anthropology, neuroscience, statistics, education, and psychology. She was part of a research lab, led by Professor Patricia Greenfield, that was beginning to look at how people were expressing their sexual identity in chat rooms. As a research assistant, she was tasked with coding the comments people were leaving online. What glared back at her from the pages of chat room conversations was how often youth were talking about race. With that epiphany, all of her experiences and training (even her early interest in computer science) coalesced behind one idea.

In 2003, she began her dissertation. It is hard now to remember a time before social media, but back then, while some teens were on Myspace, mostly teens were just hanging out in chat rooms. Almost no one thought much about the influence of social media. Merriam-Webster would not even add "social media" to their dictionary until 2011, citing 2004 as its first usage.[75] Some people were making the argument that online interactions would be "beyond race" because it was pseudo-anonymous and would bridge the divides that exist in de facto segregated real lives.[76] But Brendesha believed that social media was where teens were actually being themselves—and recognized that anonymity might just lead to more explicit bias. So, epitomizing good research methods by relying on the data, she looked at what teens were actually saying online. She popped into monitored and unmonitored chat rooms and "listened in" for thirty-minute intervals in the late spring and early summer of 2003. She found that teens mentioned race in some way in thirty-seven of the thirty-eight chat rooms and regularly "used verbal markers of race as common ground on which to start conversations." She immediately knew that race was all over their interactions.

This research was Brendesha's starting point, and her prescience in knowing the role social media would play in the lives of teens was rewarded. Now the founding director of the Center for Empowered Learning and Development with Technology at USC, her research focuses on how teens experience racism and discrimination online, what the effects are on their mental health, and how they cope with it when it occurs—research that she continues to feel a personal connection to. When she conducted a study about the impact on youth of seeing viral videos of violence toward Black people, she said, "We decided to do this study because, anecdotally, I'd talk with my friends about how hard it is to see these videos. And if I, the director of a whole center on this, was having trouble coping, then of course kids were having these challenges." With her work, she continues to draw on the lessons she learned in Detroit and as student of Black history, saying, "At the center I direct, the mission is to center the lives of people of color—their history, their culture, their development." And *that* is ultimately how social scientists effectively fight bias—by centering voices that have long been ignored.

8 Border Walls, Travel Bans, and Global Pandemics

Political Rhetoric, Immigration Laws, and Bias Toward Children of Immigrants

If we didn't allow other people to move here, people
would not have pizza, pasta, and quesadillas.
—Seven-year-old boy when asked about American immigration policy

When we start trying to unravel bias, it becomes clear how often children are the collateral damage to adults' biases and biased policies. That was true with policies about racial segregation, and it is clear now when we look at recent immigration policies and the political rhetoric around immigration. The children of immigrants, especially Latino, Arab Muslim, and Asian children, are subjected to both stereotypes and prejudices that individuals hold, plus biased policies about immigration. Operating together, those two threads of biases collectively make the children of immigrants feel othered and excluded. Children are listening to that political rhetoric, absorbing the messages, and developing definite ideas about who is included in the American in-group and who is not.

POLITICAL RHETORIC FALLS ON LITTLE EARS

Children might not be voting in elections, but that doesn't mean elections, candidates, and campaign slogans go unnoticed. Children are always listening. In the presidential election of 2016, much of the political campaigning and rhetoric was focused on immigrants and immigration policy. Although not new to 2016, anti-immigrant and anti-Mexican rhetoric was on full display when then-candidate Donald Trump brought stereotypes and discrimination toward Mexican Americans to the forefront of his campaign. "When Mexico sends its people, they're not sending their best. They're bringing drugs. They're bringing crime. They're rapists. And some, I assume, are good people," he said, though it was clear that the last sentence was not one of his core beliefs. While on stage at the University of Nevada at Las Vegas during the final presidential debate before the election, when describing his anti-Mexican immigration policies, he said, "We have some bad hombres here, and we're going to get them out."[1] Much of this anti-Mexican rhetoric coalesced, in terms of proposed policies, around his oft-discussed promise to build a wall (on Mexico's dime) along the two-thousand-mile border separating Mexico from the United States. He cited building the wall so many times that "build the wall" became a popular chant at his campaign rallies.

Even I, a researcher on how children learn stereotypes from our culture, was surprised by how much children were learning about immigrant bias from the 2016 election. I was part of a research team, led by Meagan Patterson and Rebecca Bigler, who interviewed elementary school children both before and after the election. We talked to mostly seven-, eight-, and nine-year-olds who lived in communities that spanned the political spectrum throughout Texas, Washington, Kansas, and Kentucky. We asked children, "What have you heard in the news about Donald Trump/Hillary Clinton?" and "Have you learned anything from school, or TV, or at home about Donald Trump's/Hillary Clinton's ideas for changing laws in the United States?"

The single most commonly mentioned detail about either candidate concerned Trump's policies about immigration (mentioned by more than 40 percent of the kids). One out of every third child we interviewed specifically mentioned "the wall" when asked what they knew about the candidates. The wall may have been particularly easy for children to talk about, as the immigration "policy" is so basic that it is literally and figuratively concrete enough for a child to understand. However, not only were they keenly aware of Trump's plans for the wall, they could tell that Trump held biased attitudes toward people from Mexico. For some kids, this was personal, one girl saying she doesn't "want Mexicans to move out because my mom is Mexican." But even beyond that, regardless of their race or gender, children said things like the following:

- "I don't like Donald Trump because he said he's going to build a wall, and I don't want a wall around our country."
- "He's mean to Hispanic and Latino people. He wants to build a wall so that no one comes and invades."
- "Trump is going to kick out the Mexicans."
- "Donald Trump doesn't want immigrants to come into the US, and he doesn't want people from Mexico to come into the US."
- "He wants to build a wall and make them pay for it. That's racist."

Even comments about Clinton were really comments about Trump's wall and immigration policy: "Hillary would stop the building of the wall," "She doesn't want Mexicans to move out," and as one Black eight-year-old girl supposed, "Hillary Clinton wanted to be good to all people, even Mexican people." It was clear from the phrasing of their answers that children's ideas weren't simply based on messages handed down from parents, but picked up from snippets of news and overheard conversations.

Nationwide, some children were listening and using that rhetoric as inspiration for their own biased behavior. That was evident from the behavior featured in a viral Facebook video from a week after the 2016 election— eight seconds of White children at Royal Oak Middle School in Michigan, encircling a Latino student, chanting, "Build the wall. Build the wall."[2] In a Southern Poverty Law Center survey of more than two thousand educators around the country in the days immediately after the election, they found similar trends.[3] One teacher in Oregon reported that a student was "asking two different Latina students if they were ready to move back to Mexico now that Trump is president." Another teacher, this one from Massachusetts, said, "One student went around asking, 'Are you legal?' to each student he passed. Another student told his Black classmate to 'go back to Haiti because this is our country now.'" A Tennessee teacher said, "Students have told me they no longer need Spanish (the subject I teach) since Trump is sending all the Mexicans back." It wasn't as though children were making random, nonspecific anti-immigrant comments; they were literally referencing Trump.

Beyond the middle school chants of "build the wall" and anecdotal taunts, this anti-immigrant messaging led to nationwide increases in ethnic bullying. Researchers happened to capture the before-and-after of a presidential election when they passed out surveys about racial and ethnic bullying to about 155,000 seventh and eighth graders in Virginia in 2013, 2015, and 2017.[4] They found that students reported more ethnic bullying and teasing in the spring of 2017 than the previous two (pre-Trump) years—and not in patterns that could be explained away by randomness. In 2017, students who lived in counties that voted for Trump were more likely to be bullied and to witness their peers being taunted because of their ethnicity compared to students who lived in Clinton-supporting counties. And it wasn't because those counties were meaner or more aggressive in general. In 2015, *before* the Trump campaign and election, before all of the biased rhetoric, there were no differences in the amount of bullying and ethnic teasing between the blue and red counties.[5] Simply put, the political rhetoric trickled down to schools, and students took it out on their peers.

When our leaders—the supposed adults "in charge"—make biased comments, it normalizes bias and encourages those who hear those comments to express those same biases. Children, who are clearly listening, are especially vulnerable to this influence, as they are looking to adults for guidance on how to act and to treat others. When that guidance is filled with stereotypes and prejudice, it is no wonder that children often emulate those traits.

BIASES TOWARD IMMIGRANTS AS OTHERS

Around the world, biases against immigrants have been in place as long as there have been immigrants. Although it is easy to point to President Trump's influence on stirring up ethnic biases toward Latino immigrants, he was just leaning into the biases and stereotypes that were already there.

Five years before President Trump was elected, I documented this well-entrenched anti-Latino immigrant bias in elementary school children.[6] Specifically, I showed a group of five-to-eleven-year-old White children pictures of a White American man, a Black American man, an Asian American man, and a Latino American man,* and said, "This person was born in

---

* I didn't actually label the race or ethnicity of the person when talking to the children, because that inherently makes some groups sound less American; for example, by

America. How American is he?" (This method of showing children pictures of people and asking questions about them is a direct descendent of the doll studies). Exactly like White adults respond when asked the same questions, White children rated White Americans as the most American, rating them as "very American."[7] Black Americans were rated as less American than White Americans, and Asian Americans were rated as less American still. Finally, Latino Americans were rated as the least American of all the groups, rated as "just a little American," even though every single man was described as being born in the United States.

We then went a step further and read them short vignettes about different families of immigrants. There were families from Mexico, China, and Great Britain, plus a White American "immigrant" from a small town in Kentucky and a Black American "immigrant" from Los Angeles, who were all described as "having just moved to our city for work." Each vignette was followed by questions that sought to examine children's biases and stereotypes. Like many adults,[8] children seemed to hold the most negative biases against Mexican immigrants. For example, children rated wanting to go to school with the children who moved from Kentucky and Los Angeles more than the Mexican child. In addition to that, the White American kids in our study had the most rigid boundaries over who could be a "true American," made the biggest distinction between how American White people versus Latino people are, and most wanted to avoid Mexican immigrants.

Research shows over and over, with all biases, humans prefer the groups they belong to, the in-groups.[9] "Like me" is best. When groups keep tight boundaries on who is allowed into the in-group and who is kept out (by thinking of Whites, but not Latinos, as part of the American family), biases against those out-group individuals are maintained.[10] But not only are Latino Americans and Latino immigrants often perceived to be "other than," but they are also often dehumanized.[11] Not only are they *not* an American, but they are also *not* a human. For example, in 2018, when asylum seekers approached the US border,* President Trump tweeted

---

having the word "Asian" in an ethnic label, the non-American parts of identity are made salient. Instead, I simply pointed to faces of people who were prototypical of those ethnicities. Although Latino American men can be White or Black or neither, the Latino American man in these photos had light-brown skin and black hair.

* Most were fleeing violence in the Northern Triangle, the triangular region in Central American of El Salvador, Guatemala, and Honduras that usually tops international lists of most homicides.

that we don't "want illegal immigrants, no matter how bad they may be, to pour into and infest our Country." By using *infest*, a term more appropriately applied to termites or fire ants than people, Trump was effectively indicating that these people were no better than bugs. This mindset led to the more than 474,000 asylum-seeking minor children and their families,[12] plus about seventy-six thousand unaccompanied children, being caged in detention centers and sleeping on concrete floors penned off behind chain-link fencing typically used in dog kennels, with little medical care or nutrition.* The tendency to other and dehumanize people deemed different from "us" has very real consequences for immigrant children, especially when individuals' biases support, or at least allow them to ignore, biased and dehumanizing policies.

Even though many people were upset about the detention of so many children away from their parents, I don't think there was nearly the level of outrage that would have happened had they been "American" children. Imagine what the national reaction would have been if almost one hundred thousand White children from Connecticut, who had seen their parents assaulted, captured, or murdered, were locked in a giant warehouse without medical care or mental health services. My assumption is that a different, more child-focused solution would have been quickly found. But the othering of Latino people led, as othering *always* does, to dehumanization—which led to prejudice, discrimination, and violence—at the individual level, at the community level, and at the policy level.

LATINO IMMIGRANT CHILDREN'S EXPERIENCES WITH OTHERS' BIASES

Latino children and teens—whether they are immigrants or not—having to face anti-Latino bias isn't new. In 1968, researchers Norma Werner and Idella Evans recreated Mamie Clark's doll studies with Mexican American preschoolers. They found "the same problems of identification and preference arise for the Mexican American child as for the Negro child and perhaps for all children whose personal characteristics differ from those of the majority."[13] Unfortunately, not much has changed in the past sixty years.

---

* The current policies are very much in flux with the Biden administration, and as of mid-2021, change has not happened as quickly as many would have liked.

One of the specific biases Latino immigrant children have to contend with is the strong link in the public, as discussed in chapter 3, between being a Latino immigrant and being "illegal."[14] The societal stereotype in which immigrant equates to illegal establishes a negative social mirror that distorts how immigrant children see themselves. Children, especially younger ones, often absorb the negative associations with the word "immigrant." For example, Carola Suárez-Orozco asked Mexican, Dominican, Haitian, and Chinese immigrant students to fill in the blank: "Most Americans think that most [people from the respondent's birthplace] are _____." Sixty-five percent of children filled in the blank with a negative term. Most commonly, children wrote the word *bad*, but many children elaborated, saying things like "Most Americans think that Mexicans are lazy, gangsters, drug addicts that only come to take their jobs away." Many children wrote words associated with being a criminal, and many wrote words related to incompetence or contamination, like "We are garbage." Not all children did this equally: less than half of Chinese youth used a negative term to fill in the blank, but 75 percent of Mexican, and 82 percent of Dominicans and Haitians—those whose immigration status was constantly linked to illegality in public discourse—did. In another study with Mexican immigrant children, only twenty-five of the 110 children interviewed said they were proud of their immigrant heritage; but when they were asked about being proud of their Mexican heritage, that was a different story.[15] More than 75 percent of the children were proud of where they came from—they just didn't want the immigrant label.

Beyond that specific bias focused on illegality, Latino youth in the United States (similar to the experiences of youth from other immigrant backgrounds) repeatedly experience bullying and teasing because of their ethnicity or their presumed inability to speak English. Dozens of studies with children and teens, where each person is given a list of possible experiences and asked if those things ever happened to them, shows that about 60 percent of Latino children and adolescents regularly experience some type of ethnicity-based discrimination at school.[16] Some of this comes from peers at school, usually some type of verbal insult, as I found in my own research in 2006.[17] When examining six elementary and middle schools in Los Angeles, I found that such experiences with bias at school were common. For example, one nine-year-old Mexican American boy reported about his classmates, "They call me lots of names because I am Mexican." Another Mexican American child from the same school stated, "In PE class, a lot of kids call me a beaner." Other researchers have shown that nine out of ten Mexican American teens have experienced ethnic discrimination at least once from other kids at school, about one in five have experienced it often, and seven in ten experienced post-traumatic stress symptoms as a result.[18]

When researchers interviewed more than five hundred Puerto Rican elementary and middle school students in Boston, they found that about 12 percent of the younger students felt like they had been treated badly or unfairly because of their language, color of their skin, or where they came from.[19] The rates were much higher when they asked the middle schoolers—about half had personally experienced discrimination over the past year. When asked what Whites think about Puerto Ricans, the middle schoolers said things like the following:

- "They think that we are not intelligent, that we live in dirty houses and are all on welfare."
- "We are all bad; drug dealers, thieves, and gangsters. There is no future for us, and we have babies at a young age."
- "They say we are pigs, always buying Goya products . . . and that we are not really a culture."
- "Savages, dirty thieves."
- "That we drive 'low riders,' carry knives, and that we all sell drugs."
- "Whites think that Puerto Ricans are uneducated, poor, lazy, and low class."

Latino students also experience bias from their teachers. Researchers, focusing on first-generation Dominican students, second-generation Puerto Rican students, and first- and second-generation Central American and Mexican students, have found that Latino students report that teachers have low expectations of them and often assume their English is poor. They also report that their teachers stereotype them as troublemakers and unfairly blame them when something goes wrong, or, conversely, that they are treated as invisible by the teachers.[20] Not surprisingly, Latino students who experience ethnic discrimination, especially when it comes from teachers and peers, are particularly likely to feel like they don't belong at school, do worse on tests and in class, have lower self-esteem, and are at greater risk for developing depression over time.[21] Ethnic bias espoused by teachers is a particularly important reason Mexican American teens gave for dropping out of high school.[22] However, teens who felt a strong connection to their ethnicity (who noted, for example, that they attended events that have helped them learn more about their ethnicity and reported having a clear sense of what their ethnicity means to them) had higher self-esteem and were less depressed.[23] Feeling a strong connection to being Mexican American helped protect the young people from other people's biases.*

Latino students—who are racially diverse, have a range of immigration histories, and come from a range of national backgrounds—face biases from kids at school, from teachers, and from politicians. The national dialogue that focuses on the legality of immigration, that assumes that all Latino immigrants are here without authorization, and then by extension that Latino people can never be "real" Americans, leads to damaging biases in children's lives. While navigating these individual biases, children have also had to navigate an ever-changing policy landscape, as the political decisions made affect their lives and those of their families.

FOR LATINO CHILDREN OF IMMIGRANTS, A "CULTURE OF FEAR"

Beyond the anti-immigrant biases and rhetoric, the past two decades have seen policy changes that have dramatically altered the lives of immigrant children. Through all of these twists and turns of policy changes, an overarching fear for immigrants and children of immigrants has always been deportation.[24] Living under a constant threat of deportation creates a "culture of fear" that leads to a cascade of stress, poverty, and worry about family instability.[25]

Children feel the effects of deportation fears before they are even born.[26] Epidemiologists found this when they focused on the small town of Postville, Iowa, in 2008, where a meat-processing plant was the site of the single largest federal immigration raid in US history.[27] Almost 10 percent of the town's population, mostly Mexican and Guatemalan immigrants, hundreds

---

* This powerful protection that comes from having a positive ethnic identity is not specific to being Latino, but is true for all racial and ethnic minority groups. For example, having a positive and strong sense of Black identity is also an important buffer for Black teens too. The same applies for Asian teens. (T. Yip, Y. Wang, C. Mootoo, and S. Mirpuri, "Moderating the association between discrimination and adjustment: A meta-analysis of ethnic/racial identity," *Developmental Psychology* 55, no. 6 (2019): 1274).

of them the breadwinners for their families with young US-born children, was arrested. Fear of follow-up home raids permeated the small town, with many Postville families avoiding their homes, sleeping in churches, or leaving the town completely.

The researchers looked to Iowa birth certificate data for the thirty-seven weeks following the raid and for the same thirty-seven-week period from the previous year. The found that the infants born to Latina mothers *after* the raid had a 24 percent greater risk for low birth weight compared to similar infants born the year before. This greater risk of low birth weight showed up for both the foreign-born Latina mothers *and* the US-born Latina mothers, showing that fear generalizes and spreads, even to women who weren't directly under threat. There were no greater risks for poor birth outcomes for the infants born to non-Latina White mothers, apparently because worries about deportation didn't hit so close to home.[28] The mothers' fear led to their babies being born underweight because the stress affected their neuroendocrine balance, "leaving infants vulnerable to a dysregulated endocrine environment." This matters because infants born underweight are more prone to infections in their first few days, and are more vulnerable to motor, social, and language delays and learning disabilities compared to healthy weight babies. So from the very beginning, some babies are born with an extra hurdle to jump because of the fear and discrimination their mothers faced while pregnant.*

This biological hurdle is compounded by the additional hurdles of poverty facing children of immigrants, as three-quarters of immigrant children with an unauthorized immigrant parent live at or near the poverty line.[29] One in three children with an unauthorized immigrant parent routinely experience food insecurity, which puts children at an even greater risk for poor health.[30] When local immigration enforcement is active in a community, the rate of food insecurity increases by about 10 percent.[31] This is particularly challenging because one in four undocumented immigrant children have no health insurance themselves.[32] So, they are less likely to get the medical attention they need although health problems are more likely when children are undernourished.

---

* Other studies have shown similar low birth weight effects with pregnant women with Arabic-sounding names immediately after the September 11 attacks (Diane S. Lauderdale, "Birth outcomes for Arabic-named women in California before and after September 11," *Demography* 43, no. 1 (2006): 185–201).

Children's worry about a parent being taken away is a universal fear that transcends public policy, national borders, or skin color, as one of the most necessary features of childhood is a strong emotional connection to family.[33] Since the 1950s, developmental psychologists have shown—in thousands of studies—that one of the foundational building blocks for a healthy, well-adjusted life is a stable and secure attachment to a parent or caregiver.[34] But for immigrant children, the fear that their parents will be deported and they will be separated colors much of their childhood. These fears are widespread, felt most acutely by children of undocumented parents (about 4.5 million US-citizen children have an undocumented parent[35]). Their fear is understandable, since deportation has dire consequences: If both parents are deported, children are forced into foster care. If only one parent is deported, families are often forced into more extreme levels of poverty, move from place to place, often requiring children to move out of their existing school.

Because children may not fully understand immigration policy, fear around deportation can be broad and spread out to all situations.[36] Interviews with immigrant children have shown that children begin to associate all immigrants with illegal status, regardless of their own legal status or the status of the parents.[37] For example, one mother explained that her eleven-year-old daughter, who was nine years old when she came to the United States from Mexico, "has a great fear of the police. She was afraid that they would send her back to Mexico. She used to evade people so they would not ask her questions because she was afraid that they would ask her for a social security number . . . she started biting her nails out of worry."

Teachers notice this culture of fear that children live in. In a survey of 760 schools across thirteen states, almost 85 percent of teachers said that their students were noticeably scared of ICE deportations.[38] One high school administrator from the South noted, "They are not thinking about college, or the test next week, or what is being taught in the classroom today. They are thinking about their family and whether they will still be a family; whether their family will remain intact." A school administrator in the Northeast said, "Several students have arrived at school crying, withdrawn and refusing to eat lunch because they have witnessed deportation of a family member. Some students show anxiety symptoms . . . All of this impacts their ability to focus and complete work, which further affects them academically." As one teacher, in a survey by the Southern Poverty Law Center right after the 2016 election, noted, "The highest achieving boy in my class has shown particular concern about the upcoming election. He is Hispanic and is always asking me questions about, and worrying . . . He has told me he can't sleep at night because he is worried that his family will be sent away in November . . . It is completely and utterly heartbreaking to see a 10-year-old so concerned with such adult issues."[39] Carrying these adult worries around robs children of their childhood.

For the children who are separated from their families, through either deportation or separation at the border, there will be lifelong damage done to children's psychological and physical health.[40] Their brain development is altered, and they show greater anxiety, depression, and behavior problems, as well as symptoms of post-traumatic stress disorder. Children have a harder time learning, as fear and hypervigilance take up most of their cognitive effort. These factors all contribute to the fact that, as multinational comparisons have shown, countries with supportive integration policies for immigrants are more likely to have child populations with better overall health and mental health indicators than those with less supportive approaches.[41] With this mind, we need to push this country toward collectively caring about the health and well-being of immigrant children as much as other "American" children. Currently, the biases that consistently other immigrant children are preventing that from happening.

WIDESPREAD ISLAMOPHOBIA AND THE STEREOTYPE OF A TERRORIST

Xenophobic and anti-immigrant rhetoric isn't limited to Latino immigrants. Another big target is Muslim or Arab Americans, and as a result, their children as well. In 2017, there were approximately 3.5 million Muslims living in the US, 1.3 million of them children.[42] There are also approximately 3.5 million Arab Americans in the United States.[43] Keep in mind, these are two different, albeit overlapping, groups, as people can be from Middle Eastern or Arab League countries (roughly the countries of Northern Africa and Western and, at times, Southern Asia) and not be Muslim and people can be Muslim and not from that broad region. More than a billion people in the world are Muslims, but fewer than 15 percent of Muslims worldwide are Arabs. Despite that reality, people have applied stereotypes without attention to accuracy and the prototypic image of an "Arab Muslim" has fused together in public perception. Also, because accuracy never interferes with a stereotype, people who are Sikh, Hindu, and Buddhist, and people from India and Southeast Asia, all get lumped together despite their different religious affiliations or countries of origin.

Islamophobia, the broad label applied to bias toward Muslims or anyone that "seems" Muslim, is not new. In the year after the 9/11 attacks, the FBI declared that hate crimes toward Muslims and Arabs in the United States increased by 1,700 percent. Since 2015, there has been a renewed focus on banning Muslims coming to the United States. This surge began, in part, as a reaction to both the terrorist attacks in Paris in November 2015, attacks that the Islamic State of Iraq and the Levant (ISIL) laid claim to, and to the mass shooting in December of that year in San Bernardino, California, by Syed Rizwan Farook and Tashfeen Malik. Around the same time, large numbers of primarily Muslim refugees and asylum seekers, fleeing the conflicts in Syria, Afghanistan, and Iraq, one-fifth of whom were children, made their way across Europe and many sought asylum in the United States.[44] With this large wave of displaced persons, the number of refugees worldwide reached the highest levels since World War II,[45] yet polls at the time found 60 percent of American voters believed that the United States should not accept Muslim Syrian refugees into the country because they posed a "national security threat."[46] Because they held the image of a Muslim refugee as being "threatening," many people ignored the fact that more than half of those refugee applications were for children.[47]*

Combined, those 2015 events—and the media coverage of them—led to an increase in anti-Muslim political rhetoric. For example, in December 2015, then-candidate Trump told MSNBC that he would "strongly consider" shutting down mosques in the United States as part of his response to the recent attacks.[48] When Bill O'Reilly asked Trump if there was a "Muslim problem" in the world, Trump responded, "Absolutely. I mean, I don't notice Swedish people knocking down the World Trade Center. There is a Muslim problem in the world, and you know it, and I know it."[49] He later doubled down with Fox Business Network, saying: "We're having problems with the Muslims, and we're having problems with Muslims coming into the country . . . You have to deal with the mosques, whether you like it or not.

---

* Being unaware that refugees include children involves ignoring the fact, as almost all of the news images of refugees showed pictures of children. Filippo Grandi, the United Nations high commissioner for refugees, pointed out, "Children don't flee to seek better opportunities. Children flee because there is a risk and a danger."

These attacks are not done by Swedish people."[50] Then in early 2017, he signed an executive order freezing US entry of refugees, placed travel bans on people from Muslim-majority countries, and, in case there was confusion about the basis of the bias, said the United States would prioritize Christians, rather than Muslims, coming to the United States.[51] The goal was a "complete and total shutdown of Muslims entering the United States."[52]* Because bias begets bias, anti-Muslim hate crimes, according to the Council on American-Islamic Relations' 2018 report, increased by 74 percent after Trump's election.[53]

Bias toward Arab Muslims stems from and plays into a very specific stereotype we constantly see in the media: an anti-American terrorist. The first part of the stereotype is that Arab Muslims are portrayed as anti-American. According to polls by the Public Religion Research Institute during the presidential campaigns of 2015, 76 percent of Republicans, 52 percent of Democrats, and 57 percent of Independents agreed with the statement "The values of Islam are at odds with American values and way of life," and a survey by Reuters found that 63 percent of Republicans, 47 percent of Independents, and 37 percent of Democrats agreed that "Muslims living in America have been less willing to assimilate into American society than other immigrant groups." In other words, to a large proportion of Americans, Muslims could never be "true" Americans, echoing the common theme of bias: keeping certain groups perpetually out of the in-group.

The second part of the stereotype is that Arab Muslim men are portrayed as violent terrorists. In a study analyzing how Muslims were portrayed on network and cable television news between 2008 and 2012, researchers found that Muslims were presented as terrorists 81 percent of the time, even though, according to the FBI, only 6 percent of terrorists in the United States are Muslim.[54] As a point of comparison, 94 percent of terrorists in FBI records are non-Muslims, but only 19 percent of news coverage on terrorists is about non-Muslims.

Representation, even on the news, does not match reality, but stereotypic portrayals reinforce stereotypes in the next generation. This is especially true when the representation is so centered on one singular image. When I was a child in the 1980s, almost every bad guy in every movie was Russian (the classic example is *Rocky IV*, when American Rocky battles the callous

---

* One of the first acts of President Biden's presidency in 2021 was to reverse this ban.

and cruel Russian Ivan Drago). Coming off the Cold War, they were the villains Americans were taught to fear and hate. For the past two decades, that bad guy has been an Arab Muslim man plotting to blow something up—and we see Arab Muslims in very few other roles. Given that singular pervasive stereotype, it is hard for children to not absorb that bias when it is so consistently on display.

ISLAMOPHOBIA GETS PICKED UP BY KIDS

By elementary school, non-Muslim American children are showing signs of Islamophobia. In one study, with my student Hadeel Ali, we asked 150 elementary school children if they knew what the word *Muslim* meant, and if they knew anyone who was Muslim.[55] Only 11 percent of children knew that the term *Muslim* referred to a religion, while another 24 percent were somewhere in the ballpark, thinking it had something to do with culture, ethnicity, immigration, or language—and most of the kids who knew the term had learned it because they knew someone who was Muslim. Everyone else had either no idea or thought it had something to do with "muscles."

We then showed children pictures of smiling, happy people from different ethnic groups: a White American, Black American, Latino American, Chinese American, and Arab American man with a head scarf (a kaffiyeh). We asked questions about how American the person was, how much the child liked the person, and how much the child was scared of the person. Even when children didn't know what the word Muslim meant, they reported being scared when the saw the Arab American, and they said he was the least American of the pictures. This was especially true for the younger kids, the ones from five to seven years old. When we asked more specific questions, and compared an Arab Muslim immigrant with a Scottish immigrant, we learned that elementary-aged children perceived an Arab Muslim immigrant (especially if he had on a head scarf) to be less happy living in America, to like "doing American things" less, and to like the people living near him less than the European immigrant. The children didn't know anything about the man, but their answers perfectly matched the violent, anti-American other portrayed in the media. Their stereotypes about Arab Muslim women (especially if they were wearing a hijab) were also specific, namely that they were oppressed and silenced. They thought the Arab Muslim woman needed permission to do things, enjoyed less time with her friends, and was less likely to have a job or career compared to the European woman. In short, they were forming biases with their emotions, even when they didn't know the basis of those biases, and their stereotypes were specific and media-based, even if their knowledge was incomplete.

There is an important caveat here: Children who had some knowledge of Muslims, even just the ballpark "something about culture" knowledge, showed fewer anti-Muslim biases than clueless children. This suggests that children in US elementary schools should learn what it means to be Muslim, preferably from someone who is Muslim. It doesn't need to be a deep dive into the Quran, but children should at least recognize Islam as a major religion (and for Christian and Jewish children, as a religion very similar to their own). Having a little bit of knowledge and some personal connections are important buffers from biases.

As humans, we want to describe people because we want to predict their behavior.[56] In the absence of real knowledge, a stereotype, especially one presented repeatedly and without variation, will step in to fill up the void. Actual knowledge about a group and knowing actual people in that group makes a stereotype less useful. Thus, putting a personal face on an unfamiliar category, pushing aside media images of terrorists and political rhetoric, helps humanize rather than other.

AND ISLAMOPHOBIA IS FELT BY MUSLIM KIDS

Just like Latino children feel the consequences of others' anti-Latino biases, Arab American, Arab immigrant, and Muslim children and teens feel the consequences of others' Islamophobia. Sometimes the bias directed at kids makes the news, like when, in 2015 in Irving, Texas, a fourteen-year-old American Muslim boy, Ahmed Mohamed, was arrested when he brought a homemade digital clock into school and school officials assumed it was a bomb. The skinny teen in his NASA T-shirt, who had been proud of his circuitry work on his middle school robotics teams, was taken away from the school in handcuffs.[57] More often, experiences with Islamophobia don't make headlines, but occur without fanfare every day. In a survey of more than 1,500 Muslim students between the ages of eleven and eighteen who were enrolled in public and private schools in California, 40 percent reported being bullied for being Muslim—twice the national numbers for who gets bullied at school. American Muslim children (including children born and raised in America) report being told to go back to where they came from. They report their peers make comments about them being terrorists, denigrate their religion, and publicly questioned them about specific articles of clothing.[58] As one student noted, "A lot of my classmates once in fourth grade thought that Muslims shouldn't be allowed in the country and one person said to me that Muslims are terrorists." Similarly, another student said, "I have been called a terrorist before and [told] that I did 9/11." Some teens report that other kids would often threaten to blow up the Arab immigrant students' country of origin or make references to them being a threat to the school—but the harassment didn't just come from other kids. Some Muslim students report that their teachers mock the Muslim call to prayer or ask the one Muslim student in the class to explain to the others why Muslims are terrorists.[59]

Wearing clothing markers (like a hijab for girls) often increases the likelihood that a student will experience bias. Muslim girls who wear hijabs regularly report being called terrorists and hearing negative comments about their religion from strangers.[60] As one girl remembered, "One time in elementary school, I decided to wear my hijab for cultural awareness day, and people made fun of me, tugged on it. I have never worn it to school again to this day."[61] One Muslim Canadian middle school girl told researchers, "In a basketball game when we beat them and we wear hijabs and one of the parents said, 'Well at least they didn't bomb us.'"[62] One of the Arab American Muslim college students in my own research lab had just started wearing a hijab when she moved to the city for college; as a teen in a small Southern town, her mom had discouraged her from wearing it because of fear for her safety.

Arab Muslim children know that these biases are being driven by a biased media landscape. Arab American adolescents overwhelmingly reported that Arabs were always portrayed as "enemies of the US" in the media.[63] In a study with Muslim middle school students, one boy stated, "It's hard because you cannot give them a good picture of yourself because they already have their own picture that they got from the media."[64] Another boy articulated the stereotype, "If you hear 'terrorist'. . . you automatically think of a Muslim." One girl noted how the stereotype trickles down to the individual, "There are people from different races that have done so many bad things, yet nobody's going to go and say, 'Oh, you did this and then all of your race is bad,' but one Muslim goes and does something and then they're like, 'Oh, this person did this now all Muslims are bad.'" When the media representation is so biased, every story compounds the stereotype.

The 2016 election and the rhetoric around "Muslim terrorists" led to increased bias toward Arab Muslim children and teens. In 2016, 57 percent of Muslim teens reported seeing offensive posts and comments about Islam or Muslims on social media; in 2019, when a "Muslim ban" wasn't in the news, those numbers dropped to 35 percent.[65] In a Southern Poverty Law Center survey in the days after the 2016 election, teachers of Muslim children reported a spike in negative comments made by other students, and a spike in fear on the part of the Muslim students. An early childhood teacher from Tennessee noted, "One Muslim girl clung to her kindergarten teacher on November 9 and asked, 'Are they going to do anything to me? Am I safe?'" An elementary teacher from Minnesota said, "One of my students from last year who is Muslim has not worn her hijab since the election." A middle school teacher from Pennsylvania observed, "We also have some Muslim students. Many of them were crying and so scared the day after Trump won. They are thinking of future plans just in case. My Muslim students wondered why America didn't like them. It's been tough and emotionally exhausting." This echoes the "Social Science Statement" from part I that noted that children are hit the hardest by bias when it comes from "symbols of authority, the full force of the authority of the State." It is difficult enough for a child to wonder why an individual child at school doesn't like them; it is an unbearable burden for that child to have to wonder why their country doesn't like them.

This fear was evident to me and my student when we conducted that earlier study about Islamophobia. We had planned to include interviews with children who attended a Muslim private elementary school, which my Arab American Muslim student leading the project was particularly motivated to include. We had a wonderful meeting with the principal and met many of the teachers, but, although the principal had agreed to let us conduct the study, the parents asked us not to, afraid that such a study would draw attention to the school and put their children in danger. They had already faced death threats and vandalism, and their parental worries were heartbreaking. In my career, I have interviewed thousands of children in about seventy-five schools, and not one school ever had to decline because of death threats against their elementary school children. The burden of worry that these parents carry, similar to the worries of parents of Black teens concerned for their children's safety from police violence,[66] is added to the everyday worries all parents and teachers carry around. The effects of biased media and violent political rhetoric infiltrate every aspect of the lives of children and their families.

IMMIGRANT BIAS IN THE TIME OF COVID

In times of crisis, political rhetoric often turns to blame.[67] When the COVID-19 crisis began, politicians wanted to assign blame for the global pandemic. In March of 2020, a *Washington Post* photographer captured the image of Trump's speaking notes where he scribbled out Coronavirus and hand-wrote in its place "Chinese Virus."[68] Then, at political rallies in the spring of 2020, he began calling COVID the "kung flu." With that public scapegoating, bias against Asian, specifically Chinese American, children began to swell again.

According to a Pew Research Center survey in June of 2020, three out of ten Asian Americans said they had experienced slurs and jokes since the COVID-19 outbreak.[69] Four out of ten Americans believed that it was more acceptable to express racism toward Asian people after the COVID-19 outbreak than it was before. Researcher Charissa Cheah noticed this spike in Chinese slurs and labels to talk about COVID and suspected that Chinese American kids might be facing some extra challenges.[70] Early in the pandemic, between March and May of 2020, she sent online surveys to 543 Chinese American parents and 230 of their children, who ranged in age from ten to eighteen years old. She and her coresearchers found that more than three out of four Chinese American parents and youth surveyed reported regularly witnessing online or in-person racial discrimination due to the COVID-19 pandemic. About four out of ten parents and children had been the direct target of racial discrimination either online or in person. About 65 percent of youth said that people "cracked jokes about people of my race or ethnic group online," 40 percent said someone made fun of them for being Chinese, and 58 percent said people made comments about avoiding places with Chinese people. Clearly, political rhetoric was once again filtering down into children's lives.

Of course, biases toward Asian American youth did not begin with COVID. For Asian American youth, one of the hardest struggles is trying to be treated like a typical American kid. One of the most common biases they experience is being made to feel like "always an outsider"[71] and a "perpetual foreigner."[72] When researchers analyzed interview transcripts of 120 Chinese American high school students in public schools in Boston and New York (some were born in the United States to Chinese-born parents and some immigrated themselves when they were younger), they found that more than half of the students reported being discriminated against by other kids at their school.[73] Students reported being "beaten," "bullied," "tripped," "hit," "pushed," "kicked," and having things thrown at them inside the school (such as in the hallway or in the bathroom) and outside (in parks and on the school bus). Lin, a thirteen-year-old girl, said, "I was beaten and bullied here in the US . . . the Black and White students beat me and bullied me, like when I was in a park, they'd throw things at me for no reason." Carl, a sixteen-year-old boy who emigrated from Hong Kong, said, "The most difficult thing [about immigrating] is being bullied by both Blacks and Whites. They bully Chinese and Vietnamese students. They walk by and push you deliberately. They use expletives . . . They are not targeting one individual student, they target the entire group of Chinese students."[74] Other students report being "told to go back to China" or mocked for their accents.[75]

Asian American youth also battle the double-edge sword of the "model-minority stereotype." This stereotype seems positive, designating Asian and Asian American students as strong, smart students, but the result of this stereotype is bias. Students report that they are made fun of for any mistake in class because they are "supposed to be so smart."[76] In interviews, researchers find about 15 percent of the students talked about being treated poorly or bullied for "getting good grades," "being too smart," being "geeks," "nerdy," "studying too much," and "not having fun." They also experience pressure to live up to high academic expectations, and worry about acknowledging any academic difficulties.[77] Also, being treated like a teacher's pet is not easy for a teenager trying to fit in. In many interviews, Chinese American youth said their teachers were blatant about their positive bias, saying "Chinese kids can do everything." That positive bias frustrated the non-Chinese kids and led to resentment and even more harassment. Plus, there are many Asian and Asian American students who actually need extra help in their academics, but the struggling students are overlooked because it is just assumed they "can do everything."[78] Stereotypes are always flawed because they assume all members of a group are similar to one another, so even seemingly positive or harmless stereotypes are ultimately negative for children.

Bias toward Asian Americans dates back more than a century. In 1941, following the Japanese attack on Pearl Harbor, President Franklin Roosevelt signed Executive Order 9066,[79] ostensibly to provide "every possible protection against espionage and against sabotage to national-defense," which forced 120,000 Japanese Americans—more than half of them children—to be locked away in isolated internment camps for four years. Although the United States was also at war with Italy and Germany, Italian Americans and German Americans were not forced into prison camps—only Japanese Americans. The only difference between Italian and German Americans and Japanese Americans is race. The order was not about national security. It was racism. It was also the epitome of dehumanization as three thousand adults and children were housed in the livestock pavilion of the Pacific International Livestock Exposition Facilities,[80] and 8,500 adults and children were forced to live in stables at the Santa Anita Assembly Center northeast of Los Angeles.

When we see discussions today about "national security," pay attention to the skin color of who is considered a threat.[81] You will likely find that race seems to determine government reaction and perceptions of what's threatening more often than anything else.[82] We see the combined preferences for Whites, along with the belief that immigrants of color represent threats to American safety and way of life, reflected in our history of immigration policies that allowed White Europeans to immigrate at the exclusion of everyone else. For example, in 2018, then-President Trump asked, "Why do we want all these people from shithole countries coming here?" "Shithole countries" apparently referred to Haiti and countries in Africa. Trump then wondered why there aren't more immigrants to the United States from Norway.

But objective data highlights how this is a biased perception of threat: both the FBI and Department of Homeland Security report that "racially and ethnically motivated violent extremists—specifically white supremacist extremists (WSEs)" are "the most persistent and lethal threat in the Homeland."[83] White supremacist groups actually conducted 67 percent of terrorist plots and attacks in the United States in 2020,[84] yet, despite this objective data, research shows that immigrants of color are more likely than White people to be perceived as threats to our safety, security, values, and way of life.[85]

Time and again, we see this: Japanese Americans were "threats" to "national security," Asian Americans are health "threats" by "bringing in viruses," Arab Muslims are "terrorists," and Mexican Americans are "rapists and drug dealers." We are warned by politicians that if we don't stymy immigration, "our" national identity will be destroyed. While data suggests we should be most scared of White supremacists, political rhetoric and biases point us at immigrants of color.

These biases that immigrants of color are threatening outsiders get adopted by children, who perceive immigrants of color to be less American and more aggressive than White immigrants. These biases are directed *at* children as well. Despite being the "land of immigrants," the policies and politics at the national level, combined with a singular media narrative, normalized the rejection and exclusion of millions of children. The adults in charge must stop centering policies and conversations around the race and nationality of children—and must start seeing their humanity.

THE SCIENTIST BEHIND THE SCIENCE

CAROLA SUÁREZ-OROZCO ─────────────

Carola Suárez-Orozco,* distinguished professor of counseling and school psychology at University of Massachusetts Boston, has spent her career examining how immigrant children and adolescents adapt to new experiences. Her family background taught her about the "accidents of migration"—how "who gets what and for what reason are all accidents of birth." A lot of a person's life and opportunities often happen to be based on what inch of land their mother is standing on when they are born, and what may seem like an inconsequential move can lead to a completely different life trajectory. As with the many scientists in this book, her own story has informed and enriched her research. She is intimately familiar with that experience of othering and being made to feel like an outsider. When she reads interviews with immigrant youth, she "knows exactly how that feels."

She was born in Switzerland to a Swiss-German mother and a French father. Her mother had an American passport, having been in the United States only long enough to be born. When Carola was five, she and her parents moved to the United States, sponsored by her mother's German father who had stayed behind in New York after his daughter's birth. As a child, Carola constantly moved for her father's job. She attended nine schools before graduating high school. Constantly being the new kid, plus being Swiss-French in California in the late 1960s, meant that she always felt othered. She had a complicated name no one could pronounce, didn't dress like everyone else, and was constantly reminded by her parents to not act like "an American brat." As Carola says, "Being an outsider is *always* what I am." Even now, she says that she can "pass" as an American, but there remains a deeply embedded sense of "not being an American" that was engrained in childhood.

When Carola graduated from high school, she had no concrete steps in place. Even though her father had a PhD, there was no talk of college, no thoughts about the pathway forward. Like many immigrant parents, her parents valued education but didn't know the "American game of college."

---

* The information about Carola is based on my own interviews with her, published interviews, and her publications.

So, she did what seemed familiar, attending the community college directly across the street from her high school. While she was there, she began assisting an instructor in an English-as-a-second-language class. She was bilingual, already fluent in English and French, so she was perfect for the task. In that class, she met a brand-new student, Marcelo Suárez-Orozco. He was also an immigrant, newly arrived from Argentina, sent to the United States by his parents to escape the violence of the "Dirty War." She helped teach him English. They married nine months later. They both ended up transferring their community college credits to the local university and earned degrees from University of California, Berkeley.

After graduation, like many women before her, Carola paused her own dreams for her husband to go to graduate school and pursue his. For years, her job involved counseling immigrant families from Mexico and Central America, moving to Southern California as her husband's career as an anthropologist took off. When she finally had the opportunity to earn a PhD of her own, she was interested in the ethnic identity and achievement motivation of immigrant adolescents, but she knew she could not understand the individual adolescent experience without grappling with the demographic, social, economic, and cultural characteristics of US Latinos and the "public malaise" Americans felt toward immigrants. So, she combined what she learned across her own life—what it feels like to be a cultural outsider, what she learned from sitting in on conversations with Marcelo and his anthropology advisor as they talked about their work with Central American refugees, and what she had learned from those many hours of talking to Latino families on both ends of the California coast. In doing so, she wrote a dissertation that would ultimately shed light on the immigrant experience, inspire a burgeoning field of child development, and establish her own academic identity.

In her work, Carola uncovered a seeming paradox: Mexican and Mexican American youth were more connected to their families than the White teens she compared them to. The second-generation Mexican Americans were "transitional," with strong family connections like first-generation Mexican Americans, but lower achievement motivation—like White teens. White teens were more focused on autonomy, pushing back against authority figures, had more family conflict, and despite negative stereotypes about Mexicans, they were the least motivated to do well in school. In uncovering this, Carola learned that the more "American" youth became, the less motivated they were. For the Mexican American youth, their motivation to excel in school seemed to be "poisoned" by the xenophobia and anti-immigrant policies and rhetoric they were facing every day in the United States. This work, which she had to battle her graduate advisors to consider as important, eventually won the Society for Research in Adolescence Best Social Policy Book Award in 1996.[86]

Her graduate school advisors might not have recognized the importance or innovation of her work, but the field of developmental science did. When the American Psychological Association was putting together a presidential task force on immigration, she was the obvious chair.

That is where Carola's story makes a critical divergence from Ruth's and Mamie's. Desperately wanting her own permanent academic position, her life having been on hold for so long to support her husband's rising career, she found her own faculty position at New York University. Marcelo, unlike the men of previous generations, left a beloved position at Harvard to follow her to NYU. They have since made several more moves, to UCLA, then to University of Massachusetts in Boston (for Marcelo to be chancellor). Over a lifetime, she has moved more than thirty times. But Carola's story also highlights one of the strengths that many immigrants hold: the ability to adapt to changes with resilience. She has continued to use that perspective as an outsider to inform her research questions.

9 Gender Gaps, #MeToo, and Toxic Masculinity

The Gender Biases That Persist

Anger remains the emotion that is least acceptable for girls and women because it is the first line of defense against injustice.
–Soraya Chemaly in *Rage Becomes Her: The Power of Women's Anger*

Biases affecting children are not restricted to race, ethnicity, and immigration status. The groundwork is laid by preschool for every single gender-based inequality we see in adulthood. There are biases playing out in the classrooms and the hallways of schools that leave a mark that persists long after graduation—in the jobs we pursue, the quality of relationships we have, and the ways we feel about ourselves and our bodies. Both boys and girls face biases, biases which are not independent of one another, but rather feed off each other, limiting everyone's options. Until those early biases are addressed, it will be impossible to have gender equality among adults.

Unfortunately, it seems that one of the biggest challenges in unraveling gender bias is convincing people it is bias to begin with. With race and ethnicity, living in segregated worlds makes for greater discomfort with diversity, which often leads to disliking the other group and a disinclination to interact. With gender, we mostly live in integrated worlds, and once puberty hits, (straight) boys and girls *want* to interact. The bias comes in in the *ways* in which boys and girls interact, the subtle ways teachers and adults sanction or ignore those behaviors, and the ways in which children enforce expected behaviors among each other.

MEASURED PROGRESS TOWARD GENDER EQUALITY

In the past few decades, there has been remarkable—albeit measured—movement toward gender equality.

- In 1977, two-thirds of Americans said it was better for men to be the breadwinners while women stayed home to take care of the family,[1] but by 2016, two-thirds of Americans said men and women should be equal at work and at home.[2]
- Although slightly more than one in three physicians are men, more than 60 percent of physicians under age thirty-five are women, and women are enrolling in medical school at higher rates than men.
- While only one in three attorneys overall are women, among attorneys under age thirty-five, there are equal numbers of men and women practicing law.
- Since Title IX was passed in 1972, there has been a tenfold increase in the percentage of girls who play high school sports.[3] And if you ask an American to name a famous soccer player, they will most likely name an American woman (although the female physician, attorney, *and* famous soccer player are likely to be paid less money than their male counterparts).
- When *Wonder Woman* came out in 2017, a movie not only starring a powerful woman but directed by a woman, it shattered box office records, earning around $820 million. Signing the deal for the sequel, *Wonder Woman 1984,* placed the starring actor, Gal Gadot, among the highest paid actors of the year.

But as with the movement toward racial equality, the steps toward gender equality have been halting. American women fought to earn the right to vote a hundred years ago, but women remain drastically underrepresented in national politics: Not only has the United States never had a woman in the top political position, but also, according to the United Nations, the United States ranks seventy-eighth in the world in percentage of women in legislative bodies of government,[4] though in 2021, the swearing in of Vice President Kamala Harris helped a bit with political progress. Then, while in 2020, there were more women who were CEOs of Fortune 500 companies than ever before, even with thirty-seven CEOs (up from two in 2000), women head only 7.4 percent of the country's top five hundred companies (and only three of those thirty-seven women are women of color).

The number one barrier adults see limiting real gender equality across society is sexual harassment: According to a 2020 Pew Research Center poll, of the 57 percent of adults who think the country can do more for gender equality, 82 percent of women and 72 percent of men point to sexual harassment as a major obstacle.[5] In 2017, Harvey Weinstein's predatory behavior was brought to broader public attention, and the #MeToo movement revealed that almost all women had a sexual harassment story of their own. The #MeToo movement, and the resulting public backlash toward celebrities and powerful men who sexually assaulted their female colleagues, raised awareness of the pervasiveness of sexual harassment. However, it left intact the underlying cultural biases that facilitated the toxic behavior to begin with—namely, the ones that sexually objectify, diminish, and silence women and the ones that foster aggression and dominance in men. Those cultural biases are deeply entrenched, largely because they have been encouraged since early childhood.

GIRLS CAN BE SMART, BUT NOT "BOY" SMART

Girls are in a double bind in which they are perceived (and expected) to be smart, but not *too* smart. By the time children begin elementary school, girls are already the "good" students. Teachers perceive girls in their classes as well-mannered and compliant relative to boys in class.[6] It isn't a wholly inaccurate stereotype, as girls, on average, do better in their classes. They outnumber boys 57 to 43 percent in bachelor's degrees earned in the United States, and, according to the National Center for Educational Statistics, often have higher standardized test scores than boys.[7] It also isn't surprising that teachers see girls are being better behaved than boys given that this is how parents socialize girls: to be nice, quiet, obedient, and not take up too much space.[8]

But although girls are expected to be the good students in class, they are not expected to be the best students in class. When researchers asked elementary-school-aged children who does well in school by earning good grades, children overwhelmingly said girls. But when they asked who is "really, really smart," by age six, both boys and girls said it is the boys. In other words, by first grade, kids believe that girls can be good students,[9] but only boys can be brilliant. This bias echoes that found in parents, as parents are two and a half times more likely to google "Is my son gifted?" than "Is my daughter gifted?" Similarly, they google the phrases "Is my son intelligent?" and "Is my son a genius?"[10] more than the comparable questions about daughters.

The other biased restriction for girls is that their expertise needs to be focused on certain subjects. Programs to engage girls in STEM (science, technology, engineering, and math) are increasingly common in many middle schools and summer camps, and there are thousands of studies related to gender and STEM. The reality, though, is that the gender gap in STEM, where girls supposedly lag behind boys, is more bias-driven than ability-driven. There isn't really a gap when we look at grades or standardized tests. In fact, girls earn higher grades than boys in math and science classes.[11] In a 2008 meta-analysis of statewide standardized math tests, researchers found that the differences in math that historically existed are no longer there, and boys and girls do not differ from one another in *any* domain of math performance.[12]

But children, teachers, and parents *believe* that boys are better at, and more interested in, STEM than girls. Researchers analyzed large, nationally representative data sets of children's school achievement, along with their teachers' ratings of their academic proficiency and the students' learning behaviors—behaviors such as self-direction in the classroom, organization, and showing an eagerness to learn, all the behaviors that make it easier to learn and that teachers love to see. They found that when they matched boys and girls on the same level of actual math achievement and the same level of positive learning behaviors, teachers rated girls' math proficiency lower than boys. The researchers noted that the reason the gender gap in math seems to be shrinking rather than flipped is because though girls are actually doing much better in class and on tests, they have to show extra ability and extra effort before teachers recognize their math proficiency. If this was a fair race, girls would be running ahead of boys, outpacing them by a few yards—until the teacher starts pulling the girls back, slowing them down, so that boys tie, all while the audience comments about how everyone is equal.

Parents show this bias too, even if they aren't aware of it. Parents are more likely to talk about numbers and science with their sons than their daughters,[13] and boys report that their parents encourage involvement in science, doing things like looking at science websites together and talking about science in a museum, more than girls do.[14] In one study that analyzed conversations between mothers and their toddler children, my fellow researchers and I found that parents of two-year-old sons used number words (such as "look, four crayons" and "you have two shoes.") *three times* more often in everyday conversation than parents of two-year-old daughters.[15] Also, parents and teachers assume that when boys do well in STEM, it is because they are naturally good at those subjects, but when girls do well in STEM, it is because they worked hard.[16] Because of these assumptions about how girls need extra effort to succeed, parents of girls are also more likely to offer unsolicited help with math and science home-work, implicitly suggesting they believe girls to be less capable in these subjects.[17] These subtle assumptions trickle down to children. Given all of these subtle cues, it is not surprising that children begin to internalize these messages that boys are just naturally suited for math and girls are just doing the best they can.

By first grade, children have absorbed the stereotype that boys are bet-ter at STEM than girls. They show this belief in their explicit biases, like when presented with a picture of a girl and a boy and asked, "Which one likes math more?" they point to the boy. They also show this belief in their implicit biases, like when they respond more quickly by pressing a specific key on a computer keyboard when a boy name (like Michael or Andrew) is paired with a math word (like addition or numbers), and respond more quickly when a girl name (like Emily or Jessica) is paired with a reading word (like books and story).[18] These stereotypes get more entrenched with age. In meta-analyses looking at Draw-A-Scientist studies, where girls and boys are asked to draw a scientist and the researchers record whether the child draws a man or woman, 70 percent of girls and 83 percent of boys at age six drew a scientist who was their same gender. But by the end of elementary school, more girls drew men than women scientists (slightly more than half), and by the time they were sixteen, three times more girls drew male scientists than female scientists.[19]* Because of these biases, girls

---

* This meta-analysis included studies from over four decades, and the analysis also examined how children's drawings differed over historical time. They wanted to make

eventually lose confidence, motivation, and interest in STEM subjects, even when they are doing well in the classes. Once they internalize this bias that math is for boys, they pull their academic selves away from math and toward languages.[20]

My colleague Campbell Leaper and I were interested in how all of these STEM biases might be affecting girls. To dig into that, we surveyed six hundred ethnically diverse girls in middle schools and high schools from Northern California, Southern California, and Atlanta. We found that 52 percent of girls had heard a discouraging comment about their math or science ability, usually made by their teachers or boys in their classes. The more often girls heard negative comments, regardless of how well they were doing in math and science classes, the more their belief in their own abilities dropped and the more they disliked and devalued those classes.[21] This means that negative comments from boys and teachers were more powerful influences on shaping their beliefs about their math and science abilities than their own grades. In fact, in large meta-analyses, the only places gender differences actually appear in anything related to math is not in performance measures, but in math self-confidence and anxiety. Even when their performance and abilities are the same, boys on average are more confident and less anxious about math than girls. As one teen girl noted, "Girls are told [by society], 'Oh girls are less interested in science.' So they're like, 'Well, I'm less interested in science.'"[22]

The result of these biases is that many girls opt out of the STEM subjects most associated with boys, namely computers and engineering. According to the National Science Foundation in 2020, although women earn 57 percent of all bachelor's degrees, they earn only 22 percent of bachelor's degrees in engineering and 19 percent of bachelor's degrees in computer science.[23] Within the workforce, only 13 percent of engineers and 26 percent of computer scientists are women.[24] Because starting salaries in STEM careers are 26 percent higher than non-STEM careers ($66,123 vs. $52,299)[25], girls opting out of high-paying STEM careers perpetuates wage gaps between men and women. The early biases, even if they are happening accidentally, lead to lifelong inequalities.

---

sure they captured developmental change instead of a confound with birth cohort. They found that children drew fewer male scientists in general over the decades, but the age effects, in which girls drew more male scientists as they got older, stayed strong even when controlling for the period in which they were born.

TOXIC MASCULINITY IN THE CLASSROOM: BOYS AS TROUBLEMAKERS

While girls are considered the good, albeit not brilliant, students, boys are considered the troublemakers. When teachers were asked to describe the typical boy and typical girl, they described a typical girl as an overachiever, but a typical boy as an underachiever.[26] Boys are further considered to be capable, but lazy, disruptive, unfocused, and lacking motivation, with teachers making comments like "Boys are noisier," "Boys do not take on the school ethos," and "Boys do not take education seriously." But although teachers *perceive* boys to be more disruptive than girls in the classroom, when researchers sit in class and record actual behavior, there are no differences in the misbehavior of boys and girls. Boys *do* get reprimanded for minor offenses more than girls, but that seems to be because girls' misdeeds are often ignored.[27] In fact, boys are more than four times more likely than girls to receive punishments in school. They are more likely to be sent to the principal's office for misbehaving, suspended from school, and expelled than girls.[28] This disciplinary bias is even stronger among Black and Latino boys, who are more likely to be referred to the office, suspended, or expelled—and more severely punished for the same offense—than White boys.[29]

Biases about boys being troublemaking underachievers have important consequences for them. Teachers who believe boys are more disruptive than girls end up being stricter with boys and enforcing harsher punishment in an attempt to stop future misbehaviors.[30] Then, when students are punished by being removed from the classroom—which boys are more often than girls—they begin to fall behind others as being out of the classroom makes it harder to keep up academically.[31] Not surprisingly, then, when researchers followed a group of suspended versus nonsuspended students who were matched in gender, ethnicity, and socioeconomic status, they found that the suspended group of students was nearly five grade levels behind the nonsuspended group two years after the suspension.[32] It is impossible for students to learn if they aren't even in the classroom, and once students start to lag behind, the lag starts to snowball until it is nearly insurmountable.

But what seems to harm boys the most in classrooms are the biases enforced by the boys themselves. By elementary school, boys are absorbing and enforcing the rules of toxic masculinity, which is a narrow and rigid type of manhood defined by violence and aggression, dominance over others, lack of vulnerability or emotional expression, and sexual prowess with girls (this last part, we'll come back to later).[33] Part of what makes this particular definition of masculinity so toxic is that showing emotions, vulnerability, or weakness is considered too feminine for "real" boys and can only be squashed by aggressive displays of status. The mix of traits, in which asking for help or being a conscientious student is discouraged and real emotions are not talked about but funneled into aggressive outbursts, is so rigidly enforced (by peers and parents who have been similarly socialized in this culture) that anything that doesn't fit this brand of masculine, anything close to feminine, is deemed less-than and rejected or mocked.

This bias and toxic masculinity that pushes boys toward defiance at school begins with the socialization of boys to be aggressive and angry. First, parents view aggression as more normal and acceptable in their sons than their daughters.[34] In one study, when parents read stories to their children that had androgynous characters displaying happiness, anger, sadness, and fear, the parents labeled the characters as male when they displayed anger and as female when they displayed happiness or fear.[35] Entertainment media reinforces these ideas: In one analysis of teen-oriented films across three decades, researchers found that male characters committed 86 percent of the aggressive acts in the movies.[36] In a 2020 study of the top twenty-five television programs popular among boys ages seven to thirteen, in the 447 episodes researchers analyzed, they found that male characters committed two-thirds of all the violent acts against another person, and were more likely to be victims of violence than girls.[37] Additionally, the toys that are marketed to boys, such as action figures and toy weapons, promote and model aggression.[38] Plus, commercials for those toys fill up television networks where boys are already watching male characters being violent, so boys see more modeling of aggressive play.[39] On top of that, boys are heavy consumers of sports media, and some of the most popular sports (such as football and hockey) value and reinforce physical aggression and violence.[40] They also frequently play video games,[41] the most popular of which are highly aggressive, first-person shooter games. Violent media, video games, and toys marketed to boys propagate a consistent message that boys are expected to be aggressive.

Altogether, by elementary school, boys are aware that displays of real emotion beyond anger are discouraged. This bias is reinforced by every parent who told their son that "boys don't cry." This is well internalized by adolescence: when teen boys were asked what "trait society values the most in boys, "strength and toughness" claimed the top spot.[42] High school boys admit to hiding their feelings from their male friends, and tell each other to "just suck it up" or "man up."[43] Showing emotions means "being a girl" or "being gay," and both are unacceptable because they are incompatible with masculinity. One boy observed, "People don't see [boys showing feelings] that often and they don't know what to do when they do see it, so they just make fun of the person." Another boy noted, "I think a lot of [boys] think that the more open they are [about their feelings], they're going to be called gay or girl. And I think a lot of people are scared of that."[44] As these studies evidence, boys have clearly learned that vulnerability is unacceptable. That bleeds into school as well, as admitting to struggling in school is a sign of vulnerability and thus is also unacceptable.

The norms of toxic masculinity, enforced by peers, reinforce the draw of being an underachieving troublemaker. By middle school, kids describe popular boys as strong and defiant risk-takers who blow off school.[45] If boys aspire to be cool, they are expected to reject educational success.[46] The need to be cool not only means that boys must reject teachers' authority, but also deters them from seeing help on schoolwork when they need it since only weak boys ask for help. Sociologist Edward Morris embedded himself in high schools and observed how boys were playing out the roles of masculinity, noting that boys "took great pride in their lack of academic care and effort. Their contrived carelessness took the form of a publicly displayed absence of academic diligence and planning. Boys' semipurposeful flouting of school requirement gained them notoriety but hampered their ability to succeed academically."[47] If boys aren't being defiant and "too cool for school," they face teasing by their male peers. One high school boy said, "[I have] an [overdue] paper that . . . I've been procrastinating a lot on it. I can't really think of a rational way to complain about that to my friends . . . [They] would just yell at me for being so concerned about school."[48] Toxic masculinity norms discourage boys from putting effort into school or seeking help from teachers, making it much harder for them to address any academic difficulties they encounter—which is then compounded by the fact that their behavior leads to harsh disciplinary actions from the teachers that may take them out of the classroom, pushing them even further behind academically.[49] The result is that boys face cultural pressures to intellectually and behaviorally disengage from academics as their primary route to high social status, yet these pressures cement teachers' biases about underachieving, troublesome boys.

Taken together, these cultural and individual biases tell boys they are the troublemakers at school by kindergarten, expect them to be aggressive, place them into a system of toxic masculinity where compliance and academic success are mocked by their peers, and overeagerly punish them when teachers remove them from the classroom, pushing them further behind academically.*

TOXIC MASCULINITY AND "FAG TALK"†

Beyond pushing boys to reject academic success and squashing any authentic expression of emotion, toxic masculinity norms also dictate that boys should be heterosexually assertive and dominant over girls. To preserve this valued concept of manliness, boys tease and torment a peer who might be deemed girly or gay.

One way they do this is by using homophobic insults against one another if they are not acting "manly" enough. Sociologist C. J. Pascoe calls this "fag talk." Boys assert their masculine identity "by lobbing homophobic epithets at one another."[50] As Pascoe says, "'Fag' may be used a weapon with which to temporarily assert one's masculinity by denying it to others . . . When a boy calls another boy a fag, it means he is not a man but not necessarily that he is a homosexual." And it can be a potent threat: a Latino boy in high school told her, "To call someone gay or fag is like the lowest thing you can call someone. Because that's like saying that you're nothing."[51] Masculinity and heterosexuality are treated as synonymous, and as counseling psychologist Paul Poteat shows in his research, "Many adolescent males report extreme stress and pressure to prove their masculinity and heterosexuality to peers in order to avoid rejection and homophobic ridicule."[52] In other words, in boy culture, to avoid harassment, boys are

---

* I would even argue that this cultural milieu contributes to a massive gap between violent crime for men and women in adulthood. According to the FBI's 2019 crime statistics, 88 percent of the people arrested for murder and 76.5 percent of people arrested for aggravated assault were men. While many factors play into this, a culture of fostering violence and aggression is partially culpable.

† I am not using this word lightly and considered censoring it, as I have other biased slurs in the book. This term, however, is used so pervasively, heard by almost 100 percent of middle school students, that it felt appropriate to use it for the purpose of explicitly labeling it as a form of bias.

constantly having to prove they are masculine—and the only way to do that is to prove they are heterosexual.

The most direct way to avoid ridicule and prove their heterosexuality, and thus their masculinity, is to sexually objectify and sexually harass girls. These patterns are in place by the time puberty starts to bubble up in middle school. In my own research, my graduate student and I asked middle schoolers to, in their own words, describe a hypothetical popular boy. One of the most common answers was being a "player" and "being good with girls." Then when we asked every kid in the class to confidentially rate each other for how typical they were for their gender and how popular they were, we found the more kids conformed to gender norms, the more popular they were.[53] These links were especially strong for the boys. Being good with girls, even in seventh grade, was the key to their popularity. The other boys, boys who showed any deviation from masculinity with any feminine or nonheterosexual characteristics, were rejected, teased, and bullied by their peers. We found that when boys were harassed and bullied by their peers for being not masculine or heterosexual enough, they suffered for it with lower self-esteem, more depression, and more anxiety.*

Because boys seem to perpetrate sexual harassment as a way of broadcasting and enforcing masculinity, boys are teased or bullied if they *don't* sexually objectify girls. In research with about three hundred middle school boys in New England, researchers found that some boys really bought into the ideal of masculinity that dictates boys "should be dominant in their interactions with others." If those boys were sexually harassed by a peer, their masculinity—according to the definition of it that they subscribed to—was usurped. In response, as a way to reclaim their diminished masculinity, they sexually harassed others. On the flip side, boys who didn't believe in that dominant view of masculinity didn't feel particularly threatened by others' sexual harassment. They didn't like it, but they didn't feel the need to harass others. The results paint a picture of a culture in which, when the ideal of masculinity required dominance, sexual harassment was the go-to way to assert that dominance over others. For boys, internalizing the cultural bias of toxic masculinity tells them that they must harass others to avoid being harassed.

---

* Girls who did not conform to feminine stereotypes were teased by peers too, but not as often, or as harshly, as the boys.

THE SEXUALIZATION OF GIRLS

The gender biases that boys and girls face are linked to one another, like two partners in a dysfunctional tango. While toxic masculinity is the leading partner, the sexualization of girls follows along. Whereas boys are valued for being dominant and sexually assertive toward girls, girls are valued for their appeal for boys. For girls, this pressure to be desirable, but more specifically to be a sexual object for others' pleasure, has its own costs.

The messages that girls' sole value comes from being sexually objectified begins early: every time a newly crawling girl is placed in a frilly, impractical dress, there is a focus on being pretty instead of the ability to move and be active. In the study of what parents google about their sons versus daughters that I mentioned earlier in this chapter, the same group of parents who worried about the intelligence of their sons also worried about the appearance of their daughters. Parents asked Google, "Is my daughter overweight?" twice as often as the equivalent question for their sons; asked if their daughter was "beautiful" one and a half times more often; and asked if their daughter was "ugly" three times more often than for their sons. By preschool, girls begin to internalize the stereotype that girls should be pretty and focused on their appearance. They start to ask, "Does this look good on me?" and "Do I look pretty?"[54] They begin to make negative comments about their bodies* and how they look, stating, "I don't like my hair/nose/bottom" or "I am not pretty." Among seven-to-ten-year-old girls, more than one-third report that they are made to feel that their looks are their most important quality.[55] By the time they are teens, when they are asked what "trait society values the most in girls," of all the possible traits in the world, half the teens named something about physical attractiveness. Only 1 percent of them named anything to do with competence or ability.[56]

It doesn't stop with simply being pretty, though. By the time children are in elementary school, girls have learned a very culturally specific message: the only way to be pretty, and the best way to be valued, is to be sexy—or, more accurately, sexualized. Sexualization, as researcher Monique Ward points out, "is not the same as sex or sexuality. It is a form of sexism. It is a narrow frame of women's worth and value in which they are seen only as

---

* Focusing on being pretty also means being thin. According to the National Eating Disorders Association, among first- through third-grade girls, almost half want to be thinner and half would feel better about themselves if they were on a diet.

sexual body parts for others' sexual pleasure."[57] Sixty-nine percent of girls ranging in age from ten to nineteen said they felt they had been judged as a sexual object "at least once in a while" in their daily life, and 22 percent said they feel this way "frequently."[58]

Girls learn that their worth comes from being sexualized every day. In one case, when researchers asked White and Latina elementary school girls in the United States about their favorite television shows, they found that girl characters were sexualized in every single show, and three out of four times any girl appeared on screen.[59] This means that when girls make an appearance on the screen, they are typically wearing skimpy clothing, making comments about their body, and flirting with boy characters. Given that children in elementary school watch four and a half hours of television a day, they will see approximately 78,069 examples every year of "sexy girl" role models just in children's programming alone.[60] Beyond that, sexually objectifying portrayals of women appear in 59 percent of music videos, 46 percent of young adult female characters on prime-time television, and 64 percent of ads in teen girls' magazines. By teens' own reports, half of teens (both boys and girls) say that "several times a week or more they see female TV and movie characters whose looks are more important than their brains or abilities" and "video game characters who look sexy or hot." Furthermore, one-quarter of girls' clothing is revealing or has sexually suggestive writing, and popular dolls marketed to young girls wear leather miniskirts and thigh-high boots.[61]

This cultural push to be sexy becomes an important bias in girls' lives, in part because being sexualized is supposedly incompatible with being smart, so if girls are trying to be sexy, they have to downplay being smart. In 2012, researcher Christy Starr updated Ruth and Mamie's "doll studies" for the modern era by showing a group of six- to nine-year-old girls a series of paper dolls. Some of the dolls were sexualized, dressed in a low-cut shirt with the midriff showing, wearing makeup, a complicated hairstyle, and pursed lips. The nonsexualized dolls were dressed in a sweater and long flowing skirt, had similar length but less complicated hair, wore no makeup, and were smiling. In questions very reminiscent of Ruth's and Mamie's, Starr asked the girls, "Which doll do you think looks most like you?" and "If you could look like one of these two dolls, which would you like to look like?" Starr found that 69 percent of the elementary school girls either said they currently looked like the sexualized doll or *wanted* to look like the sexualized doll. But at the same time girls say they want to look sexy, they say the sexy girl is not very smart: When Starr asked the girls, "Thalia is a scientist. She conducts important experiments in a laboratory and is well respected among other scientists. Which doll is Thalia?," 79 percent of the girls assumed the nonsexualized girl was the scientist.

In my research with elementary school children, children as young as five tell us that, compared to a nonsexualized girl wearing jeans and a blouse, a girl in skimpy clothing with heavy makeup and jewelry is popular but not smart, saying things like "Girls that dress like that aren't very smart" or that they just "act dumb."[62] Similarly, in other studies, when adults were shown images of sexualized and nonsexualized girls, the sexualized girls are described as less intelligent, capable, competent, and determined, *even when the sexualized girl was described as being an honors student and the president of the student council.*[63] Even parents of elementary-school-aged girls do this. When asked, "How certain are you that your child will reach her educational goals?" and "How far do you think your daughter will go in school?" the parents of daughters who aspired to look sexualized believed their own daughters would be less successful in school.[64] While it is hard to know whether this is driven by the parents or their daughters, it is clear that there are different academic expectations for sexy girls. When girls start to value this culturally pervasive image of the sexy girl, they apply the "sexy but dumb" stereotype to themselves, downplaying their own intelligence and ambition. Girls who prized being sexualized had worse performance in math, language arts, science, and social studies, in both their grades in school and on their standardized tests.[65]

Theoretically, one could argue that the girls who aren't doing well in school assume it is better to be successful at something, and decide to take the "sexy girl" path instead of the "good student" path. But that assumption proves false. In my research, I tried to figure out which came first: aspiring to be sexy or downplaying intelligence. I conducted a longitudinal study over the course of middle school, beginning when students were in seventh grade and returning to the same students when they were in eighth grade. I found that seventh-grade girls who believe that girls *should* be valued for their sexual appeal to boys were less motivated to learn in school and were less confident in their academic ability by eighth grade, regardless of how well they were actually doing in school.[66] Even girls who did well in school reported downplaying what they knew when they valued being sexualized, saying they didn't raise their hands even when they knew the answer and pretended to do worse on a test than they actually did. They were also more skeptical about the importance of education for their lives than the other girls. In essence, not only does believing in these stereotyped images interfere with girls' classroom participation—like when they are not raising their hand even when they know the answer to a question—but it also seems to cause them to devalue school altogether. What's more, this pressure to play dumb gets more pronounced over the course of middle school, regardless of how academically talented the girls were at the beginning, resulting in eighth-grade girls who value being sexy but looking and acting very uninterested in school (which also ironically serves to reinforce the sexy-but-dumb stereotype to their peers).[67] By culturally valuing girls' appearances over their abilities, and by inundating them with a singular image of sexy-but-dumb girls, girls absorb that bias and apply it to themselves, limiting their own academic pursuits.

This pattern, where girls downplay their intelligence, is similar to what happens with boys in the classroom: cultural biases, heavily promoted in the media that youth consume, convey what popular boys and popular girls are like. Popular boys are defiant, aggressive, dismissive of teachers, and interested in girls; popular girls are thin, sexy, appealing to boys, and not very bright. By middle school, kids are enforcing these norms within their peer groups and within themselves.

WHEN SEXUALIZATION AND TOXIC MASCULINITY MEET IN THE HALLWAY

Given the biased culture in which girls are sexualized and objectified and boys' aggressive heterosexuality is encouraged, it is depressingly predictable that, by middle school, girls are frequently sexually harassed by boys. In one study of 858 Black and White fifth, sixth, seventh, and eighth graders, researchers found that one out of four fifth graders experienced sexual harassment in the form of sexual comments, jokes, gestures, or looks—and by eighth grade, it was one in two.[68] Similarly, one in ten fifth graders had been touched, pinched, or grabbed in a sexual way; by eighth grade, it was up to one in four.[69] Since all of this happens in hallways, cafeterias, band rooms, classrooms, and school buses, almost all middle school students (96 percent) have witnessed sexual harassment happening at school.[70] Then these types of behaviors continue to ramp up as teens move from middle school to high school, and by ninth grade and tenth grade, the frequency with which teens sexually harass their peers reaches an all-time high (it becomes a little less frequent as teens reach the end of adolescence).

Sexual harassment is so common in middle school and high school, in part, because early teenagers are a biological and social mess, with little experience with one another. Puberty is rushing in like a bull, dousing a still-developing brain (one in which the regions that help with impulse control are still developing) with hormones. Boys and girls in their early teens have very little experience positively interacting with one another, as they spent much of early childhood and elementary school in gender-segregated boy groups and girl groups.[71] After all, prior to that point, most often, girls play in small groups of two or three girls on the elementary school playground, while boys play sports games on the other side of the playground; parents and teachers regularly allow for girls-against-boys games, girls-only sleepovers, and boys-only activities. So, in middle school, when (straight) kids awkwardly want to interact with one another and want to express their sexual interest in their peer, all they have to guide their behavior is a biased cultural script of toxic masculinity and sexual objectification instead of a history of real friendships. In my research with Campbell Leaper where we asked about STEM biases, we also asked about sexual harassment. We found that 90 percent of girls had experienced at least one form of sexual harassment by the end of high school.[72] The universality of that experience explains why so many adult women can say, "Me too!"

The effects of this harassment are profound. Girls feel emotional distress, embarrassment, lowered self-esteem, depression, and suicidal thoughts.[73] They start to question their potential happiness in long-term relationships. Their attitudes about their bodies become more negative, with many girls not liking their own bodies and starting to have disordered eating patterns. They also start acting out, abusing drugs and alcohol, and getting into fights.[74] They suffer in school, are absent more often, and disengage from academics. Girls describe sexual harassment as making them feel "dirty—like a piece of trash," "terrible," "scared," "angry and upset," and "like a second-class citizen."[75] Seventy-six percent of girls report feeling unsafe because they are a girl at least once in a while. (We'll discuss the effects of homophobic harassment boys experience in the next chapter.)

Despite—and perhaps because of—how common sexual harassment is in schools, schools largely ignore it. Even after the 1999 case of *Davis v. Monroe County Board of Education* ruled that sexual harassment in school violated Title IX, lax regulation by the Department of Education has meant that schools do little to address sexual harassment in a meaningful way. For instance, schools' sex education curricula rarely covers sexual harassment, or even consent.[76] An analysis of eighteen states' K–12 health education standards (where two states were randomly selected from each of the nine regions of the United States designated by the US Census) found that no—zero—states specified anything about explicit "sexual consent" in their standards.[77] These conversations aren't happening at home either, as only one-fourth of parents of boys and one-fifth of parents of girls talk to their kids about not sexually harassing others.[78]

Beyond ignoring sexual harassment in their formal education, schools also ignore what is going on in their hostile hallways. Even though Title IX requirements mandate that schools report sexual harassment occurrences, according to the Department of Education in 2016, more than two-thirds of school districts in the United States reported zero instances of sexual harassment. That stands in glaring contrast to the extremely high rates of sexual harassment documented by our research: 90 percent of teen girls report that they have experienced sexual harassment, but 75 percent of school districts never report a case. There is a clear disconnect.

Although one possibility is that schools are simply not reporting these negative events, it is also likely that schools are frankly not acknowledging—even to themselves—what is happening. When asked, some teachers say that sexual harassment is something that happens between adults, or between adults and students, but not between student peers.[79] Other teachers and staff tell researchers that there is a general lack of education and training on what sexual harassment is and how they are supposed to handle sexual harassment.[80] Even when they want to deal with it, teachers say they feel unsupported by the school administration to follow through on any consequences.[81] This attitude trickles down to students. For example, a survey with 1,447 teachers and 3,616 sixth-grade students across thirty-six middle schools in the Midwest found that when teachers and staff perceived their school to be intolerant of sexual harassment (for example, when they agreed with statements like "Boys understand that it is *not* okay to make sexual comments to girls at school"), students reported fewer instances of sexual harassment.[82] On the flip side, when teachers said their schools didn't care much about sexual harassment, students felt that too. Students, both boys and girls, know what is tolerated and what it not tolerated at the schools (and at home for that matter). When schools establish clear expectations, students learn those norms, and although they will push the limits, they ultimately know there will be consequences for violating those expectations. Thus, biased norms gradually shift.

Unfortunately, instead of there being negative consequences for teens who sexually harass their peers, many teens are rewarded with popularity. In our heteronormative culture, tough boys who are successful at sexually pursing girls (and who may often use sexual harassment as a means to that end) are the most popular. In my research with my colleagues, we asked high schoolers to confidentially indicate how often they sexually harassed others. We also gave them a roster of their school and asked them to circle the names of the people they were friends with. By analyzing their social networks of friends, we found that the boys who most often sexually harassed girls were also more likely to be the central hub of a large social circle. They were the most popular—the ones who held the most social influence over their peers.[83] This pattern is in the cultural script, the trope of the popular boy in teen movies—and it is clear in real-life headlines too. Then-candidate Donald Trump was successful in a presidential election despite being recorded bragging about his ability to, without women's consent, "grab 'em by the pussy." Brett Cavanaugh was successfully confirmed to the Supreme Court in 2018, despite Professor Christine Blasey Ford's detailed testimony about how he sexually assaulted her when they were teens. There is high tolerance of sexual harassment and assault, and it is more often than not unjustly rewarded with social status.

THE OBJECTIFICATION AND VIOLENCE THAT RESULTS

The sexualization of girls doesn't just lead to them being thought of as less intelligent or competent, or feeling unhappy with their own bodies—although both are true. The toxic masculinity of boys doesn't just lead to academic underachievement and teasing by peers—although both are true. The deeper danger of these biases are because sexualization leads to dehumanization. And as we see time and again, being dehumanized always leads to violence—especially when one group is taught to be violent.

Researchers have consistently shown that sexualized women are processed in the brain in a similar way to objects (their body parts are mentally catalogued as separate objects) and quite differently than either men or nonsexualized women (they are both processed as a "whole person").[84]

Researchers have shown that even elementary school children do this: children in elementary school who were exposed to pictures of sexualized women in experimental studies rated those women as less than fully human, with fewer human characteristics, and even less worthy of being helped when in danger, than nonsexualized women.[85]

Constantly seeing women and girls as sexual objects in media starts to shift our tolerance of violence toward women. Monique Ward conducted meta-analyses in 2016 and 2019 on the effects of watching sexualized TV shows, video games, music videos, music, and movies—not pornography, just the regular, run-of-the mill sexy-girl-lying-across-the-hood-of-a-car-in-a-music-video level of sexualization. Her findings emphatically show that youth's exposure to sexualized media, in both everyday life and in experiments, leads to increased levels of thinking of women and girls as objects and greater acceptance of sexual violence toward women. The more exposure they had to sexualized media, the more teens endorsed rape myths—the idea that girls who wear sexy clothes are "asking for it." This willingness to "blame the rape victim" is also strengthened when teens were asked to play a video game with a sexualized female character in it for fifteen minutes.[86] The effect of tolerating sexual violence toward women and blaming rape victims is even larger among boys who watch pornography—a concerning link since recent surveys show that 79 percent of adolescent boys have seen pornography, and a quarter of those report seeing it often.[87] And real-life sexual violence is often the outcome: one in four girls in college have experienced some form of sexual coercion, with one in five experiencing forced intercourse, most frequently by a boyfriend.[88]

This sexualization-to-dehumanization-to-violence link is in place by adolescence, and is exacerbated because we so heavily promote and allow for aggression in boys and promote compliance in girls. In a Plan International study, when teens were asked about the pressures they felt, boys said they felt pressure to be physically strong, be willing to throw a punch if provoked, be interested in sports, dominate others, and "hook up with" a girl. Girls felt pressure to manage other people's emotions, to be attractive, and not to brag or be too confident. As Soraya Chemaly writes in *Rage Becomes Her: The Power of Women's Anger*, "In the classroom, it was almost certainly the case that the women were managing a double bind that we face constantly: conform to traditional gender expectations, stay quiet and be liked, or violate those expectations and risk the penalties, including the penalty of being called puritanical, aggressive, and 'humorless.'" She further notes, "It is difficult for many adults to accept that boys can and should control themselves and meet the same behavioral standards that we expect from girls. It is even harder to accept that girls feel angry and have legitimate rights not to make themselves cheerfully available as resources for boys' development." The message that girls have drilled into them is never show anger and don't take up too much space. As a result of learning these lessons, more than half of girls say they would not report sexual harassment behaviors "because people would not like them if they did." So, even though sexual harassment causes substantial psychological harm, girls don't report it for fear of not being liked—all while boys perpetrate it as a way to be liked.

Gender biases are particularly difficult to unravel because they are so tangled in the accepted cultural milieu in which kids live. Girls, since infancy, are encouraged to be sweet and kind, be the "good student, but not the best student," manage others' feelings, and put others' needs first. They are heavily sexualized in all forms of media, so much so that they begin to sexualize themselves because it is so culturally valued. For their part, boys, since infancy, are encouraged to be aggressive. They are teased and harassed if they don't show aggressive, heterosexual interest in girls.

To change these norms, we have to break the connection between boys' toxic masculinity, girls' sexual objectification, and their popularity. As long as youth have to choose between popularity (which is the status currency in any middle school or high school) and not demonstrating a biased behavior, many will choose to act in a biased way. The only way to break that connection is to provide a broader range of media images of popular boys and girls (which changes the options they can aspire to be), to help boys and girls see each other as equals and friends instead of sexual conquests, to be more explicit with children about how these behaviors are damaging and harmful, and to provide consistent consequences when biased behaviors happen.

THE SCIENTIST BEHIND THE SCIENCE

MONIQUE WARD ————————————————————

Monique Ward, a professor in the Department of Psychology at the University of Michigan, has spent her career showing how the media that teens voraciously consume shapes their ideas about gender, sexuality, and relationships.* When the American Psychological Association gathered a task force on the sexualization of girls and women, she was tapped to join the efforts. Despite her standing in the research community, she never planned on being a research psychologist. However, she found that by following her passion, she could ask questions no one else thought to ask.

Growing up in Connecticut in a traditional family with seven siblings, she always knew she was good at school. She liked all of the sciences and the human body and anatomy and so everyone kept telling her, "Oh, you're good in school. You like science. You should be a doctor." She thought, "Okay, so I will be a doctor." But by her second year at Yale University, she knew that medicine wasn't her passion. Instead, she fell in love with an introductory psychology class. She assumed, as many people do when they think about psychology, that being a therapist was the only choice. At the same time that she was immersing herself in the theories and methods of psychology, she found herself fascinated by the conversations she was having with her fellow students about gender and relationships. Interacting with people from all over the world, she was shocked at how some people thought men and women were supposed to act. She kept thinking, "Where are they getting these ideas?" She noticed that, in these conversations with her peers, people would often reference movies and television as their ideal of how romantic relationships should be. This was particularly interesting to her because she loved movies. She loved the power of movies and television to draw us into their story lines and to help us emotionally connect with the characters—the way those mediums provide a shared cultural experience. The question of where people got their ideas from led to her senior thesis about how men learn about masculinity.

When she graduated from Yale, Monique became a rape crisis counselor. She found the experience "brutal" and "emotionally draining" and

---

* The information about Monique is based on my own interviews with her, published interviews, and her publications.

found herself carrying around these tragic stories of women throughout the day. She also found there was a limit to how much she could help. "It felt like you're helping people. But it is one person at a time and in a small incremental way after bad things have already happened to them." She said, "That was really rough. Okay, so you come to me because you've gotten raped at work, you're homeless, whatever it is that I could try to help you. But boy, it would be great if we could give people knowledge or power to help to see if we can stop some of these bad things happening." Although it wasn't a conscious decision, her thoughts started shifting to how we can have widespread cultural change that alters the toxic parts of gender and relationships.

Now, as a researcher, that is at the core of what she studies. After getting her PhD at UCLA, she went to University of Michigan as a new professor and began pursing these questions: How does the media, especially the television shows and movies that we all watch, teach us a cultural script about how boys and girls should act? What are the consequences for both boys and girls of watching hours of media that sexualize girls? She has repeatedly shown that boys and girls learn a specific script from the media they consume, a script in which girls are sexualized for boys' pleasure, and these scripts are reenacted in boys' and girls' interactions with each other.

One of the biggest surprises to her is that so few other developmental scientists study the effects of media on children's ideas about themselves and the world—especially considering children spend so much of their lives engaged with media. "They spend more time consuming various media than anything else except sleeping. The data show that children spend more time, on average, with media than with school, with talking to their friends or talking to their parents…anything." As she says, her research is a little like studying "the sea we are all swimming in." Media is everywhere, all the time. It is so ubiquitous it is hard to pinpoint. It is a "constantly moving target." It is everywhere, it informs so much of children's gender development, and yet whenever we think we have a handle on it, the media landscape completely shifts. For Monique, *that* is what makes it so interesting.

10

When the Authentic Is Invisible, but the Slurs Are Everyday

Bias Toward LGBTQ+ and Gender-Nonconforming Youth

In the end, everyone just deserves the right to be their authentic selves, just be who they are.
—Jazz Jennings, trans advocate and author who at age six began publicly sharing her gender identity story

The heteronormative culture described in the last chapter is so pervasive that many kids land in the cross fire. While that cultural pressure is used to police the behavior of straight cisgender boys and girls, for lesbian, bisexual, queer, and trans girls and gay, bisexual, queer, and trans boys, it is particularly damaging. Youth who don't fit into a rigid heteronormative image are targeted by homophobic and transphobic language, harassment, and bullying. Specifically, the biases facing LGBTQ+ youth are marked by contrasting themes of invisibility and severity. Invisibility both in the sense that LGBTQ+ individuals are rendered invisible in children's media and in that the biases facing LGBTQ+ youth are rendered invisible by the casual way that "that's so gay" is used as an everyday synonym for stupid in every middle school, and in how straight youth rarely consider how hurtful it is to have your identity used as an insult. Biases facing LGBTQ+ youth are also marked by their severity. LGBTQ+ teens are frequently emotionally and physically bullied and assaulted—and the mental and physical health consequences are deadly. Furthermore, the severity is strengthened because, unlike the other biases described in the book, LGBTQ+ youth often face the most severe rejection possible for a child: from their parents. Given all of this, the key to reducing LGBTQ+ bias is to make the invisible visible and to protect youth from violence and rejection.

THE BIASES CHILDREN LEARN TO HOLD

My research across the different types of biases held by children (like those described in this book) has shown that children don't need actual knowledge about a group to be biased toward them, and sometimes a lack of real knowledge leads to stronger biases. That is true when it comes to sexual orientation. Developmental psychologist Rachel Farr and I, along with our colleagues, conducted a series of studies to examine elementary-aged children's biases about same-sex families (families with two lesbian moms or two gay dads). For example, across two different studies, we found that only about one-fourth of elementary schoolkids could define what "gay" or "lesbian" meant. The kids who knew said things like "Gay is used for boys who like boys. Lesbian is used for girls who like girls," or "If a boy marries a boy or a girl marries a girl." Plenty of kids said gay means "stupid" or "weird." Most kids, though, said, "I don't know."[1]

This lack of knowledge, however, does not prevent biases from appearing. Even when they don't know what "gay" means, children still have prejudices and stereotypes about gay and lesbian couples. In one of our studies, we measured children's implicit biases about same-sex couples by looking at how often they clicked a computer key indicating "like" or "don't like" after seeing pictures of same-sex couples (like two women sitting next to one another on a sofa holding hands) versus mixed-sex couples (like a man and a woman sitting next to each on a front stoop). We found that children made more positive associations with the straight couples than the same-sex couples. Then when we explicitly asked them about pictures of same-sex couples and mixed-sex couples and their respective children, children reported liking the same-sex couples less and rating them as more "gross" (the child-friendly word for disgust) than their mixed-sex counterparts. They also said they liked the children of same-sex couples less. By the time children started elementary school, even without knowing what gay or lesbian meant, their LGBTQ+ biases were in place. As children get older, their bias around sexual orientation and gender identity—their sexual prejudice—grows, peaking across genders as they turn into adolescents.[2] That's typically the most biased age for straight girls, as their biases against lesbian women and gay men decrease across their teen years.[3] However, for straight boys, although their biases against lesbian women decrease, their biases against gay men stay steady,[4] a reflection of the strongly enforced norms of toxic masculinity that intricately link masculinity with heterosexuality.

Sexual prejudice seems to be made up of three overlapping components:[5]

1. There are a person's beliefs about homosexuality itself—such as where sexual orientation comes from, whether it is biologically innate, socialized, or a "lifestyle choice," and how acceptable being gay is. For some people, their religious beliefs factor into their attitudes about homosexuality.
2. There's how comfortable a person is in social interactions with LGBTQ+ people. Do they interact with LGBTQ+ people, and if or when they do, are the interactions positive or negative?
3. There's their beliefs about the rights of LGBTQ+ people—like whether they should have the same access and protection under the law as straight, cisgender people. These beliefs encompass a person's thoughts on marriage equality, antidiscrimination laws, and policies around LGBTQ+ couples adopting children.

When put together, sexual prejudice is some combination of believing being gay is wrong, being uncomfortable around gay people, and believing that laws should not ensure equal rights for gay people.

In general, at least on the surface, sexual prejudice has been on the decline over the past few decades. A Pew Research poll in 2020 found that, among Americans older than fifty, only 62 percent believed that homosexuality should be "accepted by society"; but among eighteen-to-twenty-nine-year-olds, 82 percent did.[6] This greater tolerance by younger generations doesn't seem to just be a reflection of youth, but a sign of chang-ing times. After all, through the 1990s and early 2000s, only 47 percent of Americans—including eighteen-to-twenty-nine-year-olds—thought homosexuality should be accepted, while 45 percent thought it should be "discouraged." Two decades later, we now see fewer than one in four Americans who think homosexuality should be discouraged. Yet this shift in public opinions toward greater acceptance of LGBTQ+ individuals in society is really reflecting greater belief in equal rights—it is not a real pushback against the overwhelming heteronormativity in our culture. That heteronormativity is still coursing through children's media and through their biased interactions with one another. These peer norms of heteronormativity and toxic masculinity seem to override other values children may hold, such as beliefs in fairness and kindness. Times are changing, but LGBTQ+ youth are still at risk.

A HETERONORMATIVE SOCIAL MIRROR AND WHAT ISN'T SEEN

Homophobic bias harms millions of LGBTQ+ children and teens. Based on national samples analyzed in 2020 by the Williams Institute, a think tank based in the College of Law at UCLA, about 9.5 percent of the US population of youth, between the ages of thirteen and seventeen, identify as either lesbian, gay, bisexual, and/or transgender (keeping in mind that transgender is a gender identity and trans youth can be either straight or LGB).[7] That's almost two million LGBTQ+ American high schoolers. When surveys ask about how many children and teens consider themselves gender nonconforming in some way, almost one in eight young people identify as gender nonconforming or transgender.[8] These numbers are likely to increase over the next decade, as greater acceptance of LGBTQ+ identities becomes more prevalent among younger generations.* A Gallup Poll from early 2021 found that one in six individuals born between 1997 and 2002 identify as LGBTQ+ (with more than half of that number identifying as bisexual).[9] Despite these growing numbers, children see a very straight and cisgender world reflected back at them through

---

*   This could be attributed to increasingly accepting environments, which means for many people, family rejection is less frequent, financial and employment security is less risky, media representation is more common, and overall safety is less of a concern when coming out. This does not mean bias is not prevalent and extreme for many individuals.

media. No doubt, LGBTQ+ individuals are represented in media overall more than ever before. A report by GLAAD (Gay and Lesbian Alliance Against Defamation) that focused on the 2018–2019 television landscape calculated that LGBTQ+ people represented almost 9 percent of television series regulars on broadcast prime-time scripted programming (an increase of 2.4 percent from the previous year).[10] That's about twice what Gallup polls estimated the population of LGBTQ+ adults in the United States to be that year.[11]

Yet the representation of LGBTQ+ people in *children's* media is much less common, and there are very few depictions of same-sex relationships. Over the past few years, there have definitely been some positive examples. In 2014, the Disney Channel featured its first openly queer character, a lesbian couple on an episode of *Good Luck Charlie*.[12] In the 2017 live-action remake of *Beauty and the Beast*, LeFou danced with a man; then Pixar produced an animated short film, *Out*, focused on a young gay man struggling with coming out to his parents; and *Toy Story 4* included a two-mom family. In 2018, Cartoon Network's *Steven Universe*, a show with multiple lesbian romances and nonbinary characters who use they/them pronouns, became the first animated program in history to depict a queer wedding when Ruby and Sapphire, two of the show's central female-presenting characters, were married.[13] And in 2019, on the live-action series *Andi Mack*, Disney's first openly gay protagonist, Cyrus Goodman, came out by saying, "I'm gay"[14]—a first for the popular network.

Likewise, public television has been slow to have positive representation of LGBTQ+ individuals, but is showing some incremental progress. *Arthur*, the long-running PBS cartoon about the anthropomorphic aardvark and his family and school friends, has a history of trying to be inclusive. In 2005, on one of their spinoffs, *Postcards from Buster*, Buster, Arthur's best friend, visits a lesbian couple in Vermont. Unfortunately, in the early aughts, showing a lesbian couple on children's television caused a national uproar. President Bush's secretary of education, Margaret Spellings, denounced the program. PBS was told they would need to shelve the episode and return the public funds used to produce it.[15] They complied. Flash-forward fourteen years: In the opening episode of their twenty-second season, Arthur's teacher Mr. Ratburn married his partner, a chocolatier named Patrick. Although the words *gay* or *lesbian* were never used, PBS stations in Alabama and Arkansas refused to air the show, saying that parents had not been properly warned about the "controversial content."[16] To state the obvious, it was a rat and an aardvark in tuxedos with corsages standing next to one another; to see the controversy, you have to want to see it.

These few exceptions, while definitely an improvement from a decade ago, prove the rule about how heteronormative children's media is. Almost every princess story involves a prince, and even when the princess rejects the potential princes, there are still the ever-present heteronormative assumptions. For example, in 2012's *Brave* by Pixar, the plot hinges on the princess's refusal to marry (boys were the only option given); in 2013's *Frozen*, Hans is Anna's love interest she eventually rejects, but by the 2019 sequel, she is in love with Kristoff. Even in nonprincess movies, if there happens to be a female character, the plot is still heteronormative (in 2004's *The Incredibles*, Violet gets a crush on a boy and changes her hair; in 2015's *Inside Out*, the movie ends with Riley capturing the attention of a boy, Jordan). We have yet to see a Disney princess fall in love with another princess.

Across children's media, if there are gay characters, they are often one dimensional. As one teen said, "If it's a gay high school character, they're normally scrawny and weak, a potential to be a bullied person and they're pushed around. They're really insecure and they have . . . girl best friends that help them out."[17] In an analysis of forty-five episodes of four of the most popular shows on Disney and Nickelodeon, when boys were portrayed as anything but hypermasculine and straight, they were the comedic counterpoint to the popular boys, the butt of jokes because of their norm-breaking behaviors.[18] "Acting gay" or feminine is played for laughs, not inclusion. And when lesbian or gay youth are shown in noncomedic roles, there is usually controversy or sadness around coming out or being rejected by their family. Trans youth are especially invisible. In a GLAAD study of all shows on broadcast, cable, and streaming television in 2018–2019, there were a total of twenty-six trans characters across all platforms.[19]

Children and teens often use fictional representations from media to help shape their identity, and this is especially important if they are in a minoritized group where they may not have access to real-life role models. Therefore, this heteronormative social mirror—in which LGBTQ+ kids don't see their reflections unless those reflections are controversial or mocking—makes it difficult for LGBTQ+ children to develop a positive sense of self. The lack of LGBTQ+ representation in children's media also harms cisgender straight kids who don't have the opportunity to learn about the diversity of sexual and gender identities. For kids, who are always listening and learning about the norms of what is valued and accepted, they pick up the idea that LGBTQ+ individuals and families are largely ignored and absent, and therefore devalued.

LGBTQ+ individuals and families are so invisible in children's media—especially compared to their relative representation in adult media—for multiple reasons. One is that people often conflate sexual orientation (an identity) with sex (a behavior). In an attempt to shy away from content about sexuality, children's media erroneously avoids representing people and families with different sexual orientations. Additionally, despite having nothing to do with either sexual orientation or sexuality, diverse gender identities are also rarely shown. The foolishness of this is apparent once you consider that, by labeling people a girl or a boy (like all children's media does), we are already talking about gender identity. Many children in preschool know their gender identities, and children in media should, like real-life children, represent a range of gender identities and forms of gender expression. Otherwise, when these heteronormative standards in media overlap with heteronormative messages at home, and are enforced as norms in the schoolyard, children easily develop biases against LGBTQ+ individuals and families.

THE BIAS LGBTQ+ YOUTH EXPERIENCE

Despite seeming declines in sexual prejudice and tentative growth in media representation, it is clear from nationwide studies that LGBTQ+ bias is still pervasive—and it doesn't take much effort to uncover those biases. As we spoke of in the previous chapter, if you walk down the hallway of a middle school, it won't take long before you hear the words *gay* or *fag* used to describe someone or something—anyone deemed stupid, feminine, emotional, studious, or small. In national surveys of middle school students, almost every single student reported hearing "gay" used negatively regularly.[20] Many of the kids who say "That's so gay" are not purposefully expressing homophobic attitudes; it is just something "everyone says." But when slurs are embedded in everyday language, it normalizes the bias—the casual use makes it harder to see the damage caused. Yet it *has* caused damage. In a national survey of 23,000 LGBTQ+ teens conducted by GLSEN (the Gay, Lesbian, and Straight Education Network) in 2017, 92 percent of the nearly 100 percent of those 23,000 LGBTQ+ teens who had heard "gay" used in a negative way were upset by it.

Beyond the everyday use of "gay" as a synonym for anything negative, LGBTQ+ youth face even more extreme forms of harassment and bullying. LGBTQ+ youth live in constant fear of extreme physical threat.[21] Seventy percent of LGBTQ+ youth report they were called names and threatened by their peers; almost 30 percent were pushed or shoved; 49 percent were cyberbullied; and 12 percent were punched, kicked, or assaulted with a weapon—all because of their sexual orientation, gender identity, or gender expression. For transgender youth, the rates were higher and the harassment even more extreme: Some studies find 83 percent of transgender youth have been physically harassed and 25 percent have been physically assaulted.

But the fact that most of this harassment occurs at school is not the only reason that LGBTQ+ students often don't feel safe there: oftentimes, teachers themselves are biased against their LGBTQ+ students. More than half of LGBTQ+ youth report hearing homophobic remarks from their teachers.[22] Teachers also punish LGBTQ+ youth, who are twice as likely to be suspended as straight kids, more than their peers.[23] Even if teachers aren't actively penalizing LGBTQ+ students, they offer very little support: The majority of youth don't report the bias and discrimination they experience because they doubt a teacher or school staff member would actually do anything to help.[24] Of the students who reported LGBTQ+ discrimination to a teacher, 60 percent said the teacher did nothing in response. As one teen stated, "The worst thing about homophobic bullying in my school is knowing that the teachers won't stop it."[25] This sentiment was echoed by another high school student who said, "Our school is very insensitive toward harassment issues toward [LGBTQ+] youth. I once tried to talk to our principal about the homophobic language rampant in our schools but he said he couldn't help because it would be too controversial."[26] Like with sexual harassment between boys and girls, many teachers view peer-to-peer homophobic bullying as "horseplay" or "messing around."[27]

This takes a toll on LGBTQ+ youth's academic life, mental health, and physical health. It hurts their school success, as LGBTQ+ youth who experience bias have a lower sense of school belonging, have lower GPAs, are more likely to fail a course, and are less likely to take demanding classes compared to their straight, cisgender counterparts.[28] They often avoid school, drop out entirely, or generally leave high school less prepared for college compared to their peers. Bias also hurts their physical health, as LGBTQ+ youth who experience bias are more likely to engage in risky behaviors that can result in harm, such as drinking and drug use and not practicing safe sex. Perhaps the most damage is exacted from their mental health. When LGBTQ+ youth experience bias, they are increasingly likely to be depressed, more anxious, show signs of post-traumatic stress disorder, have lower self-esteem and less satisfaction with life, and think about—and attempt—suicide. According to a 2015 survey of more than one thousand high school students who identified as LGBTQ+, 43 percent of all those asked had seriously considered suicide at some point in the last year, 38 percent had already planned how they would do it, and almost 30 percent had attempted suicide one or more times in that year.[29] As the parent of a gay teen myself, it is hard to wrap my mind around those numbers.

There are real kids behind every single one of these statistics. Seth Walsh was one of them. In 2010, in a rural California community about 120 miles north of Los Angeles, rumors were flying in Seth Walsh's elementary school that he was gay. In interviews, his grandmother Judy said, "He started getting teased by the fourth and fifth grade."[30] By the time he came out in the sixth grade, "the kids were starting to get mean." She said, "He was ridiculed. He was pushed into lockers, pushed to the ground, tripped . . . By the seventh grade, he was afraid to walk home from school because he was afraid he would get harassed. As he was walking by a classroom, a kid yelled out, 'Queer.' Stuff like that."

The bullying was relentless. Other kids would make comments to his face, call him on the phone to make fun of him, post comments about him on the internet. Seth's mom, Wendy, reported this harassment to the school. She talked to the teachers and school administrators. She said, "I talked to the vice principal about my concerns. He said, 'Remind me next year.'" No one at school seemed to care much, and her concerns kept being dismissed. In September of 2010, Wendy went to the back yard and found her thirteen-year-old son unconscious. After another round of bullying, he had hung himself from a tree in their yard. She pulled him down and desperately tried to resuscitate her son's small body. He was on life support for a week before he died.[31]

For all of the damages that LGBTQ+ bias leaves in its wake, the effects are especially harsh for boys, as boys seem to be most vulnerable to the bullying and harassment that comes from breaking the heteronormative "rules." As discussed in the last chapter, being a boy and being overtly heterosexual are intertwined as part of toxic masculinity. These are the rigid biased rules that benefit some boys—the straight, cisgender, hypermasculine ones—more than anyone else, and most severely and violently punish the boys who violate them.

PARENTS CAN MAKE A DIFFERENCE

As I touched on earlier in this chapter, one of the most damaging sources of LGBTQ+ biases are—unlike with racial, ethnic, or gender bias—children's own parents.* Because of the central role a parent plays in the healthy adjustment of a child, supportive parents can drastically alter the health and well-being of their kids—while sexually prejudiced parents' rejection of their LGBTQ+ child is particularly painful.

Most parents assume that their children will be straight and cisgender, and actively parent under that heteronormative assumption. Sociologist Karin Martin surveyed 641 mothers of three- to six-year-old children. She asked the moms about whether they ever wondered if their young children would grow up to be gay or lesbian. She found that *only* 6 percent of moms described themselves as "purposefully parenting to be sure that their children know that gays and lesbians exist." One of these few moms said, "Because I know that many kids do [end up gay], and I've known too many [LGBT] people who have felt very unhappy at their own response to being [LGBT]. I want to make certain my kids don't add to this in others (because I am certain that they know some kids who are [LGBT], even if the kid doesn't know it yet), and because I want them to be happy about finding love, regardless of the gender of the person." This minority of parents, as Martin said, "leave open the possibility for a wide variety of paths."[32] The inclusive parents want to proactively make sure their children feel unconditionally loved and don't only see that heteronormative social mirror.

---

* Although this book covers racial/ethnic, gender and LGBTQ+ bias, there are many important differences between those forms of bias, especially as it pertains to the role of parents. In one way, parents who are the same race/ethnicity as their children do not typically racially discriminate against their own children. In a different vein, parents may inadvertently pass along gender biases to their children because of their own internalized gender biases (often ones they are unaware of). Yet for LGBTQ+ biases, parents may more actively discriminate against their own children because of the nature of sexual prejudice in which some people may inaccurately believe it is a moral choice. For LGBTQ+ youth, parental bias can be the most harmful of all.

A much more common response, expressed in about 60 percent of parents, was to "hope for the best," and say that they would love their children "in spite of being gay." One mom said, "At this point, I don't see any difference if they are interested in [a] specific gender. And even if they are gonna be gay or lesbian, I will support them. Even [if] I don't approve of gay and lesbian." That last sentence is the real kicker, and likely to be the one that rings the loudest to their child. One mother reported that her young daughter "watches and reads a lot of Disney stories so she believes that every girl will meet a prince just like in the stories and they will find each other and fall in love, get married and have babies." This mom's underlying assumption was that having a heteronormative media diet leads to be being heterosexual, so she, like many parents, just assumed her kids would be straight, and thinking about providing an inclusive environment was moot.

In contrast to this passive approach to "inclusive-ish" parenting, one in three parents actively tried to "prevent" their child from being gay or lesbian. As one mom stated, "We model a heterosexual healthy marriage life in our family so I believe our daughter sees a correct woman's modeling as do our boys with their dad." Another mom stated, "I believe that I can teach my children that this is a sin and model a good relationship for them, and this will never be an issue." Yet another one said, "I don't believe that children are born gay [but] that it is brought on by environmental influences, or how a child is treated. I don't treat my children like fragile pieces of glass I treat him like he's a boy and expect him to act like a boy." One mom even went so far as to say, "Because he will learn that the Bible does not allow that. We will not allow it. And if he is, he will be committed to a psyc[hiatric] hospital to find out what is wrong with his mind and brain function!" To be clear, these heteronormative and homophobic messages at home do not make it any less likely that children will be LGBTQ+, as parenting strategies neither cause nor prevent any sexual orientation or gender identity (otherwise, no gay or trans kids would have to endure homophobic or transphobic parents, but many do). All that these parents are doing is ensuring that their children will try to hide their identity from and struggle to feel loved by their parents.

Some studies find one in four families are "extremely rejecting" of their children when they come out, and many more make comments about how their children express their gender (telling boys to stop being a "sissy").[33] This disapproval can be gut-wrenching, as parental rejection can make youth feel especially isolated and alone.[34] Researchers have specifically asked LGBTQ+ youth about how often their parents talked openly about their sexual orientation, how often their openly LGBTQ+ friends were invited to join family activities, how often a parent brought them to an LGBTQ+ youth organization or event, and how often a parent appreciated their clothing or hairstyle, even though it might not have been typical for their gender. They found that 57 percent of youth whose parents were not accepting and supportive of their LGBTQ+ identity had attempted suicide.[35]

On the other hand, family emotional support and acceptance, when it is felt and believed by kids, can help mitigate and alleviate the other negative experiences with bias. Supportive families lower the odds that their teen will attempt suicide, reduce depression and anxiety, and alleviate some of the stress faced at school.[36] Family support is no magic shield that protects again all societal bias and stigma, but it definitely helps.* In this way, parents play a crucial role: they can either be supportive, or they can place their children at greater risk for suicide and depression.

WHEN BIAS TOWARD LGBTQ+ PARENTS TRICKLES DOWN TO THEIR CHILDREN

Bias toward LGBTQ+ individuals doesn't stop in adulthood; it also affects them when they grow up, form families, and become parents. Then children in LGBTQ+ families sometimes experience a secondhand bias as bias against the parents trickles down to their kids.† Charlotte Patterson, a professor of

---

* One of the most well-known examples of how parents can advocate for their children against LGBTQ+ bias began in 1972 at New York's Christopher Street Liberation Day March. Jeanne Manford marched with a handwritten sign urging "Parents of Gays Unite in Support for Our Children." This was first step in the creation of what is now called PFLAG (previously Parents, Families, and Friends of Lesbians and Gays). The Christopher Street Liberation Day March was a precursor to what would become a pride march. PFLAG was originally meant as a support group for parents of gay and lesbian children, but became an effective parent advocacy group for LGBTQ+ children. In the early 1990s, a PFLAG chapter in Massachusetts helped pass the first safe schools legislation in the United States. Similar parent advocacy groups exist in the UK, Canada, Latin America, Israel, Vietnam, the People's Republic of China, and throughout Europe.

† Ironically, a key argument in the "marriage equality case" of *Obergefell v. Hodges* in 2015 was that same-sex marriage would "damage" kids. However, when the Supreme Court ruled in favor of marriage equality, citing the Equal Protection Clause of the Fourteenth Amendment, a core part of Justice Kennedy's majority opinion was focused on the inherent bias directed at children when their parents are discriminated

psychology at the University of Virginia, along with her former graduate student Rachel Farr (who would later collaborate with me on the same-sex family studies described above), compared the development of kids from lesbian mothers with the development of kids from straight mothers. They found they were equally well-adjusted.[37] Peterson has replicated these comparisons multiple times using different samples of families, examining things like children's preferences for same-gender playmates and activities, social competence, self-esteem and anxiety, behavior problems, substance use, and measures of school outcomes, such as grade point averages and trouble in school. Again and again, kids in LGBTQ+ families looked just like kids in straight families. The only real difference between the two groups favored the kids in LGBTQ+ families, as they tended to feel a greater sense of connection to people at school. Parenting style mattered, of course, but sexual orientation didn't. When parents had a warm and affectionate relationship with their child, children were equally well-adjusted.[38]

This isn't to say that children in LGBTQ+ families feel no bias. Rachel Farr interviewed children in elementary school who had been adopted by same-sex parents about their experiences in their families. More than half of the children talked about "feeling different" at times. As one nine-year-old boy with two dads noted, "I'm one of the only people in my school that has two daddies." A six-year-old girl, when describing how her family is "not like other families," said, "Like a lot of families have moms and dads and some families have two moms and two dads." However, the most common form of bias that kids experienced was the subtle assumption of heteronormativity. As one ten-year-old girl with two dads said, "If they're like, 'Where's your mom?' or 'Is your mom coming?' and I'm like, 'Oh, I have two dads.'" A

---

against, saying that "The marriage laws at issue here thus harm and humiliate the children of same-sex couples." Once again, children were at the center of an equal rights debate. Kennedy cited an amicus brief which said, "Children of same-sex couples, like the victims of racial segregation [decided in *Brown v. Board of Education*] and immigrant children excluded from educational opportunities [decided in *Plyler v. Doe*], suffer the harmful psychological effects of the condemnation of their families, which, as the Court noted in *Brown*, is compounded by the law's sanction of this discrimination." In other words, when families are discriminated against, children suffer psychologically. Kennedy also noted that "As all parties agree, many same-sex couples provide loving and nurturing homes to their children, whether biological or adopted." The research he referenced was Patterson's and Farr's. This statement, dropped into one of the most important Supreme Court cases of this century, represented another moment when the courts relied on developmental science to learn about the lives of children.

seven-year-old remarked, "My friends sometimes [say] 'you tell your mom, then'—but I'm like, 'Dude, I have two dads.'" One kid even said his friends "didn't know same-sex couples existed."[39] Different strains of research have consistently shown that many of the key biases facing kids are rooted in the invisibility of LGBTQ+ individuals and families.*

LGBTQ+ bias is simultaneously invisible and severe. It seems as though attitudes are getting less biased, based on national surveys and representation in the media that adults see. Yet every middle schooler we talk to hears "gay" used as a slur every day at school, trans youth are physically assaulted regularly, parents are still kicking kids out of the house when they come out as gay or trans, and suicide rates among teens because of LGBTQ+ biases and harassment remain high.

To reduce LGBTQ+ bias, we must make LGBTQ+ identities less invisible to children. The fact that more elementary school children thought "gay" meant "stupid" than could give an accurate definition of the word underscores that lack of visibility. But when identities are rendered invisible, they are treated as shameful. That shame is compounded when parents reject or shun children for who they are. And shame about having an LGBTQ+ identity, in part, contributes to why suicide rates are so high for children who experience LGBTQ+ bias compared to other types of bias. While we try to make the culture less biased for LGBTQ+ youth, there must also be serious attention paid to inclusive mental health services for youth. No child should ever question their worth because they represent a natural part of human diversity.

---

* Even though they experience bias, most children in this study felt personally very positive about their families. One girl exclaimed, "It's like I have two times the loving because I have two of my moms." Another child said, "[My parents] are really kind and awesome . . . flawless." One nine-year old with two moms poignantly said, "I have a rainbow family that always sticks together."

THE SCIENTIST BEHIND THE SCIENCE

CHARLOTTE PATTERSON ———————————————

Charlotte Patterson,* like most of the scientists who study bias, felt a personal connection to what she studies. After earning a PhD in developmental psychology from Stanford University in 1975, she began her career as a professor at UVA. Her early research was focused on self-control in children and how they nonverbally communicated with parents. She slowly started looking at how families were influential in the peer relationships children were having, but never focused on children of same-sex couples. Then, in the late 1980s, as a lesbian thinking about starting her own family, she started looking for research on how children in same-sex families fared and found herself frustrated by the lack of studies out there. There had never been a systematic look at how children with LGBTQ+ parents were developing. As a researcher, she decided she should fix that gap.

In 1992, she wrote a paper titled "Children of Lesbian and Gay Families" that critically reviewed the research on children in LGBTQ+ families that had been done so far. As Charlotte said, "Information was strewn across many fields—some in social work, psychology, psychiatry—a few people here and there who didn't seem to know one another. It wasn't a coherent field at that point in time. I realized there were lots and lots of interesting things that nobody had studied, to put it mildly." In the era before you could do an online search of everything ever published, she literally drove from campus to campus in search of doctoral dissertations and unknown studies. But all of this effort led to an important discovery. By reviewing the existing research, she was able to debunk the myths that children in same-sex-parents families were being harmed. They seemed to be developing the same as everyone else.

This wasn't an easy topic to tackle in the late 1980s. She said, "In those days, and still today, if you write something on an LGBTQ+ topic as a professional research psychologist, people will assume you have some connection to the topic. I was frankly worried that . . . it would be a real problem for my career. Would people let me work with their children?" She remembers thinking, "Well, who else is going to do it if not me?"[40] Charlotte said, "A

---

* Information about Charlotte is taken from my personal interviews with her, from published interviews, and from her publications.

lot of people were shocked that I wrote it. People saw that article as a kind of professional coming out. That won me some friends and lost me some, as you can imagine." But beyond the personal worries, very little research on children in same-sex families had been conducted at that point. When she first started presenting her research at the meeting of the Society for Research in Child Development (SRCD), all of the researchers who studied anything related to LGBTQ+ issues were crammed into one single session, regardless of the topic. But that paper changed things.

Charlotte had also long recognized the importance of her work in educating public policymakers. She knew from the beginning that the judicial system was biased against LGBTQ+ parents and that bias was, in part, driven by fears about how children would develop. She knew that research could help address those fears and demonstrate with data how children were actually being affected by same-sex parents—so that's what she researched. Her work has played a central role in advancing equal rights for LGBT parents over the past two decades. Her research was cited in the amicus briefs filed by the American Psychological Association (APA) for the *Obergefell* Supreme Court cases guaranteeing marriage equality, plus the 2000 Supreme Court case of *Boy Scouts of America v. Dale* (the case in which the Boy Scouts dismissed a scoutmaster for being gay), and the 2003 case of *Lawrence v. Texas*, which overturned state laws criminalizing private consensual sexual behaviors. Her research has also been cited in amicus briefs and majority decisions in the Supreme Courts of Virginia, Maryland, Oregon, New Jersey, New York, Iowa, and Illinois. Peterson has also testified as an expert witness in a number of high-profile cases, such as *Bottoms v. Bottoms*, when a lesbian mother was sued by her own mother for custody of her child, and *Baehr v. Miike*, a 1996 same-sex marriage case in Hawaii.

Beyond informing policymakers and the judicial system, sometimes her work lands directly in the hands of families. She said, "I sometimes see that my research has made an impact when people tell me that they used the work in many ways when they were considering having children." She continued, "Most people my age in the gay community grew up assuming they wouldn't have kids. A lot of us were affected with what I would call internalized homophobia." She explains, "If you've heard people around you forever telling you that you'd be a terrible parent you wonder, maybe I shouldn't have children. A lot of people told me they read my articles and said, 'Hey, maybe I could be a good parent!' Or they used the findings to reassure worried grandparents-to-be."

She—and her research—also inspired an entire field to follow along. In 2019, when the newly formed LGBTQ+-based caucus of developmental researchers met for the first time at the biennial meeting of SRCD research- ers, about one hundred young researchers were crammed into a convention center meeting room. Many of the people in the room weren't even born when her 1992 paper came out, but they were all researchers who either studied LGBTQ+ youth and families or were themselves LGBTQ+ schol- ars. The new caucus was celebrating their official recognition as part of the organizational structure of the largest professional group of developmental scientists in the world. When Charlotte entered the room, running late because she had been presenting her latest research as part of a symposium on the other side of the large convention center, she was met with a standing ovation. A lot had changed in the twenty-seven years she had been working on this topic. Rather than "ruining her career," as she had worried, she had not only helped change the laws of the land and ignite an entire field of research, but also inspired a generation of scholars who could see themselves in her. Representation always matters. For kids and for researchers.

PART III

MOVING FORWARD

*What We Need to Do Today and
Tomorrow to Unravel Bias*

11 Unraveling Bias Can Start at Home

It is not enough to be compassionate. You must act.
—Dalai Lama

Changing bias is hard: bias is embedded within our institutions and within individuals, two threads existing in a feedback loop and sustaining one another. Biased beliefs and attitudes allow us to justify and endorse biased policies, and biased policies keep inequalities in place that rationalize biased beliefs—we've seen that time and again throughout this book. Neither form of bias exists in isolation, so, in order to unravel bias, as bell hooks writes, "there must exist a paradigm, a practical model for social change that includes an understanding of ways to transform consciousness that are linked to efforts to transform structures." In short, because bias occurs at multiple levels, we have to take a multilayered approach to address and eradicate bias in *all* of those places—changing both our thinking and our institutions.

Think of the efforts to unravel bias in terms of what aspect of bias that effort is changing—a heart, a mind, or an institution. Think of things that change a heart as things that appeal to the feelings and emotions about others—things that we can change by focusing our and our children's attention on compassion, empathy, and fairness. Other efforts and actions will focus on changing minds—which are actions that seek to change the stereotypes we believe about others, what we think is true, and what we've been told by biased cultural scripts. Then there are things which change institutions—actions that focus on changing policies and practices that don't value children equally. Changing institutions requires the most coordination and cooperation—but changing both hearts and minds starts at home, in the everyday interactions between caregivers and children.

We'll talk in detail about all three of those aspects in part III, but we'll begin with the first two. While helping the children in our lives reduce their own biases, we *also* want to protect children who are being harmed by bias. Most children (because they belong to multiple groups) both hold biases about others *and* experience bias from others. So, this chapter also offers science-backed suggestions for what we can do within our own homes and families to help protect children from the biases they experience.

REDUCE YOUR OWN BIASES

Just as the flight attendant reminds us to secure our own oxygen mask before helping our children, we have to honestly evaluate and address our own thoughts, feelings, behaviors, and implicit biases about race, immigration, gender, and LGBTQ+ status before we can address our children's biases. Implicit biases are created by seeing biased "inputs" (such as the thousands of television scenes linking Black men as criminals, Arab Muslims as terrorists, and sexy girls as airheads), and by adulthood we have seen millions of these biased examples. It is particularly difficult to change our own implicit biases because of those millions of examples across our entire lives—they are well entrenched in our neural structures (specifically, in the brain's amygdala, prefrontal cortex, and temporal lobes).[1] Implicit biases did not develop overnight, so there is no magic bullet to reduce them overnight either.

There are steps, however, people can take to reduce their implicit biases.[2] First, determine what your implicit biases are. The easiest way to do that is to take one of the tests listed as an Implicit Associations Test (https://implicit.harvard.edu/implicit).* It is important to keep in mind

---

* If you don't want to take an online test, try an imagination exercise. Imagine a "Black man." What image instantly comes to mind? How does he dress, how does he talk? Imagine a "White man." What image instantly comes to mind? How does he dress and

that *most* people show implicit biases: because we are clever as humans, our minds detected patterns in the world—but those patterns emerged from a biased cultural landscape. As a result, these implicit biases are where the heart and mind are on different tracks. So while, yes, people who are in a group that is stigmatized or marginalized in our culture often have implicit biases that reflect that stigma (for example, Black Americans often hold pro-White implicit biases), those patterns of bias do *not* mean that you don't feel proud of your group, feel love for your group, or feel a deep sense of solidarity with other members of your group. Similarly, for people who hold implicit biases against others, those patterns do not mean that you do not believe in equality or desire to be unbiased. You may want to recoil from your results because they feel at odds with what your heart believes—but we have to understand what our brains are doing before we can retrain our minds to match what our hearts are feeling.

Once you are aware of where your implicit biases are, the next step is to learn strategies for reducing them.[3] One of those strategies (called *stereotype replacement*) involves learning to replace stereotypical responses with nonstereotypical responses. This includes noticing when you make a stereotypical response, labeling it as a bias, and thinking about why it happened—then imagining what an unbiased response would be and visualizing using that instead. An example of this would be to reflect on your reaction when a Black man gets onto an elevator with you. Do you tense up, feel afraid, or step away?* Those are responses reflecting the stereotype that a Black man is dangerous,[4] a pervasive bias that is largely driven by media images and the systemic mass incarceration of Black men, and which contributes to deadly race-based police violence. If your initial response reflects this stereotype, think about how you could react differently next time. Perhaps look at his face, notice his clothes, relax your breathing. Think about how you might have reacted had it been a White man.

Another effective strategy (called *counterstereotypic imaging*[5]) is to imagine, in detail, counterstereotypic examples.[6] They can be abstract examples (such as smart Black people), famous examples (such as President

---

talk? How are those two images different? Do the same process for other social groups.

* Claude Steele, a Black social psychologist and expert on the effects of stereotypes, tells the story in his book *Whistling Vivaldi* of how he would whistle classical music when he got on an elevator as a means of avoiding this very reaction from others.

Obama), or non-famous examples (such as a friend or neighbor). Do this frequently—the goal is to make positive examples more salient and mentally accessible, so that they can override some of the negative biased examples your brain has encoded over the years. A third strategy (called *individuation*[7]) involves finding personal and specific information about group members. This could involve asking about shared interests or finding out about hobbies or family members. This allows you to use accurate personal information instead of relying on stereotype-based inferences. A fourth strategy (called *perspective taking*) involves considering experiences from the other person's point of view. Doing this helps people feel psychologically close to another person, and that makes it harder to respond with bias. This may take the form of consuming media (especially books, movies, and television) about the experiences of diverse people. Media is a great place to start so that you are not burdening an individual by asking them to do this mental and emotional labor for you.

Finally, focus on slowing down your thinking and reminding yourself daily that you don't want to be biased. Think of implicit biases as the autopilot of your brain. Implicit biases are most likely to bubble up and affect our behavior when we are stressed out, moving quickly, and not paying attention.[8] They take over when the other more thoughtful parts of your brain (the ones opposed to bias) are busy rushing around through the day. We have to keep the motivation to remain unbiased mentally front and center and slow down enough to prevent that autopilot from making decisions for us. This is one reason that people who have completed general mindfulness exercises have shown a subsequent decrease in implicit biases.[9] A two-minute meditation every morning reminding yourself to focus on people's unique characteristics and to intervene when you see biases can help keep antibiased goals more salient than the biased associations in your mind.

Beyond these specific strategies that have been shown to reduce implicit biases, all of the suggestions listed below that are focused on reducing children's biases and protecting children from bias are also helpful for adults. Reducing biases is a lifelong process, so it is natural for adults and children to learn and change together. Talking to children about your own learning process also reinforces that this is an imperfect journey. This is the time to take a growth mindset approach: we can all get better, it is never perfect or finished, and it just takes work.

FOCUS ON EMPATHY AND OTHER PEOPLE'S PERSPECTIVES

Feeling empathy toward others, focusing on connecting with the humanity of others, is an important way to reduce biases. At its most basic, empathy is defined as the ability to experience the same feelings as those of another person. Empathy is part cognitive: children have to be able to take another person's perspective in a situation. Very young children struggle with this because it is mentally complicated to see the world from a different set of eyes. But empathy is also part emotional: children have to appreciate how the other person feels and feel something (sympathy, compassion, worry, etc.) in return. The more we feel empathy for another person, the more we can imagine ourselves in that situation, the closer we feel to them. And we don't show biases toward people we feel close to or who feel similar to us.

Studies have shown how feeling greater empathy and being able to take the perspective of others helps reduce all types of bias. For example, when empathy and perspective taking (meaning the ability and motivation to take another person's point of view) is boosted, teens have more positive attitudes toward immigrants.[10] And even though showing LGBTQ+ bias is often associated with being popular among teens, teens who are good at taking others' perspectives, teens who can "personally understand and relate to lesbian and gay individuals," are able rise above and attenuate that social norm (and their popularity was not linked to showing LGBTQ+ bias).[11] Some of the most effective prejudice reduction interventions involve exercises to practice both empathy and the ability to take another person's perspective.[12]

Exercises to boost empathy in children begin with simply talking to them. Children sometimes need some help to feel empathy toward others. When researchers read a hypothetical story to elementary school children and asked if they would be willing to help the child in the story, children were more likely to say they would help only *if* the child was described as a friend. But when the researchers pushed on their empathy abilities a little more, and asked the kids to think about the girl and how sad or upset she was likely to be, the children were equally likely to help, regardless of whether she was described a friend or not.[13] Parents, caregivers—anyone who wants to positively influence a child—should model empathy and walk children through understanding others' emotions. Ask children, "How would you feel if this happened to you?" "What do you think you would feel if someone did that to you?" In one study of elementary school kids, children, after reading a book about a girl who was frustrated, had conversations with an adult about the nature of emotions ("How did Maria feel?"; "Have you ever felt that way?"), the causes of the emotions ("Why did Maria feel that way?"; "What might make you feel angry?"), and how to control and regulate emotions when needed ("What kinds of things can we do when we feel angry?"; "What can we do to feel happier?"). After these types of conversations, children were better at understanding emotions and taking other peoples' perspectives, and were more empathetic.[14] Even though that study focused on elementary-aged children, similar conversations—talking about others' emotions and perspectives, talking about how to cope with complex emotions—works for any age child or teen. That ability to connect with and relate to the feelings of others helps us see the humanity, rather than the otherness, of people who differ from us.

LEARN TO SEE THE INDIVIDUAL

Biases are, in part, cognitive and can literally change our perceptions of others. As described in chapter 1, because many people have limited exposure to diverse others when they are infants, they lose the ability to see the difference between out-group individuals, instead thinking out-group individuals "all look alike." This perceptual bias of thinking all out-group members *look* alike leads to a social bias of assuming that all out-group members *are* alike.[15] After all, it is hard to treat someone as an individual if we can't recognize them as an individual. Researchers have shown that helping children perceive people as individuals can actually reduce their social biases in a phenomenon known as *perceptual-social linkage*.[16] For example, in experimental studies, when five-year-olds were trained to recognize the names of different-race individuals, the children's implicit racial biases went down.[17]

Therefore, one strategy to help reduce biases is to help children process people from different racial groups as individuals. As early as possible, children need to see a variety of diverse faces and see them regularly. If necessary, use pictures in books or media and point out the differences in faces, such as, "See her glasses," "See his braids," "Look at the shape of her eyes," "Look at the freckles on her nose," "He has a dimple in his chin." I've done similar things in my own life, like when my three-year-old White daughter pointed to a picture of a Black D-list female celebrity whose headshot was framed on the wall of a Los Angeles restaurant and loudly shouted, "Oprah!" It wasn't Oprah. My daughter was clearly showing the impact of this out-group homogeneity effect. However, despite my acute embarrassment,* instead of letting the moment pass, we walked to the wall of photos, and I pointed to and read each name of each celebrity, and we talked about each picture. My goal in that—and every—moment was to make sure she recognized that each person was unique and not simply a member of a group.

INCREASE KNOWLEDGE OF OTHER GROUPS AND INCORPORATE THEM INTO A COMMON IN-GROUP

Social groups are distinct and provide meaning for our lives—it's important to teach children about them and help them learn about the different types of groups we belong to. Conversations about ethnicities, religions, gender identities, and sexual orientations help increase children's knowledge of groups so that they are not simply relying on stereotyped caricatures to evaluate an individual. As my research has repeatedly shown, children who are knowledgeable about a group show fewer biases toward that group compared to children who only parrot back the stereotype, as accurate knowledge can crowd out the stereotypes.[18] Having a little bit of knowledge, having some personal connections, helps humanize rather than other. Helping children learn about different groups can involve going to museums and cultural fairs, and finding educational books that convey accurate information.

At the same time that it is important to recognize what distinct groups represent, it is also vital to see that different groups can share a common identity. This doesn't mean denying the importance of groups, heritage, culture, or identity—just seeing that there are similarities as well as differences.

---

* Whenever our children publicly express biases, it can be embarrassing. It is pretty embarrassing when our children make any public comment about anyone's physical appearance (this is also true when the comments are based on age, weight, or ability). But because I know those comments reflected a perceptual bias that could lead to a more meaningful bias, I knew I couldn't let it go. Even though I was not comfortable (because it was so public, we were the only White family in the restaurant, and people did turn to look), in my position as a White parent of White children, I can't allow race to be a taboo topic or something we don't name and address. Sometimes these moments involve me giving myself a pep talk to "just get over yourself."

For example, in our Muslim-stereotype study, we found that the children who felt very American *and* who rated White Americans and Arab Americans equally "real Americans" extended the positive feelings they had about their own group to Arab Muslims, making them "part of the family." This is called a common in-group identity. Finding a common identity helps reduce bias.

Children may need help to find those shared identities. There are an infinite number of common identities, and at some point, all humans belong to some shared groups. This isn't about erasing groups (messages like "We are all humans" do *not* help), but it is about redefining groups and changing the boundaries to include more people. Those common identities can be based on shared communities ("We may have been born in different countries, but we are all Bostonians"), schools or teams ("We may be different religions, but we are all Wildcat fans!"), nations or regions ("We may be from the United States, and they are from Mexico, but we are all North Americans"), or religions ("We may be different races, but we are all Baptists"). Seeing the common threads between diverse people makes it easier to feel empathy toward others, to take others' perspectives, and to feel motivated to intervene in moments of bias.

TALK OUT LOUD ABOUT STEREOTYPES, DISCRIMINATION, AND PRIVILEGE

Ibram X. Kendi writes in *How to Be an Antiracist*, "Only racists shy away from the R word. Racism is steeped in denial." I would like to expand that and say that *all* biases are steeped in denial. Therefore, to change the stereotypes embedded in our minds, children need to be able to identify and label stereotypes. Research has shown that, to reduce bias, people first must be aware of their biases and *then* must be motivated to eliminate them.[19] They must reflect on when biased responses are likely to happen and think about how to replace them with a nonbiased response. This doesn't happen automatically—and it means we have to talk more, not less, about all types of biases with children of all ages.

As Riana Anderson and I wrote in a paper called "It's Never Too Young to Talk about Race and Gender," it is helpful to meet children where they are. Ask them questions about what they notice and why it happens. These conversations may be uncomfortable at first, but it gets easier with practice.

And adults do not need to set aside a special time to have "the Talk" with children; these conversations should occur as part of daily life—while driving or walking to school, while cooking dinner, while watching television. They should definitely occur when the adult sees inequalities. When you see something, pause and ask about it: what is happening, who is it affecting, when and where does this happen, and why is race or gender or sexual orientation important in this situation? This tip also means helping children spot racism, sexism, and LGBTQ+ bias in the quantity and quality of media representations too. It can sometimes be difficult to recognize the absence of something, but that is a powerful bias we need to help kids recognize. So, when there is a lack of representation, say something.

For kids in marginalized groups, these conversations about bias should be balanced with conversations about how to cope with bias that they experience ("What can you do when that happens? What can you say? Who can you tell?"). For kids in privileged groups, these conversations need to include discussions of their privilege in clear terms.* This is especially the case for parents of White children and parents of cisgender straight boys. Conversations with kids in privileged groups should be focused on reducing their biases, but also understanding unearned privilege ("Do you think the same thing would have happened if someone that looks like you did it?").

For many children, these collective conversations help them learn to recognize the different biases that harm people and to recognize that they may belong to one group that needs help coping with bias and one group that needs help to see their privilege. For example, in the summer of 2020 when police violence toward Black men and women was very public, I asked my teenaged, White, lesbian daughter how she thought a police officer would treat her if *she* was pulled over for speeding. This led to a powerful conversation about how she could leverage that privilege when she saw others at risk (for example, how she could safely insert herself into the situation). But not long after that conversation, we talked about her frustration with seeing only straight relationships in romantic comedies and her sadness about never seeing a story she could connect with.

The key elements of a conversation about bias differ depending on the bias being discussed, but for conversations about racial bias (which seem to be the most uncomfortable for White parents), it means explicitly

---

* The onus of changing bias should not be on the shoulders of those being targeted by bias (it is asking too much to both survive *and* reduce bias).

mentioning race (we have to explicitly use racial labels if we are going to move past bias), discussing who was responsible when racist acts take place, empathizing with the target of racism, and explicitly labeling it as prejudice. These conversations don't have to be perfect. Research with White mothers who were assigned to talk to their children about implicit racial bias found those conversations reduced their children's implicit racial biases, and actually reduced the parents' own implicit biases—*even* when parents were visibly tense, anxious, and physiologically stressed.[20] In other words, even if you are nervous and bumbling, these conversations are still helpful.

Media, especially books and movies, are excellent starters for conversations about bias, civil rights, sexism, and discrimination.* Media that involves storytelling is emotionally engaging and captures children's attention. This is also a great way to learn about key figures and moments in the fight for social justice. These books should go beyond Martin Luther King Jr. or Rosa Parks, as such figures are necessary, but not sufficient. Many children think Martin Luther King Jr. fixed all racial inequality, so the conversation needs to include both historical examples and *current* examples. For historical examples, connect them to children's current lives. For example, after a story about Rosa Parks, ask children, "Do you know anyone who went on strike or went to a protest?" Find books or movies about Black Lives Matter, about the immigration crisis, or about coping with poverty. Find media about women's equal rights and the fight for suffrage. In the study we did about the election in 2016, when asked, only one child could name a woman who had fought for women's rights (naming Susan B. Anthony).[21] Eleven kids said Hillary Clinton, as she was the only representation they knew, but no other child could name anyone even close. Don't let your child be ignorant of the world they live in: books and movies can help children and adolescents learn about historical and current bias and injustice in the world and the people who helped us make progress.†

A lot of people, instead of explicitly talking about bias, want to simply present counterstereotypical examples of people, hoping that will sink in.

---

* Learning for Justice, EmbraceRace, Welcoming Schools, Smithsonian, and A Mighty Girl all have extensive lists of books that can help with conversations about bias for children of all ages.

† Rachel Ignotofsky's wonderfully illustrated *Women in Science: 50 Fearless Pioneers Who Changed the World* (2016) even includes a biography and illustrations of Dr. Mamie Clark.

This is the approach schools often take because it seems less "controversial." The problem is, this doesn't work. One reason stereotypes are hard to change is that stereotypes reinforce themselves because we register and accept information that confirms our existing stereotypes and forget, ignore, or misremember the times our biases don't work. So, when children are simply shown periodic counterstereotypical examples, they skip over those counterintuitive details. For example, when children were read stories in which a White child was being lazy and a Black child was being hardworking, younger children misremembered the Black child as the one being lazy. So, instead of changing their stereotypes because they heard about a hardworking Black child, they changed their memory to fit their existing stereotype.[22] These examples of breaking the stereotype have to be pointed out and explicitly discussed. Our brains take as many shortcuts as possible, and actually changing those biased patterns takes explicit effort.

The key issue to remember is that bias is everywhere, all the time. If a biased world is the only input children hear and see, children will pick up those biases and internalize them. It is up to adults to be a louder voice in their ear. Give them another explanation for the structural inequalities they are seeing, one that doesn't allow them to rely on biased stereotypes as the explanation. The only way to reject a stereotype is to recognize it for what it is: a biased and simplistic, often inaccurate representation of a person. The best way for children to recognize a stereotype for what it is to talk about it.

DEVELOP A POSITIVE GROUP IDENTITY

Bias is deeply personal. Its impact is personal. It shapes how children think of themselves, altering their mental and physical health, restricting their relationships with others. For kids in groups targeted by bias, we have to help them protect their identity when confronted with negative stereotypes and discrimination. For children of color, for example, a positive racial/ethnic identity, one in which they value and feel proud of their race or ethnicity and feel connected to other people in their racial/ethnic groups, is a powerful buffer against bias. A sense of self connected to racial/ethnic identity provides both the acknowledgment that other people's biases exist but also the resolute belief that one can be resilient against them. Study after study shows that holding a strong, positive racial/ethnic identity (for example, strongly agreeing with statements like "I am proud to be Black" and "Being

Black is an important part of who I am") helps kids and teens do better in school, get along better with their peers, be less depressed and anxious, and be more resistant to negative stereotypes.[23] A 2019 meta-analysis, which combined more than eighteen thousand teens over fifty studies, found that a secure, positive racial/ethnic identity buffers Black, Asian, and Latino youth from the negative effects of experiencing discrimination.[24] Parents can help by discussing their family's cultural heritage, family traditions, and the importance of ethnic pride.

Having a positive group identity works for other social groups too. My research with Campbell Leaper has shown that for girls, having a feminist identity—defined as a belief that men and women are equal and should be treated equally—helps buffer the negative effects of academic bias and sexual harassment.[25] For LGBTQ+ youth, it can be important to feel proud of that identity, to know about the important people in history who were LGBTQ+, and to find positive cultural role models. Ultimately, feeling part of something bigger helps people feel less alone in the face of bias.* Across different types of groups, it is important to help children who belong to marginalized groups to believe "we have done great things, and we can do great things."

For kids in groups who benefit from bias, we have to help them develop a healthy, positive identity rooted in antibias goals. For example, the best way to feel proud of yourself in the context of Whiteness is to transform your privileged identity into one of allyship. This sense of self integrates acknowledging unearned privilege and centering Whiteness around being an antiracist. The same type of antibias identity applies to boys and to straight or cisgender kids. One way to do this is to help them learn about allies who fought for the social justice of others and think about concrete ways to address injustice whenever they encounter it. This can mean help-ing children endorse the idea that "I can and will do something when I see unfairness—this includes telling an adult." But this also means helping them identify as an ally who works *with* others from a place of humility and self-awareness—for example, being able to say, "I will be a good listener to people who are different from me, I will learn from them, and I will ask them

---

* I highly recommend the *ReVisioning History for Young People* book series. There is *Queer History of the United States for Young People, An Indigenous Peoples' History of the United States for Young People,* and *An African American and Latinx History of the United States.* These capture influential people in the fight for social justice, but beyond that, they include people who were talented in the arts, science, business, sports, and culture.

how I can be most helpful." Ultimately, it involves children embracing the sentiment that "We can be helpers. It is up to all of us." Most importantly, this identity frames feeling good about oneself by enacting the mantra "When we see bias, we stop bias."

Intertwined with developing a positive sense of self is fostering an appreciation of diversity. Feeling secure in oneself is the first key to accepting and embracing the differences among us. Children can build on their understanding of their own identities to express comfort and joy with human diversity, use accurate language for human differences (for example, by knowing what transgender means), and form deep, caring connections across all dimensions of human diversity. Parents and schools can help children develop positive group identities beyond conversations: physical space can help children see the value of themselves and a diverse world. Does the child's environment have

- culturally diverse toys;
- pictures, posters, or artwork from people from different ethnic groups;
- children's books focused on children of color;
- books about/from people of different ethnic groups;
- toys to facilitate learning about diverse people or a culture different from your own; and
- pictures of friends or family different from your child's ethnicity?

Be mindful that there are different goals for different kids, but the end result is the same. For children in privileged groups, most of what society reflects back to them are images of themselves. So diversify their space with information and images of non-White, noncisgender male, nonstraight people. For children in marginalized groups, they need to see themselves reflected back, so their spaces should also be filled with images of non-White, noncisgender male, nonstraight people.

LEARN ABOUT AND AFFIRM YOUR CHILDREN'S GROUP IDENTITIES

When parents and their children belong to different social categories, it can be more difficult for parents to help foster a positive group identity.

It is hard to help prepare our children for biases that we don't personally experience. For example, one challenge unique for multiracial children is that although they face bias just like other kids of color, their parents may be less equipped to help them cope with it. Parents who are Black or Latino or Asian can talk to their Black and Latino and Asian kids about the racial and ethnic bias they may experience, because they've experienced it too. But in multiracial families, everyone's experiences may differ in profound ways. A White mom cannot fully understand the lived experience of her Black-presenting son. Parents of color regularly prepare their children for bias and foster pride in their cultural heritage, and these conversations help children and teens cope with discrimination. But White parents rarely talk about race. For multiracial children in particular, their parents have to figure out how to have those conversations.

A lot of White moms raising children of color, despite their own experiences and comfort zone, seem to be stepping up. In research with White mothers raising Black-White biracial children,[26] one mom, Nora, embraced her role: "I feel like I've been really committed to raising my biracial kids [to be] knowledgeable [about] Black stuff ... I've been really committed to [teaching them about their Black heritage]. Kind of my path in life is just really caring about interracial relations ..." Another mom fully recognized how being forced to choose one identity was problematic, stating, "First, I think it's important for my child/children to feel secure and confident in their own identity, regardless of the label they choose to identify with. Second, but also important, I believe it is healthiest if my children identify as biracial, to relate to both sides of their family, and to not feel like they must choose one over the other or that one side of their family is less a part of them than the other." One now-adult child reflected back on her childhood and agreed that her mom's efforts to nurture all of her identities helped, especially appreciating that "having [her] mom go out of her way to make sure [she and her siblings] had peers that looked like us." To a large degree, this really involves parents recognizing that race and ethnicity are important social identities and that parents are important for helping children develop all parts of their identity.

Similar efforts to fully embrace all aspects of our children's identity is also critical for LGBTQ+ youth. This should start before a child ever indicates their sexual orientation by making sure language and assumptions are not heteronormative. For example, don't presume a child will grow up to date or marry someone of the other gender (for example, don't say, "When you grow up, your husband . . ." to your daughter). By being inclusive in language, you help normalize a range of sexual orientations and convey that you are accepting of your child regardless of who they will love. If your child comes out, express affection when your child tells you (or when you learn) about their identity. Support their identity even if you feel uncomfortable. If you are uncomfortable, do your own research until you become comfortable. Remember that your support can make an enormous difference in their mental health. Advocate for your child if they are mistreated because of their LGBTQ+ identity and require that other family members respect your LGBTQ+ child. Also help your child have a robust support system, connect them with LGBTQ+ adult role models, and bring them to LGBTQ+ organizations or events. Explicitly welcome your child's LGBTQ+ friends and partner to your home and family events. Ultimately, it is the easiest parenting act there is: just respect, love, and support children for who they are.

PROMOTE GOOD SLEEP HABITS AND HEALTHY COPING STRATEGIES

Coping with bias is hard. Recent research shows some things can help—and a big one is a good night's sleep. There is a complex two-way relationship between the HPA axis, which includes cortisol (the stress hormone) levels and regulation, and sleep.[27] At its most basic, too much cortisol or dysregulated cortisol impairs the quality and quantity of sleep, and poor sleep can, in turn, elevate cortisol and dysregulate the HPA axis. One thing that helps bring down cortisol and keep the system on track is a good night's sleep. Research has shown that when adolescents had slept longer the night before, they were less likely to ruminate on what was bothering them, less likely to turn the negative thoughts over and over again in their head.[28] Beyond the general benefit of sleep for reducing overall worrying, when teens slept well the night before, they were also more likely to use positive problem solving and seek more peer support on the days they specifically experienced discrimination. And both of those coping strategies (reminding themselves it would get better and talking to their friends) led them to have more positive well-being the next day. In other words, a good night's sleep helped teens cope with the bias they experienced because it left them better equipped to seek out friends and family for support, helped them come up with positive ways to reframe the bias, and helped them not keep focusing on the negative event.

While we are all working to reduce the bias that occurs in the world, families and those with children in their circles of care can help protect children from the damage caused by that bias. Families can also lay critical groundwork, fostering change in children's hearts and minds, to help children fight the bias out there.

12

How Schools and the Community Can Help

A child is a child of everyone.
—Sudanese proverb

B eyond their own families, children and teens are also part of a broader community. First, children in the United States spend, on average, 6.5 hours a day at school. Barring snow days or global pandemics, they attend school about 180 days a year. If we add up the hours spent from kindergarten through their senior year, US children are spending more than fifteen thousand hours of their lives in school. Teachers and school staff, school board officials, and PTA members have an extra responsibility to ensure that schools are bias-free spaces for children to learn. Children are also part of neighborhoods and local communities. They go to after-school activities, churches, and summer camps. They also go to shopping malls, downtown festivals, and children's museums. All of these contexts matter. As members of communities, we must work to reduce the biases that affect children beyond our own families. This means ensuring that the environments children spend time in, as well as the policies that affect children, are bias-free. This chapter offers science-backed suggestions for what we can do within our schools and communities to help prevent children from developing biases, and to protect children from the biases they experience.

ENSURE OPPORTUNITIES FOR INTERGROUP CONTACT

The past seventy years of research have shown that contact with diverse people is the single best way to reduce bias. Intergroup contact needs to be positive, cooperative, and involve working toward a common goal. When we interact with someone, we become comfortable with them. When we become comfortable with them, we feel less anxious around them, we empathize with them more easily, and we ultimately like them more. This means you need to develop friendships with people who are different from you. It also means that you should help kids develop friendships with people who are different from them.

Finding opportunities for positive intergroup contact may not happen readily in our segregated world, so many of you will have to actively seek out these opportunities. It's also important that we can facilitate these in schools and communities. We need to join, and make it easier for others to join, activities that attract a diverse group of kids. One important space to focus on is the after-school activities students participate in. In extracurriculars, diverse students share equal status, unlike in classes where there is often a racially linked, track-based hierarchy. In after-school programs, students share a common goal and develop a shared common identity.[1] And it is all endorsed by authority figures like coaches and teacher sponsors. Schools can make changes to make sure these spaces reflect all of their students. This may mean recruiting diverse students to join and (given the overlaps between race and socioeconomic status) finding ways to reduce the costs associated with these extra activities (for example, by organizing and participating in fundraisers that offset participation costs or by asking the organizers to add a button to the online registration that allows those who can to donate extra to make participation more affordable for others).

We also need to promote, attend, and fund schools that are diverse. Children in diverse schools—truly diverse schools with no ethnic majority—feel safer and have more cross-group friendships than children in less diverse schools. This is true across all types of bias. We see it with race: racial diversity helps reduce racial bias. We see it with gender: gender diversity reduces gender bias.[2] We see it with sexual orientation and gender identity: LGBTQ+ diversity reduces LGBTQ+ bias.[3] Contact matters because it opens up the opportunity to make friends with diverse others. Knowing people, caring about people, changes both the heart and mind. Being able to do this may, however, require structural changes to schools and spaces; we'll talk about that in the next chapter.

CHANGE THE NORMS FOR WHAT IS ACCEPTABLE

We can't just change bias for the individual child. For most youth, especially middle schoolers and high schoolers, their daily goal is simply to fit in with other kids. Walk down a hallway at a middle school or high school and see how they are dressed the same, have the same haircuts, and talk the same. Conformity is valued in adolescence—teens care about what other teens think about them. Trying to convince teens to loudly go against the status quo won't work—so we need to first change the status quo. If we help nudge the norms of what's acceptable, we will likely be far more successful in reducing bias.

Research has shown that peer norms—the typical behavior and attitudes that establish the status quo within a group of peers at school—influence bias, for both good and bad. In my research on sexual harassment in high schools, my colleagues and I used social network analysis to examine whether there were different norms surrounding sexual harassment in different peer groups. We asked every ninth grader to circle the names of their ten closest friends from a roster of all of the ninth graders in their school. They then answered a series of questionnaires about how often they sexually harassed their peers. After that, we connected each student to their friends, creating a network within the school of who was friends with who. We found that the sexual harassment behaviors of teens were consistent with the sexual harassment behaviors of their friends. There were clusters of friends who reported perpetrating a lot of sexual harassment, and clusters of friends who rarely, if ever, engaged in sexual harassment. Each peer group had their own norms of what was acceptable behavior.[4]

Friends select similar friends (birds of a feather indeed flock together), and people seek out like-minded peers to befriend. Indeed, research finds that teens that started out xenophobic befriended other teens who were equally xenophobic.[5] Youth engage in bias when that is the norm. They seem to sink to the lowest common denominator when there are no other options. But tolerance is contagious. While friends' biases did not spread and reduce tolerance in their friends, teens who were a little more tolerant of immigrants, over time, started to influence their friends who were a little more xenophobic—and their friends' xenophobia decreased.[6] Other studies find similar trends: when kids were asked to have conversations about stereotypes, biased kids became less prejudiced after having conversations with unbiased kids.[7] The unbiased kids were the influencers, not the other way around. It seems that arguments for tolerance might be more convincing than biased arguments, because tolerant attitudes are more aligned with facts than biased attitudes (for example, immigrants do not increase crime, so the facts simply do not support that bias). It seems that teens' rational tolerance will win over their friends and reduce their friends' fear-based biases. This research shows ways that peer norms can be leveraged to reduce bias.

Adults can help that process by being more proactive in changing norms. Teachers and school staff are in excellent positions to do so, as the most effective way to change norms is to set, advertise, and enforce clear rules. This works for lots of behaviors. For example, when I was in high school in the late 1980s, kids used to congregate behind the school to smoke. Smokers knew it, the kids who didn't smoke knew it, and teachers knew it; it was the accepted norm. At some point, the school decided to change that norm, so they posted No Smoking signs in the area, a teacher would walk by periodically to shoo any smokers away, and students would get in trouble if they kept going out there. Within a few years, that norm completely changed. I'm not sure what it did to teen smoking in general, but the smokers definitely didn't do it at school anymore. Imagine if we banned harassment and bias with as much fervor as teen smoking.* Both are damaging, both are driven by peer norms, but one is heavily sanctioned at schools, and one is tolerated. We just have to change the expectation away from "kids will be kids" to one in which "kids must show kindness."

PROMOTE BEING AN UPSTANDER AND AN ADVOCATE

As part of their series on racial justice called "The Power of We," *Sesame Street* asks "What's an upstander?" Their answer: "An upstander is someone who

---

* This analogy can be expanded, because to prevent teen smoking, smoking was also banned in movies and media children watched and laws were passed outlawing teen smoking. Thus, we needed changes to both the culture and the law.

uses their kind words and actions to help themselves and their friends." That answer works for preschoolers, but it also works for adults. Changing bias at the individual level is an important step, but we also have to help others cope with bias and change how we all respond as bystanders to bias—then we need to teach our children to do the same. Most examples of bias or harassment happen in front of other kids. When a bystander intervenes, there is more than a 50 percent chance of stopping the negative behavior.[8] We have to teach all children to be upstanders—to be the kids who step in and do something rather than watching passively as bystanders. Such actions can not only stop the immediate experience with bias, but also help to change the peer norms of what it accepted behaviors.

There are five concrete steps that we can use to teach children to be upstanders who intervene when they see an instance of bias:[9]

1. Children have to notice the incident and recognize it as discrimination. This is why conversations about stereotypes, discrimination, and privilege are so important. Children have to know what they're looking for and at to be able to spot bias happening.
2. Children need to define it as an emergency, something that has to be stopped immediately. The incident doesn't need to be physical harassment to be an emergency; it is just as much of an emergency even if it is verbal harassment or social exclusion. This is where empathy is helpful. If children are adept at feeling empathy toward others, they can recognize that being called a name or being left out can be just as painful as anything physical.
3. Children need to assume personal responsibility to help. They need to know that watching bias happen to others and doing nothing is the same as contributing to the bias—that to do nothing is to be part of the problem.
4. Children need to have enough confidence in their own abilities to help. To help them do that, you should come up with scenarios, brainstorm ways to intervene, and then role-play and practice with them until they feel confident.
5. Children have to actually help. They can help the targeted child escape the situation, tell a teacher about the incident, use humor to defuse the situation and/or distract the perpetrator, or tell the

perpetrator to stop. Every situation is different, but it is helpful if they have several strategies in their pocket.

For parents and teachers to be an upstander, you must be an advocate for your child or children in your care. This can include advocating that the child in your circle of care be placed in appropriate classes at school, talking to the principal if the child is unfairly disciplined, and filing complaints with the school district if the school is not protecting the child. If the principal doesn't listen, go to the district-level administrators. Be the squeaky wheel. Bias is real. It happens to children. It happens at schools. It is okay—it is necessary—to stand up for them.

SCHOOLS SHOULD SHOW EXPLICIT VALUE OF DIVERSITY

Schools (for the most part) do not control who attends; they do not draw their own zoning boundaries. But schools *can* make a lot of choices—and those choices reflect their values: they can make the experience of going to their school better or worse by showing that they value diversity. Libraries and hallways can be decorated with only old White men—the Albert Einstein, George Washington, Abraham Lincoln posters everyone can envision. Or they can be decorated with flags from around the world, faces of ethnically diverse children, messages about "Acceptance and Tolerance." My younger daughter's elementary school has a large bulletin board at the entrance, decorated in rainbow colors, claiming, "Everyone is Welcome Here, Everyone Belongs" in multicolored letters (this is especially poignant because it welcomed them back after a year away because of COVID). All schools have decorated bulletin boards, but it's up to the school to choose what kinds of messages they convey.

Kids notice these clues to inclusion, even if they don't realize they notice. In my research, my graduate students and I walked the halls of the schools and recorded how often schools displayed positive messages about diversity and tolerance across an entire school district. We found that when individual schools take the old-White-man approach to decorations, their Latino students assumed their community thinks more poorly of them.* Specifically,

---

* This study was focused on Latino children, but I imagine that the effects would generalize to other groups as well.

Latino students perceived more community-level bias when their schools displayed few images that reflected multicultural values. On the other hand, students of color seem to feel better about themselves when they can literally see that their school values them.[10] These changes cost a little money, but schools are already spending money on other decorations—so why not redirect that money to décor that will make for a better environment, especially since posters cost much less than other changes to school-funding models? You can ask that the PTA earmark $100 to be spent at the school supply store—or have the students do creative inclusive artwork.

Teachers can also show that they value diversity, no matter which students sit in their classrooms. In my research with Latino third and fourth graders, I also surveyed how much teachers enjoyed diversity, how much they believed diversity enriched their lives, how much they enjoyed being around people different from themselves, etc. Then I connected the teachers' answers with the answers of the Latino students in their classes and found the teacher attitudes trickled down to their students. If the teacher valued diversity, the children in their class independently reported having more positive attitudes about their own ethnic group and experienced less peer discrimination. In other words, the kids felt better about themselves and had more positive interactions with their classmates when their teacher valued a diverse world.[11] Teachers are clearly teaching much more than academics, so if you're a teacher, keep that in mind. And if you're not a teacher, talk to them about the importance of diversity in their classrooms and ask what they are doing to show they value diversity. Ask what you can do to help convey messages of inclusion in the classroom, whether that's helping organize a book drive to donate diverse books for the reading corner or asking a speaker from an underrepresented background to come to talk to the class about their area of expertise (perhaps they have an interesting career, are knowledgeable about the history of the community, or can demonstrate an attention-grabbing hobby).

SUPPORT YOUTH VOICES

Teens who get adults to listen and reevaluate biased policies have always been a powerful engine for social justice. This was evident in the 1951 school-wide boycott led by Barbara Johns and Dorothy Davis that we spoke of in chapter 2; it was evident in the perseverance of both Jamie Nabozny and Gavin Grimm that we spoke about in chapter 5; and it was certainly on display in 2020. In the summer of 2020, in the wake of the deaths of George Floyd, Breonna Taylor, Ahmaud Arbery, and Daniel Hambrick, outraged protesters in cities around the world marched to have their voices heard. That summer, a group of six teens who met online—Jade Fuller, Nya Collins, Zee Thomas, Kennedy Green, Emma Rose Smith, and Mikayla Smith—organized a Black Lives Matter protest in Nashville, Tennessee.[12] On June 4, 2020, more than ten thousand people gathered at the courthouse in downtown Nashville to protest police violence toward Black people. Thomas summed up what led the six teens to organize this protest: "As teens, we are tired of waking up and seeing another innocent person being slain in broad daylight. As teens, we are desensitized to death because we see videos of Black people being killed in broad daylight circulating on social media platforms. As teens, we feel like we cannot make a difference in this world, but we must."

In California, seventeen-year-old Tiana Day noticed a call to action on Instagram from nineteen-year-old Mimi Zoila, and together, they led a Black Lives Matter protest across the Golden Gate Bridge. Day said, "For me, I was never really an activist before. But this movement lit a fire in me . . . When I was marching, I just felt a mass amount of empowerment."[13] Youth like Day, Zoila, Thomas, Smith, Green, Smith, Collins, and Fuller who speak out about social justice are not only helping to change the public conversation—they are engaging in one of the most powerful coping mechanisms for thriving in the face of bias: instead of internalizing the negative feelings that come from bias (for example, by feeling shame), turn the negative emotions outward and turn them into action, especially actions that help others. The students are a great model of helping themselves in the process of helping others.

In 2020, I led a webinar for the Society for Research in Adolescence focused on teens who were involved in activism. The teens were ethnically diverse and Zoomed in from around the country to be part of this panel, each talking about the social justice causes they were working on. While juggling school work and college applications, they were running petition drives to change voting rights for felons, raising awareness of toxins in water that were disproportionately affecting people of color, and protesting police violence. When I asked them what adults should be doing to help, one teen quickly quipped, "Get out of the way!"

He went on to explain that, yes, adults are important, as youth need school sponsors for projects or organizations, often need financial support (for example, to help buy poster board or pay organizing fees), and may need logistical help (for example, driving a carpool). But he emphasized that adults often try to take over, change the issues, and affect change in ways they think are right. What these teens advised was for adults—for you—to simply ask teens how you can help. Then listen to what they say and help in *that* way. Provide support, but then stand in the background and let them take the lead. Sometimes, reducing bias in childhood means handing youth the megaphone—you just provide the batteries.

13 Changing the Bigger Picture

*Never doubt that a small group of thoughtful, committed citizens
can change the world: indeed, it's the only thing that ever has.*
—Margaret Mead, cultural anthropologist

While we try to change the hearts and minds of children who hold biases, and protect the hearts and minds of children experiencing bias, we also have to change the culture, structures, and policies that entrench biases and maintain inequalities. This is the third, but most unwieldy, aspect of bias to change. Making deep structural changes takes collective effort and advocacy: it involves voting with your pocketbook and time, getting engaged in local and national politics, and making sure your voice and children's voices are heard.

SUPPORT INCLUSIVE MEDIA

Media acts like mirrors and windows, reflecting back to us what we are like and informing us of what other people's lives are like. At its best, media images and messages can validate our own experiences, bodies, and lives, and can help us feel empathy and a sense of connection to those who differ from us. But when media is not at its best, when those mirrors and windows are made with biased glass, the reflection and view are skewed and harmful. Most of the stereotypes children learn come from biased media images, which is why children's stereotypes in urban Los Angeles and rural Alabama are basically the same. But knowing that media can be problematic isn't enough—and changing media is no easy task, as media is fractured, segmented, small, sneaky, and, especially for kids, wrapped in innocent packages. Media includes children's books and magazines; television and movies; magazine covers at the grocery checkout line; Instagram and Snapchat filtered pictures; TikTok and YouTube videos; billboards on the side of buses, bus stops, and highways; radio ads and music lyrics; news programs on in the background; and posters in the school library. Children lump together magazine ads designed to sell perfume with award-winning literature, not differentiating the purpose and intended audience of one for any other: it all conveys who is valued and why and, insidiously, it appears to represent reality. *All* media is educational, but it is difficult for us to notice the lessons it teaches because we ourselves are immersed in and desensitized to the media culture. It is like trying to notice the air we breathe—but once we notice it, it quickly becomes clear how toxic the media air is.

Although representation has improved over the past few years, only about one in four children's books in 2016 depicted people of color (which is about half of what it should be given the population). Similarly, in terms of gender representation, on *Time*'s list of the 100 Best Children's Books of All Time, only 19 percent of books featured a female protagonist. A lack of authentic representation in media is especially pronounced for some groups of kids, such as American Indian kids or Indian American kids. For example, in 2017, less than 2 percent of children's books featured a significant American Indian or First Nations character. When media representation is especially sparse, each image is forced to be a cultural ambassador. As author Chimamanda Ngozi Adichie said, "The single story creates stereotypes, and the problem with stereotypes is not that they are untrue, but that they are incomplete. They make one story become the only story."

It's not just about the quantity of representation though—it is the quality of that representation. This is especially problematic when the single story that the stereotype is born from is itself already biased. For example, the documentary *The Problem with Apu* discusses the impact of the Indian character on the long-running show *The Simpsons*. Apu was "the only Indian . . . on TV at all"—but that sole source of representation was biased. Hari Kondabolu, the creator of the documentary, said, "After a while, you'd watch *The Simpsons* on a Sunday and you'd get a sense of how you'd be made fun of at school on Monday, based on what Apu did in the latest episode." In a similar vein, for Native Americans, the singular image is historical (when researchers conducted an internet image search for "Native Americans," they found that 97 percent of images were historical representations[1]), so children only see teepees and feathered headdresses in books about Christopher Columbus and Thanksgiving, and images that reflect modern children are largely erased. Children feel devalued and invisible when they can't find images of themselves and their *real* lives reflected in the world.

Content is more likely to be authentic and stereotype-free when the person creating the media is from the same group they are representing. Yet, only one-fourth of children's books written *about* Black people are written or illustrated *by* Black people, one-third of books about Latino people are written or illustrated by Latino people, and a little over one-third of books about Asian/Pacific Islander people are written or illustrated by Asian people.[2]* All that being said, none of this is to discredit other work or to imply that no one can create media that's not nearly autobiographical. I am, after all, a White woman who writes about race. But I put in a lot of work (more than twenty years of a career) to learn from and listen to others, check my own assumptions and preconceptions, and constantly monitor myself to make sure I am not speaking *for* others, but rather amplifying their voices (that is a main reason for having the sidebars in the book). I try to make sure that I am privileging (i.e., buying the work of, and depending on what other positions they may hold, featuring, nominating, awarding, and just widely uplifting) people who are telling their own stories. In other words, when evaluating media or buying new media, check out who wrote it or produced it. This is one way to make sure the stories are portrayed authentically.

The benefits of improving representation go society-wide: It is just as important for White children as children of color to see racially and ethnically diverse others represented in media. White children need to accurately understand that the world is indeed diverse. It is important for all children, girls or not, to see brave and bold girls. They need to learn that girls are interesting as individuals and worthy of being a main character. Similarly, seeing children show a range of gender identities and expressions

---

* I highly recommend We Need Diverse Books, "a nonprofit and a grassroots organization of children's book lovers that advocates essential changes in the publishing industry to produce and promote literature that reflects and honors the lives of all young people" (diversebooks.org).

is important for gender-typical kids, as they need to learn that children express their gender in an array of ways and there is no "right" way to be a boy or girl (and that some people may not identify as either a boy or girl). The world *is* diverse, by race, ethnicity, nationality, gender, gender identity, and sexual orientation. We do a disservice to all children when their media does not reflect that diversity.

Since we are so desensitized to the media we see, I recommend you take some time to conduct an audit of the media children consume. Pull out every book, DVD or Netflix account, and Spotify playlist your child has. What does it teach? Do you agree with the messages? For teachers and school staff, imagine every book in your classroom educates a child about how they should be and how others should be. Inspect the classroom, library, and school building. Look at who is represented and who is missing. Are characters of color well represented? Are Black, Latino, Asian (including South Asian or Indian), Middle Eastern, Pacific Islander, and Indigenous children present? Are girls, boys, and nonbinary children represented? Are diverse families represented? How many of the story lines assume everyone is heterosexual? There is more diverse media out there than ever before and if any of these categories aren't up to par, try to fill in the gaps.

For parents and teachers, talk to children about social media. Talk to children and teens about what apps they have, who they follow on social media, and what websites they visit. Make use of parental control functions. Parenting was easier in 1982 when there were three television channels all approved by the FCC, but now the media environment is so fractured that children and teens may be accessing images on their smartphones that adults are unaware of. In my research in middle schools in 2017, my student stumbled onto a student watching pornography on their smartphone during class. Although 75 percent of parents believed their children had not seen online porn, 53 percent of their kids reported that they had, in fact, encountered it. Parents need to talk to children about this media too (Children and Screens and Common Sense Media have great resources for conversations about social media, sexting, and pornography).

For teachers, evaluate children's textbooks and the books in school libraries. Whose history is told, and whose is excluded? Black history and women's history should not be covered in a single month, but woven throughout children's and teens' curricula. There are many resources available that can extend educational material to include all groups (for example, the 1619 Project by the *New York Times* and Learning for Justice from the Southern

Poverty Law Center have many excellent resources). Sex ed and health curricula should include the full range of sexual orientations and gender identities—and there are many resources available to help schools develop more inclusive curricula here too (for examples, look at GLSEN and Welcoming Schools). If educational materials are centered around straight White men, talk to students about why that is—don't just let them believe that "is" equates with "should be." Point to and talk about the absences and fill in the gaps. Then talk to the principal about why that book was chosen and who you can talk to about changing it.

Beyond sheer representation, look at whether the story lines in books, television, and movies show diverse people being friends with one another. Seeing diverse characters interact with one another (sometimes referred to as vicarious or extended intergroup contact) can help children feel more comfortable with interacting with diverse peers in real life and can reduce some of their biases.[3] For children who live in a world in which most people look like them (such as White kids who attend a primarily White school), it is especially important to see people who are different from themselves. If diversity can't happen in real life, then it can happen through books, movies, and television. It helps children become comfortable with a diverse world. If you find that the media messages foster stereotypes, seriously evaluate what the value of that media is. There are plenty of books today that show a diverse and inclusive world, and there is no excuse for teaching stereotypes simply because it is a "classic."

Ultimately, one of the most impactful things you can do is remember that media is driven by the market and profits, and if people buy it, companies will make more of it. So, when you see positive media examples, spread it to your social network. Hashtag the book you find or the television show you stumble onto. Often, inclusive media is produced by smaller companies without large marketing budgets, and they could use the PR help. This a pocketbook issue. Make inclusive, bias-free media popular and profitable.

AUDIT SCHOOL POLICIES FOR INEQUITIES

Schools should be safe and bias-free spaces. Outside of the home, that is where children spend most of their lives. One way to make sure schools are safe and bias-free for everyone is to do an audit of school policies.

Most schools have their policies written in student codes of conduct or handbooks, which are usually available online, and if they aren't, you can ask to see it. When you've gotten ahold of these rule books, look for descriptions of bias, harassment, and discrimination to see what the consequences are.

Check for things such as whether the school explicitly bans sexual harassment and LGBTQ+ harassment. What are the consequences for the harasser? Schools *should* have enumerated policies banning sexual and LGBTQ+ harassment, but about half of the schools don't.[4] In nationally representative samples, fewer than one-quarter of students thought their schools and teachers adequately addressed sexual and LGBTQ+ harassment.[5] The research is clear that enumerated policies explicitly banning sexual and LGBTQ+ harassment help schools reduce these forms of harassment. Schools should spell out policies for all types of harassment—and if they don't, as an adult, go to them and push for change.

While you're looking for procedures around how schools treat bias and harassment, take some time to evaluate whether dress codes are equitable. Oftentimes, when girls do report sexual harassment, they are the ones who get punished, with teachers pointing to their clothes as the reason for the sexual harassment.[6] Currently, students are more aware of the school policies enforcing dress codes banning short shorts and tank tops than policies banning sexual harassment.[7] As Soraya Chemaly writes, "Adults genuinely want to make sure that girls know they are more than just sex on legs, but dress codes that disproportionately target girls with developing bodies or for showing skin [turn women into sexual objects] by centering the gazes of the heterosexual boys and men around them." Dress code inequities also appear along racial lines. In 2019, Andrew Johnson, a Black high school wrestler, was told by the White referee that his hair did not conform to the rule book and forced to either have his dreadlocks cut or forfeit his match.[8] New Jersey Governor Phil Murphy summed it up well when he tweeted that "no student should have to needlessly choose between his or her identity & playing sports."

Policies about school sports should be equitable for children regardless of their gender identity or sexual orientation. If your student plays a sport, check into what qualifies (or disqualifies) students for teams. Make sure that students can determine their gender identity and that that is respected in their sports teams, bathrooms, and locker rooms. Check into how schools indicate the gender of students (school records should only acknowledge the chosen name and pronouns of the students, not the ones on the birth certificate that may be misgendered) and how teachers are trained to respond to discrimination and victimization.

Safety and fairness at school for *everyone* is a basic right—and, given the life-and-death consequences for many students, it is a moral imperative. But schools often don't make changes until parents or other adults complain. On one very negative hand, sometimes that means that, like with Gavin Grimm, who couldn't use his correct restroom until adults called the school to complain, things can go awry. But if outside input can make the school become more biased, it can also help the school become less biased. So make a phone call or send an email; ask to see their policies; ask other parents to do the same. Help schools realize that people are committed to making sure their policies are fair for everyone—and get those policies to *be* fair for everyone.

PUSH FOR BETTER TRAINING FOR PEOPLE WHO INTERACT WITH CHILDREN FROM DIVERSE COMMUNITIES

As a society, we have to ensure that we have unequivocal conversations about bias and procedures for reducing that bias. Specifically, the criminal justice system and the health-care system are two domains where children face biases and where training on bias must be improved. To do so, communities should push for better training for people within the criminal justice system, from police to judges, and for better training for health-care providers.

When it comes to the criminal justice system, one thing that needs a drastic change is the "adultification" of Black and Latino youth, youth who are thought of and treated like adults before adulthood. For example, research finds that when police officers are shown photos of Black, Latino, and White children labeled as potential crime suspects, the police officers are pretty good at guessing the age of the White children, but overestimate the ages of the Black and Latino children.[9] These are not small miscalculations either. Black thirteen-year-olds were estimated to be seventeen to eighteen years old—as nearly adults rather than middle schoolers. Black children are eighteen times more likely than White children to be sentenced as adults and represent 58 percent of children sentenced to adult facilities, far out of proportion given that they make up only 14 percent of children in America.[10] Clearly, all people within the criminal justice system need to be better trained about their own biases and those that might lead them to be called to a scene in the first place. Investigate whether your local law enforcement agency has a civilian review board or whether there are community organizations dedicated to building coalitions with police (an online search of civilian review board and your city will typically get you to the right place). For more detailed advice on how to push for a bias-free police department, look at the Center for Policing Equity's (policingequity.org) "Toolkit for Equitable Public Safety."

When it comes to health care, as a community member, push your system and its members to be aware of the physical and psychological harm that bias causes to children, particularly bias on the basis of race, immigration status, and gender identity. The American Academy of Pediatrics (AAP) suggests that pediatricians be trained in "culturally competent care" and assess patients for stressors (e.g., bullying and/or cyberbullying on the basis of race) and social determinants of health often associated with racism (e.g., neighborhood safety, poverty, housing inequity, and academic access).[11] Health-care providers should also be trained on the range of gender identities and suggest inclusive and affirming medical care for gender-nonconforming, gender-expansive, and transgender children and their families.[12] Ask your pediatricians' office how they ensure their doctors and nurses are providing culturally competent and gender inclusive care. If they aren't actively engaged in that training, suggest they look at the AAP's guidelines for some good strategies. For detailed advice on advocating for LGBTQ+ youth within health care, Human Rights Campaign, Gender Spectrum, TransYouth Families Allies, and PFLAG offer specific strategies and advocacy approaches.

These may feel like very bold moves to make, but I am often surprised at how receptive people are to specific suggestions. It is helpful to go into these conversations, which may feel far outside your comfort zone, with the assumption that people in these positions are doing their best and do indeed want to have equitable and inclusive practices. Working from that assumption helps the conversation stay on finding solutions rather than assigning blame.

VOTE (AND WRITE, AND CALL, AND EMAIL, AND ENGAGE)

Policies, as we've seen, matter. Politicians, obviously, make policies. Local school boards establish disciplinary plans and can make adjustments if schools are showing racial and gender biases. School boards also select textbooks for schools to use that either do or do not reflect diverse people and their stories. Elected judges can sentence Black youth more severely than White youth. Presidents nominate secretaries of education, who offer guidance on how to implement Title IX and submit a budget for their office of civil rights. Senators confirm Supreme Court justices, who decide if transgender youth get equal protection to cisgender youth under the Constitution. Justices determine what constitutes equal protection and for whom.

So, the first step in ensuring policies are not biased is voting for politicians who are not biased. Check out their policy stances and make sure they don't support biased policies. This is especially important at the local level, as it is usually much easier to change local policies than national policies. For example, the week that I wrote this chapter, my local city council was voting to ban conversion therapy (an outdated and harmful process of trying to change someone's gender identity or sexual orientation). Community members had the opportunity to speak up in support of this important ban—so we did. In May of 2021, the city council unanimously voted in support of the ban. Another time, when I noticed my school district had "Mother" and "Father" on the all the school forms parents must complete at the beginning of the year, I realized they were biased against same-sex families and needed to be changed. I asked a colleague if they knew anyone in the school district who might be responsive to LGBTQ+ issues, and I sent an email to the person they suggested. I was prepared for a long fight and multiple phone calls. But, because I asked around, I stumbled into the right ally, and one email led to an immediate change. The lesson I want to share with you is to tap into your local networks, send out requests, and be prepared to follow up. You may not spark a revolution—after all, modifying a form won't guarantee equal rights for all children in America. But every change moves the needle just a bit closer to equality. Plus, maybe you *will* be the catalyst for major social improvement—you won't know how vital a role you play in unraveling bias until you begin to try.*

As second-wave feminist Carol Hanisch wrote in 1970: "Personal problems are political problems. There are no personal solutions at this time. There is only collective action for a collective solution." This is true of bias. It is both a personal problem and a collective problem, so we need more collective action to have collective social justice. When people are fighting for social justice, be an accomplice in the fight. Decisions are made by those who show up; to unravel biased policies, we all have to show up.

---

* And, if you keep hitting roadblocks, the local media is only a phone call away. If nothing else works, every state has a branch of the ACLU.

14 What to Leave With

L ooking back at the history of this country and reading about all of
the studies documenting how bias affects children at every turn can
be overwhelming. Bias is so pervasive it is difficult to know where
to start trying to make things better. Bias is also as diverse as the people it
impacts; sometimes it's face-to-face, sometimes accidental, and sometimes
embedded within our laws. Entrenched structural biases and the stereotypes
and prejudices held by children and adults interact to funnel Black kids to
underfunded schools; send Black girls to detention for being "disrespectful"
and place boys in the pipeline to prison; allow children to chant "Build the
wall!" in the cafeteria; blame Asian American teens for COVID; keep refugee
children locked in cages away from their parents; punish a girl for wearing
a tank top while ignoring the boy who is sexually harassing her; and cause
transgender youth to develop urinary tract infections because they are afraid
to use the bathroom at school. Bias ignores that these are just kids trying
to feel safe and loved; trying to learn and make friends; trying to navigate
homework, puberty, and social media.

Most people believe in equal rights and the American dream, but oftentimes, that explicit belief in fairness makes it more difficult to change biases
within ourselves and our institutions. It is difficult to recognize that you
can be a good person who believes in fairness, while simultaneously holding
biases. But we have to start somewhere. Start with the biases that enrage
you the most. Start at home in the small conversations at the dinner table or
in the car. Start by going to the library and getting some new books. Then

226

move to a conversation with a neighbor who might be different from you. Have a conversation with your child's teacher about the classroom. Get your children involved in activities outside of their comfort zone with new kids. Role-play being an upstander for when they see harassment. Then start to look at the bigger picture. Talk to the school librarian about media for the whole school. Look at the upcoming debates in front of the city council. Get informed about policies and advocate for ones that effectively reduce bias.

But don't stop with the biases that most affect the children in your life. We have to collectively work to reduce bias that is affecting all children. We also have to care about the kid who seems completely different from our own; otherwise, we are contributing to bias. Desmond Tutu said it well: "If you are neutral in situations of injustice, you have chosen the side of the oppressor." None of us can say we care about children unless we care about *all* children because bias is too entrenched. It will take us all to unravel it.

Acknowledgments

This book has taken a career to fully write. Throughout the book are references to my own research, and that is completely indebted to Rebecca Bigler and Campbell Leaper, mentors and colleagues who have supported my work throughout my career and deeply shaped my research and thinking about stereotypes and bias.

It is also indebted to my graduate students through the years in the Children's Social Inequality in Development Lab who have collaborated with me on this research, Hui Chu, Jenna Jewell, Ellen Stone, Ilyssa Salomon, Michelle Tam, and Sharla Biefeld. When I describe a study "I" did, at least one of them was involved somewhere along the way.

Thanks also to Hannah Gieger, who helped compile the glossary and references.

Thanks to my colleagues and friends who have read drafts of this work and offered their own feedback, insights, and encouragement, especially Melynda Price, Rachel Farr, Jennifer Kotler Clarke, Rashmita Mistry, Mary Beth McGavran, Ellen Usher, and Mandy Watts.

Thanks to my literary agent, Linda Konner, for providing helpful advice and advocacy at every stage of this process.

Immense thanks to editors Vy Tran and Alyn Wallace at BenBella Books for helping turn a monster of book that tried to cover so much into something both readable and impactful.

Portions of this book were written while I was the scholar-in-residence for the Society for Research in Child Development. My time there allowed me to hang out at Howard University, Kenneth and Mamie Clark's alma mater, and at the Library of Congress, and read everything Kenneth and

Mamie Clark ever wrote. An entire book could be written of just their love letters to one another while in college.

Special thanks to the staff of SRCD for listening to sections of this book, and especially to Laura Namy for her support and encouragement during my tenure there.

I am extremely grateful to Brendesha Tynes, Carola Suárez-Orozco, Monique Ward, and Charlotte Patterson, who gave of their time and themselves to let me interview them about their lives and careers. Their careers are very time-consuming, but they were generous and kind and the book is better for it. Developmental science is a better field because of them.

I am also very grateful to Galen Sherwin, senior staff attorney for the ACLU Women's Rights Project. I appreciate the time she spent talking to me about equal protection laws and the lessons I have learned from her and her work. I have seen firsthand what Galen and her ACLU colleagues do to protect students' equal rights in schools (I served as an expert witness on a years-long North Carolina case, *Peltier v. Charter Day School*, in which girls were forced to wear skirts to public school on the premise that enforcing gender stereotypes is positive for development). The stamina and persistence it takes to fight bias through the courts makes writing a book seem easy.

I am especially grateful to Wendy Hartley, Ruth Hartley's daughter, and her husband, Steve, who let me intrude on them at home while Wendy told me stories of her mom. Looking through the photo albums her mother and father assembled based on their 1930s research trips to Tennessee was a privilege.

Finally, I am extremely thankful for the three people in my house. This book was written over the COVID pandemic while coordinating remote learning for my two daughters, Maya and Grace. They spent twelve months of quarantine watching me focus on my laptop instead of them. I appreciate their graciousness.

Special thanks to my oldest daughter and newest research assistant, Maya Kearns, for organizing all of the citations and references that I haphazardly gave her.

I am enormously grateful for my husband, Kris Kearns, for running the household while I left to write, for twice sending me away to write, and for listening to the entire book as it was written. In a book about bias, it is important to note the COVID-era research showing that male scientists, forced to stay at home because of the pandemic, saw boosts in their productivity and submitted papers to journals at higher rates than before. Women, however, were struggling to keep up because of the extra childcare burdens women had to assume during the pandemic. The inequality in childcare and domestic tasks exacerbates the wage gap between men and women and limits women's career trajectories. I am eternally thankful for a spouse who values my career and my mental health, and realizes that taking care of children and the home is not "women's work."

Timeline

1849	*Roberts v. City of Boston* rules that racially segregated schools are legal.
1855	Because of Black parents' advocacy efforts in Boston following the *Roberts* decision, Massachusetts becomes the first state to pass laws banning racial segregation.
1868	The Fourteenth Amendment of the Constitution guaranteeing "equal protection" is ratified.
1884	*Tape v. Hurley* rules it unlawful to ban Mamie Tape from a White school due to her Chinese ancestry. The California legislature quickly passes laws mandating separate schools for "Mongolians."
1896	*Plessy v. Ferguson* case in the US Supreme Court rules, citing *Roberts*, that racially segregated schools are lawful.
1929–1936	Mass deportation of almost two million Latinos from the United States.
1935	In *Pearson v. Murray* case, regarding University of Maryland School of Law, Charles Houston and Thurgood Marshall win the first legal challenge to desegregate schools.
1936	Ruth Horowitz and Eugene Horowitz begin their research on children's biases.
1939	World War II begins. Public opinion poll finds only 39 percent of Americans think Jewish people should be treated like other people.

1939	Ruth Horowitz publishes her pioneering research on projective tests on racial identity. Mamie Clark discovers Ruth's doll studies and begins her own doll studies research.
1941	Japan attacks Pearl Harbor; President Franklin Roosevelt signs an executive order that forces 120,000 Japanese Americans to be locked away in internment camps for four years.
1945	World War II ends. Reeling from the Holocaust, social psychological research begins to focus on prejudice and bias.
1947	*Mendez v. Westminster School District of Orange County, California* rules that segregation of Mexican American students is unconstitutional.
1947	Doll studies by Mamie Clark and Kenneth Clark are published and covered in popular media.
1951	Social science research is used in *Briggs v. Elliott* to argue that segregated schools psychologically harm children.
1951	In *Brown v. Board of Education of Topeka, KS*, NAACP attorneys sue on behalf of Black parents of children assigned to underfunded, faraway, segregated schools. Although the NAACP loses, the judge acknowledges research showing that segregation psychologically harms Black children.
1951	*Davis v. County School Board of Prince Edward County, Virginia*, organized via student protest and aided by the NAACP Legal Defense Fund, challenges school segregation.
1951	In *Bolling v. Sharpe*, NAACP attorneys argue that segregated schools violate the Fourteenth Amendment, but lose the case because of *Plessy* precedent.
1952	In *Bulah v. Gebhart* and *Belton v. Gebhart*, two class action lawsuits challenging school segregation in Delaware; the NAACP attorneys see their first victory. But the cases only allow the twelve named students to integrate, leaving the bigger decision about desegregation up to higher courts.

1954	A collection of cases, labeled *Brown v. Board of Education,* reaches the Supreme Court and is argued by Thurgood Marshall. The Supreme Court rules segregated schools are unconstitutional. This is the first time social science research is referenced in a Supreme Court decision.
1955	United States deports 1.3 million Latinos, including American citizens, in a policy referred to as Operation Wetback.
1963	Equal Pay, Vocational Education, and Higher Education Facilities Acts all pass.
1964	Patsy Mink of Hawaii is elected as the first woman of color to the US House of Representatives.
1964	Civil Rights Act passes, followed by Voting Rights Act.
1965	Elementary and Secondary Education and Higher Education Acts pass.
1969	Joseph Hraba and Geoffrey Grant revisit the doll studies and find the inverse of the Clarks' study: that "Black is Beautiful."
1970	Women's Strike for Equality takes place in New York City.
1972	Title IX of the Education Amendments is signed into law, banning gender discrimination in public schools.
1972	*Journal of American Medical Association* conducts groundbreaking study documenting that one-third of gay teens attempt suicide.
1973	Jeanne Manford, the mother of a gay son, who marched in a precursor to pride marches, founds PFLAG (Parents, Families, and Friends of Lesbians and Gays).
1973	American Psychiatric Association stops considering homosexuality a mental disorder.
1973	*Roe v. Wade* legalizes abortion.

1982	In *Plyer v. Doe*, Supreme Court rules that public schools are required to admit all children, regardless of their immigration status.
1988	The peak of racial integration of schools.
1991	*Board of Education of Oklahoma City Public Schools v. Dowell* rules that schools no longer need government oversight to ensure integration.
1991	Anita Hill testifies about sexual harassment by Clarence Thomas, bringing the term "sexual harassment" into the vernacular.
1992	Charlotte Patterson publishes the first review of research on children with gay and lesbian parents, which indicates that they do not substantially differ from children with heterosexual parents.
1992	In *Franklin v. Gwinnett County Public Schools*, a case of sexual harassment of a student by a teacher, the Supreme Court rules that sexual harassment in school can create a hostile school environment.
1993	American Association of University Women and *Seventeen* magazine, in nationwide surveys, document the widespread prevalence of sexual harassment in schools. First case of peer-to-peer sexual harassment is decided in *Doe v. Petaluma City School District*.
1995	In *Bottoms v. Bottoms*, a lesbian mother loses custody of her child to her own mother, primarily due to her sexual orientation.
1996	In *Nabozny v. Podlesny*, with Lambda Legal arguing on behalf of Nabozny, the US Court of Appeals rules that gay students are protected from homophobic harassment at school.
1996	Carola Suárez-Orozco publishes new research comparing the achievement motivation of Mexican teens, Mexican American teens, and White American teens, showing that the more American children are, the less academically motivated they are.
1996	Department of Education begins providing guidance to schools on how to handle peer sexual harassment.

1996	Three same-sex couples from Hawaii sue for the right to marry in *Baehr v. Miike.*
1997	Regulations about sexual harassment intervention, although vague, begin to be distributed to schools.
1998	Judges in *Bruneau v. South Kortright Central School District* and *Doe v. University of Illinois* rule that preventing sexual harassment among teens is impossible, and that courts should not intervene.
1999	In *Davis v. Monroe County Board of Education,* the Supreme Court rules that sexual harassment at school is a form of gender discrimination and thus falls under Title IX.
2000	In *Boy Scouts of America v. Dale,* the Supreme Court rules that private organizations can legally exclude LGBTQ+ individuals from membership.
2002	Patsy Mink dies; Title IX is renamed the Patsy T. Mink Equal Opportunity in Education Act.
2003	Monique Ward conducts a systematic review of more than sixty studies documenting that exposure to sexually oriented media in television is associated with a stronger belief in gender stereotypes.
2003	*Lawrence v. Texas* overturns state laws criminalizing private consensual sexual behaviors.
2004	Brendesha Tynes conducts groundbreaking research showing that 60 percent of teens experience racial discrimination in unmonitored chat rooms, the early form of social media.
2008	Largest federal immigration raid in US history occurs at a meat-processing plant in Pottsville, Iowa.
2010	A new version of the doll study, filmed by CNN, finds that although Black children don't show racial preferences, White children strongly favor images of other White children.
2011	Under President Obama, new recommendations for school-based sexual harassment interventions are published.

2012	President Obama creates Deferred Action for Childhood Arrivals (DACA) to offer legal protection for immigrants who arrived in the United States as children.
2015	In *Obergefell v. Hodges,* Supreme Court guarantees equal rights to same-sex marriage, informed by research by Charlotte Patterson and Rachel Farr.
2016	Betsy DeVos becomes Secretary of Education under President Trump and withdraws Obama-era recommendations about sexual harassment.
2017	Many states try to pass "bathroom bills" preventing trans individuals from using bathrooms aligned with their gender identity.
2017	#MeToo movement showcases the widespread impact of sexual harassment.
2019	The Safe Schools Improvement Act of 2019, which would prohibit harassment and bullying based on race, sex, disability, sexual orientation, etc., in schools nationwide, is introduced in Congress.
2020	In *Grimm v. Gloucester County School Board,* with the ACLU arguing on behalf of Grimm, courts rule that schools cannot bar transgender students from bathrooms aligned with their gender identity.
2020	*Soule et al. v. Connecticut Association of Schools* challenges whether transgender student athletes can participate on teams that match their gender identity.
2021	Kamala Harris is the first woman and the first person of color elected as vice president of the United States.

Glossary/Directory

Ambrose Caliver—the first Black person to be employed by the US Office of Education, and in 1930, served as a "Specialist in Negro Education"

Andraya Yearwood—transgender student athlete targeted in *Soule et al. v. Connecticut Association of Schools*

Anthony Kennedy—Supreme Court Justice who ruled in such major cases as *Davis v. Monroe County Board of Education, Boy Scouts of America v. Dale,* and *Obergefell v. Hodges*

Barbara Johns—eleventh-grade student from Moton High in Prince Edward County, Virginia, and key organizer in the Manhattan Project

Betsy DeVos—secretary of education under President Trump; ushered in changes limiting protections for victims of sexual harassment

Betty Friedan—feminist author and activist; wrote *The Feminine Mystique* and led the 1970 Women's Strike for Equality

Beulah King—fourteen-year-old Dine Hollow student who was interviewed by Dr. Charles Johnson's team of researchers

Campbell Leaper—developmental and social psychologist who studies gender inequality across the lifespan

Carola Suárez-Orozco—developmental psychologist who studies the experiences of immigrant children and adolescents

Charles Hamilton Houston—Black civil rights lawyer who designed the NAACP strategy to desegregate schools

Charles Johnson—Sociologist whose research on the poor conditions of (and resilient students within) rural Black schools was used in court cases arguing against school segregation

Charlotte Babcock—psychiatrist and one of the four women who provided expert testimony in the *Brown v. Board of Education* Supreme Court case

Charlotte Patterson—psychologist who studies children raised by LGBTQ+ parents

Christine Franklin—student plaintiff in *Franklin v. Gwinnett County Public Schools* sexual harassment case

David Krech—social psychologist who provided expert testimony in the *Brown v. Board of Education* Supreme Court case

Doll studies—groundbreaking social science research studies conducted by Mamie and Kenneth Clark in which Black children showed a preference for White baby dolls; at the center of the social science testimony used in the *Brown v. Board of Education* school segregation case

Dorothy Davis—student plaintiff in *Davis v. County School Board of Prince Edward County, Virginia*

Earl Warren—chief justice of the Supreme Court involved in the decisions to ban school segregation in California (*Mendez v. Westminster*) and nationwide (*Brown v. Board of Education*)

Edith Green—congresswoman who proposed the Equal Pay Act, authored the Higher Education and Higher Education Facilities Acts, and co-authored Title IX

Else Frenkel-Brunswik—psychologist and one of the four women who provided expert testimony in the *Brown v. Board of Education* Supreme Court case

Ethel Belton—student plaintiff in Delaware school segregation case *Belton v. Gebhart*

Eugene (Horowitz) Hartley—pioneering research psychologist who was among the first to study children's social biases, and husband of Ruth Horowitz

Felicitas and Gonzalo Mendez—parent plaintiffs in *Mendez v. Westminster*, which ruled school segregation for Mexican American students unconstitutional

Felix Frankfurter—Supreme Court Justice who voted in favor of school integration due to changes in public opinion on the issue

Floyd Allport—social psychologist who provided expert testimony in the *Brown v. Board of Education* Supreme Court case

Fourteenth Amendment—1868 constitutional amendment that guarantees "equal protection of the law" to all citizens of the United States

Gardner Murphy—psychologist who provided expert testimony in the *Brown v. Board of Education* Supreme Court case

Gavin Grimm—student plaintiff in *Grimm v. Gloucester County School Board* transgender bathroom case

Geoffrey Grant—sociologist who recreated the doll studies in 1969

GLAAD (Gay and Lesbian Alliance Against Defamation)—nonprofit organization fighting LGBTQ+ discrimination in media

GLSEN (Gay, Lesbian, and Straight Education Network)—nonprofit organization working to promote awareness of LGBTQ+ issues and end discrimination in K–12 schools

Gordon Allport—personality psychologist who provided expert testimony in the *Brown v. Board of Education* Supreme Court case

Harry Briggs—parent who sued on behalf of their child in *Briggs v. Elliott*

Harvey Milk—gay-rights activist and the first openly gay elected official in the state of California

Henry B. Brown—US Supreme Court Justice who wrote the majority opinion in *Plessy v. Ferguson*

Henry Floyd—Court of Appeals judge who ruled in favor of the right of transgender individuals to use the bathroom aligned with gender identity in *Grimm v. Gloucester County School Board*

Henry Garrett—doctoral advisor of Mamie Clark and noted segregationist and eugenicist who testified against Clark in *Briggs v. Elliott*

Homer Plessy—Creole man who, after intentionally sitting in a White railway car and being arrested, became the plaintiff in *Plessy v. Ferguson*

Idella Evans—researcher who recreated the doll studies with Mexican American preschoolers in 1968

Isidor Chein—psychologist who provided expert testimony in the *Brown v. Board of Education* Supreme Court case

Jack Greenberg—NAACP attorney who argued against school segregation

James Wynn—Court of Appeals judge who wrote a concurring opinion in *Grimm v. Gloucester County School Board*

Jamie Nabozny—student plaintiff in *Nabozny v. Podlesny* homophobic harassment case

John Marshall Harlan—US Supreme Court Justice and the sole dissenter in *Plessy v. Ferguson*

Joseph Hraba—sociologist who recreated the doll studies in 1969

Kenneth Clark—psychologist, key expert in NAACP school segregation cases, and husband of Mamie Phipps Clark

Lambda Legal—oldest gay-rights organization in the United States, focused on arguing for LGBTQ+ rights in court

LaShonda Davis—student plaintiff in *Davis v. Monroe County Board of Education* sexual harassment case

Leo Frank—Jewish businessman from Atlanta who was lynched in 1915, as part of rising anti-Semitism in the United States

Louis Redding—first Black attorney in the state of Delaware; argued on behalf of parents and students in *Bulah v. Gebhart* and *Belton v. Gebhart*

Maggie Red—fifteen-year-old Dine Hollow student who was interviewed by Dr. Charles Johnson's team of researchers

MALDEF—Mexican American Legal Defense and Educational Fund, founded in 1968, a leading Latino legal civil rights organization

Mamie Phipps Clark—pioneering social psychologist who studied children's perceptions of race; key expert in NAACP school segregation cases and creator of the doll studies

Mamie Tape—Chinese American child whose parents sued for her right to attend the nearby White school in *Tape v. Hurley*; though her parents won the case, the California legislature soon mandated separate schools for "Mongolians"

Manhattan Project, The—committee created by Barba Johns and other Moton High students that organized a school boycott and protests in the spring of 1951

Marcelo Suárez-Orozco—cultural psychologist, anthropologist, and husband of Carola Suárez-Orozco

Margaret Beale Spencer—professor of Urban Education at the University of Chicago who led a new version of the doll study with CNN in 2010

Mary Podlesny—school principal and defendant in *Nabozny v. Podlesny*

Monique Ward—developmental psychologist who studies how media shapes teens' ideas about gender, sexuality, and relationships

Norma Werner—researcher who recreated the doll studies with Mexican American preschoolers in 1968

Oliver Hill—NAACP attorney who argued on behalf of students and parents in *Davis v. County School Board of Prince Edward County, Virginia*

Otto Klineberg—psychologist who provided expert testimony in the *Brown v. Board of Education* Supreme Court case

Patsy Takemoto Mink—first woman of color elected to Congress and the coauthor of Title IX; posthumously awarded the Presidential Medal of Freedom in 2014

Paul McCormick—district court judge who ruled in favor of the parents in *Mendez v. Westminster*, citing the importance of social equality

Rachel Farr—developmental psychologist who studies LGBTQ+ parent families and adoption

Robert Carter—NAACP attorney who led the legal fight against school segregation

Robert Redfield—lawyer turned anthropologist who testified in school segregation cases

Ruth (Horowitz) Hartley—pioneering research psychologist who was among the first to study children's social biases, inventing many new research methods in order to do so; her work inspired that of Mamie Clark

Sandra Day O'Connor—first woman to serve on the Supreme Court and author of the majority opinion in *Davis v. Monroe County Board of Education*

Sarah Roberts—Black child whose parents were plaintiffs in *Roberts v. City of Boston*, which ruled that racially segregated schools were legal

Shirley Bulah—student plaintiff in Delaware school segregation case *Bulah v. Gebhart*

Spottswood Bolling—twelve-year-old student plaintiff in *Bolling v. Sharpe*, which ruled school segregation in the District of Columbia unconstitutional

Spottswood Robinson—NAACP attorney who led the legal fight against school segregation

Stanley Reed—Supreme Court Justice who was largely in favor of continuing segregation during the *Brown* case in 1954. He was the last Justice to agree to desegregate.

Sylvia Mendez—eight-year-old student who helped end school segregation in *Mendez v. Westminster*, awarded the Presidential Medal of Freedom in 2011

Terry Miller—transgender student athlete targeted in *Soule et al. v. Connecticut Association of Schools*

Thomas Blauert—assistant principal and defendant in *Nabozny v. Podlesny*

Thomas Garth—prolific race psychology researcher who, in 1939, acknowledged the issue of race bias in the field

Thurgood Marshall—NAACP attorney who was the lead attorney in the *Brown v. Board of Education* Supreme Court case and the first person to integrate the Supreme Court

Viola Wertheim Bernard—psychiatrist and one of the four women who provided expert testimony in the *Brown v. Board of Education* Supreme Court case

Walter A. Huxman—judge whose "Findings of Fact" in the Kansas District Court decision on *Brown v. Board of Education* stated that school segregation psychologically harmed Black children; this became critical once the case made it to the Supreme Court

Wendy Hartley—daughter of Ruth and Eugene (Horowitz) Hartley

William LePre Houston—prominent Black Washington, DC, lawyer and father of Charles Houston

Notes

CHAPTER 1: A PRIMER ON BIAS

1   "Race and Ethnicity," American Sociological Association, https://www.asanet.org/topics
/race-and-ethnicity.

2   Christia Spears Brown et al., "Ethnicity and gender in late childhood and early adolescence:
Group identity and awareness of bias," *Developmental Psychology* 47, no. 2 (2011): 463–471.

3   "Unequal Education Federal Loophole Enables Lower Spending on Students of Color,"
Spatig-Amerikaner Center for American Progress, 2012.

4   David J. Kelly et al., "Three-month-olds, but not newborns, prefer own-race faces,"
Developmental Science 8, no. 6 (2005): F31–F36.

5   Yair Bar-Haim et al., "Nature and nurture in own-race face processing," *Psychological Science*
17, no. 2 (2006): 159–163.

6   Paul C. Quinn et al., "Representation of the gender of human faces by infants: A preference
for female," *Perception* 31, no. 9 (2002): 1109–1121.

7   Naiqi G. Xiao, et al., "Older but not younger infants associate own-race faces with happy
music and other-race faces with sad music," *Developmental Science* 21, no. 2 (2018): e12537.

8   Tobias Raabe and Andreas Beelmann, "Development of ethnic, racial, and national
prejudice in childhood and adolescence: A multinational meta-analysis of age differences,"
Child Development 82, no. 6 (2011): 1715–1737.

9   Christia Spears Brown, Agnieszka Spatzier, and Mollie Tobin, "Variability in the intergroup attitudes of White children: What we can learn from their ethnic identity labels,"
Social Development 19, no. 4 (2010): 758–778.

10 Clark McKown and Rhona S. Weinstein, "The development and consequences of stereotype
consciousness in middle childhood," *Child Development* 74, no. 2 (2003): 498–515; Stephanie
J. Rowley et al., "Social status as a predictor of race and gender stereotypes in late childhood
and early adolescence," *Social Development* 16, no. 1 (2007): 150–168.

11 Judith E. Owen Blakemore et al., *Gender Development* (Psychology Press, 2008); Christia
Spears Brown, Sharla D. Biefeld, and Michelle J. Tam, *Gender in Childhood* (Cambridge
University Press, 2020).

12 Nancy K. Freeman, "Preschoolers' perceptions of gender appropriate toys and their parents'
beliefs about genderized behaviors: Miscommunication, mixed messages, or hidden truths?,"
Early Childhood Education Journal 34, no. 5 (2007): 357–366.

13 Hanns M. Trautner et al., "Rigidity and flexibility of gender stereotypes in childhood:
Developmental or differential?," *Infant and Child Development: An International Journal of
Research and* Practice 14, no. 4 (2005): 365–381.

14 Rebecca S. Bigler, and Lynn S. Liben, "A cognitive-developmental approach to racial stereotyping and reconstructive memory in Euro-American children," *Child Development* 64, no. 5 (1993): 1507–1518.

15 Raabe and Beelmann, "Development of ethnic, racial, and national prejudice in childhood and adolescence: A multinational meta-analysis of age differences."

16 Raabe and Beelmann, "Development of ethnic, racial, and national prejudice in childhood and adolescence: A multinational meta-analysis of age differences"; Brown et al., "Ethnicity and gender in late childhood and early adolescence: Group identity and awareness of bias."

17 Lynn S. Liben, and Rebecca S. Bigler, "The Developmental Course of Gender Differentiation: Conceptualizing, Measuring, and Evaluating Constructs and Pathways," *Monographs of the Society for Research in Child Development* 67, no. 2 (2002): vii–147, doi:10.1111/1540-5834.t01-1-00187.

18 Rebecca S. Bigler, Christia Spears Brown, and Marc Markell, "When groups are not created equal: Effects of group status on the formation of intergroup attitudes in children," *Child Development* 72, no. 4 (2001): 1151–1162.

19 Raabe and Beelmann, "Development of ethnic, racial, and national prejudice in childhood and adolescence."

20 Richard A. Fabes et al., "Gender-segregated schooling and gender stereotyping," *Educational Studies* 39, no. 3 (2013): 315–319.

21 Rachel H. Farr, Ilyssa Salomon, Jazmin L. Brown-Iannuzzi, and Christia Spears Brown, "Elementary school-age children's attitudes toward children in same-sex parent families," *Journal of GLBT Family Studies* 15, no. 2 (2019): 127–150.

22 Christia Spears Brown et al., "US children's stereotypes and prejudicial attitudes toward Arab Muslims," *Analyses of Social Issues and Public Policy* 17, no. 1 (2017): 60–83.

23 Gizelle Anzures et al., "Developmental origins of the other-race effect," *Current Directions in Psychological Science* 22, no. 3 (2013): 173–178.

24 Gizelle Anzures et al., "Categorization, categorical perception, and asymmetry in infants' representation of face race," *Developmental Science* 13, no. 4 (2010): 553–564; Michelle Heron Delaney et al., "Perceptual training prevents the emergence of the other race effect during infancy," *PloS One* 6, no. 5 (2011): e19858.

25 Saul Feinman and Doris R. Entwisle, "Children's ability to recognize other children's faces," *Child Development* (1976): 506–510.

26 Sandy Sangrigoli et al., "Reversibility of the other-race effect in face recognition during childhood," *Psychological Science* 16, no. 6 (2005): 440–444.

27 Rebecca S. Bigler and Lynn S. Liben, "Developmental intergroup theory: Explaining and reducing children's social stereotyping and prejudice," *Current Directions in Psychological Science* 16, no. 3 (2007): 162–166.

28 Anthony G. Greenwald and Linda Hamilton Krieger, "Implicit bias: Scientific foundations," *California Law Review* 94, no. 4 (2006): 945–967.

29 Greenwald and Krieger, "Implicit bias: Scientific foundations."

30 Tobias Brosch, Eyal Bar-David, and Elizabeth A. Phelps, "Implicit race bias decreases the similarity of neural representations of black and white faces," *Psychological Science* 24, no. 2 (2013): 160–166.

31 Brosch, Bar-David, and Phelps, "Implicit race bias decreases the similarity of neural representations of black and white faces."

32 Greenwald and Krieger, "Implicit bias: Scientific foundations."

33 Brigitte Vittrup et al., "Parental perceptions of the role of media and technology in their young children's lives," *Journal of Early Childhood* Research 14, no. 1 (2016): 43–54.

34 Brigitte Vittrup and George W. Holden, "Exploring the impact of educational television and parent–child discussions on children's racial attitudes," *Analyses of Social Issues and Public Policy* 11, no. 1 (2011): 82–104.

35 Evan P. Apfelbaum et al., "Learning (not) to talk about race: When older children underperform in social categorization," *Developmental Psychology* 44, no. 5 (2008): 1513.

36 Anita Jones Thomas and Sha'Kema M. Blackmon, "The influence of the Trayvon Martin shooting on racial socialization practices of African American parents," *Journal of Black Psychology* 41, no. 1 (2015): 75–89.

37 Diane Hughes and Lisa Chen, "When and what parents tell children about race: An examination of race-related socialization among African American families, " *Applied Developmental Science* 1, no. 4 (1997): 200–214.

38 Juliane Degner and Jonas Dalege. "The apple does not fall far from the tree, or does it? A meta-analysis of parent-child similarity in intergroup attitudes," *Psychological Bulletin* 139, no. 6 (2013): 1270.

39 Sylvia Perry, Allison L. Skinner-Dorkenoo, Jamie L. Abaied, Adilene Osnaya, and Sara Waters, "Initial evidence that parent-child conversations about race reduce racial biases among white U.S. children," PsyArXiv, preprint, created May 18, 2020, https://psyarxiv. com/3xdg8/.

40 Luigi Castelli, Cristina De Dea, and Drew Nesdale, "Learning social attitudes: Children's sensitivity to the nonverbal behaviors of adult models during interracial interactions," *Personality and Social Psychology Bulletin* 34, no. 11 (2008): 1504–1513.

41 Mark L. Hatzenbuehler et al., "Proposition 8 and homophobic bullying in California," *Pediatrics* 143, no. 6 (2019).

42 Hatzenbuehler et al., "Proposition 8 and homophobic bullying in California."

43 Gene H. Brody et al., "Perceived discrimination and the adjustment of African American youths: A five-year longitudinal analysis with contextual moderation effects," *Child Development* 77, no. 5 (2006): 1170–1189; Celia B. Fisher, Scyatta A. Wallace, and Rose E. Fenton, "Discrimination distress during adolescence," *Journal of Youth and Adolescence* 29, no. 6 (2000): 679–695; Melissa L. Greene, Niobe Way, and Kerstin Pahl, "Trajectories of perceived adult and peer discrimination among Black, Latino, and Asian American adolescents: patterns and psychological correlates, " *Developmental Psychology* 42, no. 2 (2006): 218; Jennifer M. Grossman and Belle Liang, "Discrimination distress among Chinese American adolescents," *Journal of Youth and Adolescence* 37, no. 1 (2008): 1–11; Virginia W. Huynh and Andrew J. Fuligni, "Discrimination hurts: The academic, psychological, and physical well-being of adolescents," *Journal of Research on Adolescence* 20, no. 4 (2010): 916–941; Vanessa M. Nyborg and John F. Curry, "The impact of perceived racism: Psychological symptoms among African American boys," *Journal of Clinical Child and Adolescent Psychology* 32, no. 2 (2003): 258–266; Eleanor K. Seaton et al., "The prevalence of perceived discrimination among African American and Caribbean Black youth," *Developmental Psychology* 44, no. 5 (2008): 1288; Ronald L. Simons et al., "Discrimination, crime, ethnic identity, and parenting as correlates of depressive symptoms among African American children: A multilevel analysis," *Development and Psychopathology* 14, no. 2 (2002): 371; Paul R. Smokowski and Martica L. Bacallao, "Acculturation, internalizing mental health symptoms, and self-esteem: Cultural experiences of Latino adolescents in North Carolina," *Child Psychiatry and Human Development* 37, no. 3 (2007): 273–292; Laura A. Szalacha et al., "Discrimination and Puerto Rican children's and adolescents' mental health," *Cultural Diversity and Ethnic Minority Psychology* 9, no. 2 (2003): 141; Adriana J. Umaña-Taylor and Kimberly A. Updegraff. "Latino adolescents' mental health: Exploring the interrelations among discrimination, ethnic identity, cultural orientation, self-esteem, and depressive symptoms," *Journal of Adolescence* 30, no. 4 (2007): 549–567; Wong, Carol A., Jacquelynne S. Eccles, and Arnold Sameroff. "The influence of ethnic discrimination and ethnic identification on African American adolescents' school and socioemotional adjustment." *Journal of Personality* 71, no. 6 (2003): 1197–1232.

44 Michael T. Schmitt et al., "The consequences of perceived discrimination for psychological well-being: a meta-analytic review." *Psychological Bulletin* 140, no. 4 (2014): 921.

45 For review, see Kathy Sanders-Phillips et al., "Social inequality and racial discrimination: Risk factors for health disparities in children of color," *Pediatrics* 124, no. Supplement 3 (2009): S176–S186.

46 Gregory E. Miller, Edith Chen, and Eric S. Zhou, "If it goes up, must it come down? Chronic stress and the hypothalamic-pituitary-adrenocortical axis in humans," *Psychological Bulletin* 133, no. 1 (2007): 25.

47 Rodney Clark and Philip Gochett, "Interactive effects of perceived racism and coping responses predict a school-based assessment of blood pressure in black youth," *Annals of Behavioral Medicine* 32, no. 1 (2006): 1–9.

48 Katharine H. Zeiders, Leah D. Doane, and Mark W. Roosa, "Perceived discrimination and diurnal cortisol: Examining relations among Mexican American adolescents," *Hormones and Behavior* 61, no. 4 (2012): 541–548; Virginia W. Huynh et al., "Everyday discrimination and diurnal cortisol during adolescence," *Hormones and Behavior* 80 (2016): 76–81.

49 David J. Lick, Laura E. Durso, and Kerri L. Johnson, "Minority stress and physical health among sexual minorities," *Perspectives on Psychological Science* 8, no. 5 (2013): 521–548.

CHAPTER 2: WHEN THE COURTS FIRST LISTENED TO SOCIAL SCIENTISTS

1   Michael J. Klarman, *From Jim Crow to Civil Rights: The Supreme Court and the Struggle for Racial Equality* (Oxford University Press, 2006).

2   Charles Thompson, "Plessy v. Ferguson: Harlan's Great Dissent," Louis D. Brandeis School of Law Library, University of Louisville, 1996, https://louisville.edu/law/library/special -collections/the-john-marshall-harlan-collection/harlans-great-dissent#:~:text=The%20 one%20lonely%2C%20courageous%20dissenter,the%20races%20in%20rail%20coaches.

3   Peter H. Irons, *Jim Crow's Children: The Broken Promise of the Brown Decision* (Viking Press, 2002).

4   Peter H. Irons, "Jim Crow's Schools," American Federations of Teachers, https://www.aft. org /periodical/american-educator/summer-2004/jim-crows-schools.

5   Irons, "Jim Crow's Schools."

6   Irons, "Jim Crow's Schools."

7   Charles Spurgeon Johnson, "Growing up in the black belt," *American Council on Education* (1941), 113.

8   Johnson, "Growing up in the black belt," 113.

9   Fredrick P. Aguirre et al., "Mendez v. Westminster: A living history," *Michigan State Law Review* (2014): 401.

10 John P. Jackson Jr. *Social Scientists for Social Justice: Making the Case Against Segregation* (NYU Press, 2001).

11 Thurgood Marshall, "An evaluation of recent efforts to achieve racial integration in education through resort to the courts," *The Journal of Negro Education* 21, no. 3 (1952): 316–327; Klarman, *From Jim Crow to Civil Rights*; Richard Kluger, *Simple Justice: The History of Brown v. Board of Education and Black America's Struggle for Equality* (Vintage, 2011); Jackson, *Social Scientists for Social Justice*.

12 Kluger, *Simple Justice*.

13 *Westminster School District of Orange County v Mendez*, Brief for NAACP, amicus curiae.

14 William Hastie to Thurgood Marshall, NAACP Papers, Series IIB, Box B136, Folder "California-Mendez v Westminster School District of Orange County, 1946–1947"; see also Jackson, *Social Scientists for Social Justice*.

15 John P. Jackson Jr., and John P. Jackson, *Science for Segregation: Race, Law, and the Case Against Brown v. Board of Education* (NYU Press, 2005).

16 Robert V. Guthrie, *Even the Rat Was White: A Historical View of Psychology* (Pearson Education, 2004); Ben Keppel, *The Work of Democracy: Ralph Bunche, Kenneth B. Clark, Lorraine Hansberry, and the Cultural Politics of Race* (Harvard University Press, 1995).

17   Jackson, *Social Scientists for Social Justice*.
     Kluger, *Simple Justice*.
18   Kluger, *Simple Justice*.
19   Kluger, *Simple Justice*.
20   Cheryl Brown Henderson et al., *Recovering Untold Stories: An Enduring Legacy of the Brown v. Board of Education Decision* (University of Kansas Libraries, 2018).
21   Robert Redfield Paper, Box 23, Folder 4, University of Chicago Archives, Regenstein Library, Chicago, IL.
22   Klarman, *From Jim Crow to Civil Rights*, 295.
23   Aguirre et al., *Mendez V. Westminster: A Living History*.
24   Floyd H. Allport et al., "The effects of segregation and the consequences of desegregation: A social science statement" (Supreme Court of the United States, October 1952), https://www.naacpldf.org/wp-content/uploads/Brown-v.-Board-A-Social-Science-Statement.pdf.

CHAPTER 3: ALL OF AMERICA'S CHILDREN

1   Abby Budiman, "Key findings about US immigrants," *Pew Research Center*, 2020, https://www.pewresearch.org/fact-tank/2019/06/17/key-findings-about-u-s-immigrants/.
2   Monica Muñoz Martinez, *The Injustice Never Leaves You: Anti-Mexican Violence in Texas* (Harvard University Press, 2018).
3   Russel Contreras and Cedar Attanasio, "Mexican Americans faced racial terror from 1910–1920," *The Associated Press,* July 26, 2019, https://apnews.com/article/b8516a3d80ef40da97afd3a9e4f7d706.
4   Mae M. Ngai, "The architecture of race in American immigration law: A reexamination of the Immigration Act of 1924," *The Journal of American History* 86, no. 1 (1999): 71.
5   Ngai, "The architecture of race in American immigration law."
6   "Section 1325: The 90-year-old law that defines border crossing criminality," *USA Facts*, last modified January 20, 2020, https://usafacts.org/articles/section-1325-90-year-old-law-defines-border-crossing-criminality/.
7   Alex Wagner, "America's Forgotten History of Illegal Deportations," *The Atlantic*, March 6, 2017, https://www.theatlantic.com/politics/archive/2017/03/americas-brutal-forgotten-history-of-illegal-deportations/517971/.
8   Erin Blakemore, "The Largest Mass Deportation in American History," *History.com*, June 8, 2019, https://www.history.com/news/operation-wetback-eisenhower-1954-deportation?li_source=LI&li_medium=m2m-rcw-history.
9   "Prosecuting People for Coming to the United States," American Immigration Council, January 10, 2020, https://www.americanimmigrationcouncil.org/research/immigration-prosecutions.
10   "Immigration and Nationality Act," US Citizenship and Immigration Services, last modified June 10, 2019, https://www.uscis.gov/laws-and-policy/legislation/immigration-and-nationality-act.
11   Douglas S. Massey, *Categorically Unequal: The American Stratification System* (Russell Sage Foundation, 2007), 14.
12   Wyatt Clarke, Kimberly Turner, and Lina Guzman, "One quarter of Hispanic children in the United States have an unauthorized immigrant parent," *National Research Center on Hispanic Children & Families*, https://www.hispanicresearchcenter.org/research-resources/one-quarter-of-hispanic-children-in-the-united-states-have-an-unauthorized-immigrant-parent/.
13   Texas Education Code Ann. § 21.031 (Vernon Supp. 1981).
14   *Plyler v. Doe*, 457 U.S. 202 (1982).

15 "Public education for immigrant students: Understanding Plyler v. Doe," American Immigration Council, October 24. 2016, https://www.americanimmigrationcouncil.org /research/plyler-v-doe-public-education-immigrant-students.

16 "Preliminary Analysis of HB 56, 'Alabama Taxpayer and Citizen Protection Act,'" American Civil Liberties Union, https://www.aclu.org/other/analysis-hb-56-alabama-taxpayer-and -citizen-protection-act.

17 Thomas E. Perez, *Letter from Assistant Attorney General Thomas E. Perez to Alabama State Superintendent of Education Dr. Thomas R. Bice*, May 1, 2012, http://media.al.com/bn/other /DOJ%20Letter%20May%202012.pdf.

18 *Hispanic Interest Coalition of Alabama v. Bentley*, 691 F.3d 1236 (11th Cir. 2012).

19 "The Dream Act: An Overview," American Immigration Council, March 16, 2021, https://www.americanimmigrationcouncil.org/research/dream-act-overview.

CHAPTER 4: BOYS AND GIRLS WEREN'T SEGREGATED, BUT THE SCHOOL DAY WASN'T EQUAL

1 Sascha Cohen, "The Day Women Went on Strike," *Time Magazine*, August 26, 2015, https://time.com/4008060/women-strike-equality-1970/.

2 Paula England, Andrew Levine, and Emma Mishel, "Progress toward gender equality in the United States has slowed or stalled," *Proceedings of the National Academy of Sciences* 117, no. 13 (2020): 6990–6997.

3 Edith Green, Oral History Interview, U.S. Association of Former Members of Congress, Manuscript Room, Library of Congress, Washington, DC: 62.

4 Education Amendments Act of 1972, 20 U.S.C. §§1681–1688, https://www.govinfo.gov /content/pkg/STATUTE-86/pdf/STATUTE-86-Pg235.pdf.

5 Jane Gross, "Schools Are Newest Arenas for Sex-Harassment Issues," *New York Times*, March 11, 1992, https://www.nytimes.com/1992/03/11/education/schools-are-newest- arenas-for-sex-harassment-issues.html.

6 "The AAUW Report: How Schools Shortchange Girls: A Study of Major Findings on Girls and Education," The American Association of University Women Educational Foundation, 1992; Anne L. Bryant, "Hostile hallways: The AAUW survey on sexual harassment in America's schools," *Journal of School Health* 63, no. 8 (1993): 355–358.

7 Bryant, "Hostile hallways."

8 Jodi Lipson, *Hostile Hallways: Bullying, Teasing, and Sexual Harassment in School* (AAUW Educational Foundation: 2001).

9 *Meritor Savings Bank, FSB v. Vinson et al.*, 477 US 51 (1986).

10 *Franklin v. Gwinnett County Public Schools*, 503 U.S. 60 (1992).

11 *Doe v. Petaluma City School District*, No. 94-15917 (1995).

12 Jodi L. Short, "Creating peer sexual harassment: Mobilizing schools to throw the book at themselves," *Law & Policy* 28, no. 1 (2006): 31–59.

13 Short, "Creating peer sexual harassment: Mobilizing schools to throw the book at themselves."

14 *Davis v. Monroe County Board of Education* (97–843) 526 U.S. 629 (1999).

15 Joan Biskupic, "Schools Liable for Harassment," *The Washington Post*, May 25, 1999, https://www.washingtonpost.com/wp-srv/national/longterm/supcourt/stories/court052599 .htm.

16 *Davis v. Monroe County Board of Education* (97–843) 526 U.S. 629 (1999).

17 *Davis v. Monroe County Board of Education*, Justice Kennedy dissent.

18 R. Shep Melnick, "Analyzing the Department of Education's final Title IX rules on sexual misconduct," Brookings Institute, June 11, 2020, https://www.brookings.edu/research /analyzing-the-department-of-educations-final-title-ix-rules-on-sexual-misconduct/.

19 Melnick, "Analyzing the Department of Education's final Title IX rules on sexual misconduct."

20 "Any perceived offense can be turned into a full-blown Title IX investigation. If everything is harassment then nothing is," DeVos. CBS News: https://www.cbsnews.com/news/devos -to-rescind-obama-era-title-ix-order-on-withholding-school-funds-for-assault-inaction/.

21 34 C.F.R. § 106.45(b)(1)(iv). (o 470–71).

22 334 C.F.R. § 106.45(b)(1)(iv).

CHAPTER 5: CIVIL RIGHTS ARE NOT JUST BLACK AND WHITE

1   Peggy T. Cohen-Kettenis and Friedemann Pfäfflin. "The DSM diagnostic criteria for gender identity disorder in adolescents and adults," *Archives of Sexual Behavior* 39, no. 2 (2010): 499–513.

2   "Queer Representation in Film and Television," Media Smarts, https://mediasmarts.ca/ digital-media-literacy/media-issues/diversity-media/queer-representation/queer -representation-film-television; Stephen Tropiano, *The Prime Time Closet: A History Of Gays and Lesbians on TV* (Applause Books, 2002).

3   P. Finn and T. McNeil, "The response of the criminal justice system to bias crime: An exploratory review (Contract Report submitted to the National Institute of Justice, US Department of Justice)" Abt Associates, 1987: 02138–1168.

4   Gregory M. Herek, "Hate crimes against lesbians and gay men: Issues for research and policy," *American Psychologist* 44, no. 6 (1989): 948.

5   Joyce Hunter and Robert Schaecher, "Stresses on lesbian and gay adolescents in schools," *Children & Schools* 9, no. 3 (1987): 180–190.

6   Martin, A. Damien, "Learning to hide: The socialization of the gay adolescent," *Adolescent Psychiatry* (1982).

7   Hunter and Schaecher, "Stresses on lesbian and gay adolescents in schools."

8   National Gay Task Force, "Anti-Gay/Lesbian Victimization: A Study by the National Gay Task Force in Cooperation with Gay and Lesbian Organizations in Eight U.S. Cities" (NGTF: 1984), 1. As reported in Hunter and Schaecher (1987).

9   Carlos A. Ball, *From the Closet to the Courtroom: Five LGBT Rights Lawsuits That Have Changed Our Nation* (Beacon Press, 2010).

10 Gary Remafedi, "Adolescent homosexuality: Psychosocial and medical implications," *Pediatrics* 79, no. 3 (1987): 331–337.

11 Marcia R Feinleib, "Report of the Secretary's Task Force on Youth Suicide. Volume 3: Prevention and Interventions in Youth Suicide," *United States Department of Health and Human Services* (1989).

12 Neil W. Pilkington and Anthony R. D'Augelli, "Victimization of lesbian, gay, and bisexual youth in community settings," *Journal of Community Psychology* 23, no. 1 (1995): 34–56; Andi O'Conor, "Who gets called queer in school? Lesbian, gay and bisexual teenagers, homophobia and high school," *The High School Journal* 77, no. 1/2 (1993): 7–12.

13 GLSEN, https://www.glsen.org/.

14 "Understanding anti-gay harassment and violence in schools: A report of the five-year research project of the safe schools coalition of Washington state," *Safe Schools Coalition* (January 1999), http://www.safeschoolscoalition.org/ExecutiveSummary -fromTheyDontEvenKnowMe.pdf.

15 Donna I. Dennis and Ruth E. Harlow, "Gay youth and the right to education," *Yale Law & Policy Review* 4, no. 2 (1986): 446–478.

16 Ball, *From the Closet to the Courtroom*; William P. McFarland and Martin Dupuis, "The legal duty to protect gay and lesbian students from violence in school," *Professional School Counseling* 4, no. 3 (2001): 171; *Nabozny v. Podlesny*, No. 95-3634 (7th Cir. 1996).

17 *Nabozny v. Podlesny*, No. 95-3634 (7th Cir. 1996).

18 *Nabozny v. Podlesny*, No. 95-3634 (7th Cir. 1996).

19 *Nabozny v. Podlesny*, No. 95-3634 (7th Cir. 1996).

20 Ball, *From the Closet to the Courtroom.*

21 Ellen Ann Andersen, *Out of the Closets and into the Courts: Legal Opportunity Structure and Gay Rights Litigation* (University of Michigan Press, 2009).

22 Based on interviews with Patricia Logue, in Ball, *From the Closet to the Courtroom.*

23 Ball, *From the Closet to the Courtroom.*

24 "No Promo Homo Laws," GLSEN, https://www.glsen.org/activity/no-promo-homo-laws.

25 Alabama State Code § 16-40A-2(c)(8).

26 S.C. Stat. § 59-32-30(5).

27 Laura A. Szalacha, "Safer sexual diversity climates: Lessons learned from an evaluation of Massachusetts safe schools program for gay and lesbian students," *American Journal of Education* 110, no. 1 (2003): 58–88.

28 Russell B. Toomey and Stephen T. Russell, "Gay-straight alliances, social justice involvement, and school victimization of lesbian, gay, bisexual, and queer youth: Implications for school well-being and plans to vote," *Youth & Society* 45, no. 4 (2013): 500–522; Carol Goodenow, Laura Szalacha, and Kim Westheimer, "School support groups, other school factors, and the safety of sexual minority adolescents," *Psychology in the Schools* 43, no. 5 (2006): 573–589.

29 Russell B. Toomey et al., "High school gay–straight alliances (GSAs) and young adult well-being: An examination of GSA presence, participation, and perceived effectiveness," *Applied Developmental Science* 15, no. 4 (2011): 175–185.

30 Joseph G. Kosciw et al., "The 2011 National School Climate Survey: The experiences of lesbian, gay, bisexual and transgender youth in our nation's schools," *GLSEN*, 2012; Jacqueline Ullman, "Free2Be?: Exploring the schooling experiences of Australia's sexuality and gender diverse secondary school students," *Western Sidney University* (2015), 31.

31 Stephen T. Russell et al., "Safe schools policy for LGBTQ students and commentaries," *Social Policy Report* 24, no. 4 (2010): 1–25.

32 Stephen T. Russell and Jenifer K. McGuire, "The school climate for lesbian, gay, bisexual, and transgender (LGBT) students," *Toward Positive Youth Development: Transforming Schools and Community Programs* (2008): 133–149.

33 M. O'Shaughnessy et al., "Safe place to learn: Consequences of harassment based on actual or perceived sexual orientation and gender non-conformity and steps for making schools safer," *San Francisco: California Safe Schools Coalition and 4-H Center for Youth Development* (2004); Stephen T. Russell et al., "Are school policies focused on sexual orientation and gender identity associated with less bullying? Teachers' perspectives," *Journal of School Psychology* 54 (2016): 29–38; Stephen T. Russell, Anna Muraco, Aarti Subramaniam, and Carolyn Laub, "Youth empowerment and high school gay-straight alliances." *Journal of youth and adolescence* 38, no. 7 (2009): 891–903; Goodenow et al., "School support groups, other school factors, and the safety of sexual minority adolescents," *Psychology in the Schools* 43, no. 5 (2006): 573–589; Mark L. Hatzenbuehler and Katherine M. Keyes, "Inclusive anti-bullying policies and reduced risk of suicide attempts in lesbian and gay youth," *Journal of Adolescent Health* 53, no. 1 (2013): S21–S26.

34 Cole Thaler, Flor Bermudez, and Susan Sommer, "Legal advocacy on behalf of transgender and gender nonconforming youth." *Social Work Practice with Transgender and Gender Variant Youth* 27 (2009): 139–62.

35 Joseph G. Kosciw et al., "The 2019 National School Climate Survey: The experiences of lesbian, gay, bisexual, transgender, and queer youth in our nation's schools," *GLSEN*, 2020.

36 Dennis P. Carmody and Michael Lewis, "Brain activation when hearing one's own and others' names," *Brain Research 1116*, no. 1 (2006): 153–158.

37   Stephen T. Russell et al., "Chosen name use is linked to reduced depressive symptoms, suicidal ideation, and suicidal behavior among transgender youth," *Journal of Adolescent Health* 63, no. 4 (2018): 503–505.

38   Russell et al., "Chosen name use is linked to reduced depressive symptoms, suicidal ideation, and suicidal behavior among transgender youth."

39   Julie Compton, "Trans students face 'detrimental' health effects without fed protection," *NBC News*, February 25, 2017, https://www.nbcnews.com/feature/nbc-out/without-federal -protections-trans-students-face-potential-health-crisis-n725156.

40   "Separation & stigma: Transgender youth & school facilities," *GLSEN*, 2017, https://www .glsen.org/sites/default/files/2019-11/Separation_and_Stigma_2017.pdf.

41   S. E. James, J. L. Herman, S. Rankin, M. Keisling, L. Mottet, and M. Anafi, "The Report of the 2015 U.S. Transgender Survey," Washington, DC: National Center for Transgender Equality (2016).

42   Michael Gordon, Mark S. Price, and Katie Peralta, "Understanding HB2: North Carolina's newest law solidifies state's role in defining discrimination," *The Charlotte Observer,* March 26, 2016, https://www.charlotteobserver.com/news/politics-government/article68401147. html.

43   Jolene Kralik, "'Bathroom bill' legislative tracking," *National Conference of State Legislatures*, October 24, 2019, https://www.ncsl.org/research/education/-bathroom-bill-legislative -tracking635951130.aspx.

44   *Grimm v. Gloucester County School Board,* No. 19-1952 (4th Cir. 2020).

45   Moriah Balingit, "Gavin Grimm just wanted to use the bathroom. He didn't think the nation would debate it," *The Washington Post*, August 30, 2016, https://www.washingtonpost. com /local/education/gavin-grimm-just-wanted-to-use-the-bathroom-he-didnt-think-the-nation -would-debate-it/2016/08/30/23fc9892-6a26-11e6-ba32-5a4bf5aad4fa_story.html?itid=lk _inline_manual_12.

46   American Civil Liberties Union, "Gavin Grimm at Gloucester County School Board Meeting," September 1, 2016, YouTube video, https://www.youtube.com/watch?v=My0GYq _Wydw&feature=youtu.be.

47   *Grimm v. Gloucester County School Board*, No. 19-1952 (4th Cir. 2020).

48   Majority Opinion by Floyd, *Grimm v. Gloucester County School Board*, No. 19-1952 (4th Cir. 2020).

49   Concurring Opinion by Wynn, *Grimm v. Gloucester County School Board*, No. 19-1952 (4th Cir. 2020). https://www.ca4.uscourts.gov/opinions/191952.P.pdf.

50   Soule, et al. v. CT Association of Schools, et al., Case No. 3:20-cv-00201-RNC, ACLU https://www.acluct.org/sites/default/files/field_documents/soule_et_al_v._ct_association_ of_schools_et_al_-_motion_for_preliminary_injunction.pdf.

51   Dave Zirin, "Transphobia's new target is the world of sports," *The Nation*, March 5, 2019, https://www.thenation.com/article/archive/trans-runner-daily-caller-terry-miller-andraya -yearwood-martina-navratilova/.

52   Katrina Karkazis "Stop talking about testosterone – there's no such thing as a 'true sex,'" *The Guardian*, March 6, 2019, https://www.theguardian.com/commentisfree/2019/mar/06 /testosterone-biological-sex-sports-bodies.

53   Zirin, "Transphobia's new target is the world of sports."

54   Priya Krishnakumar, "This record-breaking year for anti-transgender legislation would affect minors the most," CNN, April 15, 2021, https://www.cnn.com/2021/04/15/politics/anti -transgender-legislation-2021/index.html.

55   H.R.5 – Equality Act, 117th Congress (2021–2022), https://www.congress.gov/bill/117th-congress/house-bill/5?text?q=%7B%22search%22%3A%5B%22sexual+orientation%22%5D% 7D&r=1&s=6.

CHAPTER 6: FIRST FORAYS INTO
THE SOCIAL SCIENCE OF BIAS

1 Jackson, *Social Scientists for Social Justice*; James R. Acker, "Thirty years of social science in Supreme Court criminal cases," *Law & Policy* 12, no. 1 (1990): 1–23; Abraham L. Davis, *The United States Supreme Court and The Uses of Social Science Data* (Ardent Media: 1973); Paul L. Rosen, *The Supreme Court and Social Science* (University of Illinois Press, 1972). See also Kenneth B. Clark, *Desegregation: An Appraisal of The Evidence* (Association Press, 1953); Kenneth K. Wong and Anna C. Nicotera, "Brown v. Board of Education and the Coleman Report: Social science research and the debate on educational equality," *Peabody Journal of Education* 79, no. 2 (2004): 122–135.

2 Kenneth B. Clark, Isidor Chein, and Stuart W. Cook, "The effects of segregation and the consequences of desegregation: A (September 1952) social science statement in the *Brown v. Board of Education of Topeka* Supreme Court case," *American Psychologist* 59, no. 6 (2004): 495.

3 Guthrie, *Even the Rat Was White*.

4 Graham Richards, "Reconceptualizing the history of race psychology: Thomas Russell Garth (1872–1939) and how he changed his mind," *Journal of the History of the Behavioral Sciences* 34, no. 1 (1998): 15–32.

5 Thomas Russell Garth, "A review of racial psychology," *Psychological Bulletin* 22, no. 6 (1925): 343.

6 Vonnie C. McLoyd and Suzanne M. Randolph, "Secular trends in the study of Afro-American children: A review of child development, 1936–1980," *Monographs of The Society for Research in Child Development* (1985): 78–92.

7 Graham Richards, "Of what is history of psychology a history?," *The British Journal for the History of Science* 20, no. 2 (1987): 201–211; Fran Samelson, "From 'race psychology' to 'studies in prejudice': Some observations on the thematic reversal in social psychology," *Journal of the History of the Behavioral Sciences* 14, no. 3 (1978): 265–278.

8 Richards, "Of what is history of psychology a history?"; Samelson, "From 'race psychology' to 'studies in prejudice.'"

9 Shafali Lal, "Giving children security: Mamie Phipps Clark and the racialization of child psychology," *American Psychologist* 57, no. 1 (2002): 20.

10 Richards, "Reconceptualizing the history of race psychology."

11 Gordon W. Allport, Kenneth Clark, and Thomas Pettigrew, *The Nature of Prejudice* (Addison-Wesley: 1954).

12 Eugene L. Horowitz and Ruth E. Horowitz, "Development of social attitudes in children," *Sociometry* (1938): 301–338.

13 Bigler and Liben, "Developmental intergroup theory."

14 Ruth Horowitz and Lois Barclay Murphy, "Projective methods in the psychological study of children," *The Journal of Experimental Education* 7, no. 2 (1938): 133–140.

15 Matthew Pelowitz, "Profile of Ruth (Horowitz) Hartley," *Psychology's Feminist Voices Multimedia Internet Archive*, ed. Alexandra Rutherford (York University: 2012).

16 Ruth E. Horowitz, "Racial aspects of self-identification in nursery school children," *The Journal of Psychology* 7, no. 1 (1939): 94.

17 Beverly Daniel Tatum, *Why Are All the Black Kids Sitting Together in The Cafeteria?: And Other Conversations About Race* (Basic Books, 2017).

18 Mamie Phipps Clark, oral history interview by Ed Edwin, New York, 1976, Columbia University Libraries Oral History Research Office, http://www.columbia.edu/cu/lweb/digital/collections/nny/clarkm/transcripts/clarkm_1_1_10.html.

19 Mamie Phipps Clark, "An investigation of the development of consciousness of distinctive self in pre-school children," Master's thesis (Howard University, 1939).

20 Lawrence Nyman, "Documenting history: An interview with Kenneth Bancroft Clark," *History of Psychology* 13, no. 1 (2010): 74–88.

21 Nyman, "Documenting history."

22 Judith R. Porter and Robert E. Washington, "Black identity and self-esteem: A review of studies of Black self-concept, 1968–1978," *Annual Review of Sociology* 5, no. 1 (1979): 53–74.

23 Laura Smith, "When a Jewish man was lynched for murdering a little girl, the Klan was reborn," *Timeline*, January 5, 2018, https://timeline.com/when-a-jewish-man-was-lynched -for-murdering-a-little-girl-the-klan-was-reborn-a48d30374942.

24 Wendy Hartley, interview by author, October 15–16, 2018.

25 Wendy Hartley, interview by author, October 15–16, 2018.

26 James Grossman, "Bigotry stopped Americans from intervening before the Holocaust. Not much has changed," *Los Angeles Times*, April 29, 2018, https://www.latimes.com/opinion /op-ed/la-oe-grossman-holocaust-exhibit-20180429-htmlstory.html.

27 Matthew Pelowitz, "Profile of Ruth (Horowitz) Hartley"; Alexandra Rutherford, "Mamie Phipps Clark: Developmental psychologist, starting from strengths," *Portraits of Pioneers in Developmental Psychology* (2012): 261–275.

28 M. P. Clark, "Mamie Phipps Clark," in A. N. O'Connell and N. F. Russo (Eds.), *Models of Achievement: Reflections of Eminent Women in Psychology* (New York: Columbia University Press), 267–277.

29 Mamie Phipps Clark, oral history interview by Ed Edwin.

30 Rutherford, "Mamie Phipps Clark."

31 Mamie Phipps Clark, oral history interview by Ed Edwin.

32 Letters from Mamie Phipps Clark to Kenneth Clark, Kenneth Bancroft Clark Papers, Library of Congress, Box 1, Folder 4.

33 Letters from Mamie Phipps Clark to Kenneth Clark, Kenneth Bancroft Clark Papers, Library of Congress, Box 1, Folder 4.

34 Letter from Mamie Phipps Clark to Kenneth Clark, October 1, 1936, Kenneth Bancroft Clark Papers, Library of Congress, Box 1, Folder 7.

35 A. Karera, "Profile of Mamie Phipps Clark," *Psychology's Feminist Voices Multimedia Internet Archive* (2010).

36 Rutherford, "Mamie Phipps Clark."

37 Mamie Phipps Clark, oral history interview by Ed Edwin.

38 Mamie Phipps Clark, oral history interview by Ed Edwin.

39 Leila McNeill, "How a psychologist's work on race identity helped overturn school segregation in 1950s America," *Smithsonian Magazine*, October 26, 2017, https://www. smithsonianmag.com/science-nature/psychologist-work-racial-identity-helped-overturn -school-segregation-180966934/.

40 Elizabeth Johnston and Ann Johnson, "Searching for the second generation of American women psychologists," *History of Psychology* 11, no. 1 (2008): 40; Alexandra Rutherford, "Making better use of US women: Psychology, sex roles, and womanpower in post-WWII America," *Journal of the History of the Behavioral Sciences* 53, no. 3 (2017): 228–245; Laurel Furumoto and Elizabeth Scarborough, "Placing women in the history of psychology: The first American women psychologists," in *Evolving Perspectives on the History of Psychology*, ed. W. E. Pickren and D. A. Dewsbury (2002), 527–543; Mary Frank Fox, "Women, science, and academia: Graduate education and careers," *Gender & Society* 15, no. 5 (2001): 654–666.

41 Johnston and Johnson, "Searching for the second generation of American women psychologists."

42 Clark, "Mamie Phipps Clark," in O'Connell and Russo, *Models of Achievement*.

43 Wendy Hartley, interview by author, October 15–16, 2018.

44 Clark, "Mamie Phipps Clark," in O'Connell and Russo, *Models of Achievement*.

45 Rutherford, "Mamie Phipps Clark"; Gerald Markowitz and David Rosner, *Children, Race, and Power: Kenneth and Mamie Clark's Northside Center* (Routledge: 2013).

46 "Northside Center's Programs," Northside Center, https://www.northsidecenter.org /programs/.

47 Wendy Hartley, interview by author, October 15–16, 2018.

48 Nyman, "Documenting history."

CHAPTER 7: RACIAL BIAS INTO THE NEW CENTURY

1   Walter Goodman, "Dr. Kenneth B. Clark: Bewilderment Replaces 'Wishful Thinking' on
    Race," *The New York Times*, December 27, 1984, https://www.nytimes.com/1984/12/27/us/dr
    -kenneth-b-clark-bewilderment-replaces-wishful-thinking-on-race.html.
2   Klarman, *From Jim Crow to Civil Rights*.
3   Herman Talmadge, *You and Segregation* (Vulcan Press, 1955); Kluger, *Simple Justice*.
4   Kristen Green, *Something Must Be Done About Prince Edward County* (HarperCollins: 2015).
5   Gary Orfield et al., "Brown at 60: Great progress, a long retreat, and an uncertain future,"
    The Civil Rights Project at the University of California (2014).
6   Erica Frankenberg et al., "Harming our common future: America's segregated schools 65
    years after Brown," *The Civil Rights Project at the University of California* (2019), https://www
    .civilrightsproject.ucla.edu/research/k-12-education/integration-and-diversity/harming-our
    -common-future-americas-segregated-schools-65-years-after-brown/Brown-65-050919v4
    -final.pdf.
7   Chinh Q. Le, "Racially integrated education and the role of the federal government," *North
    Carolina Law Review* 88 (2009): 725.
8   Le, "Racially integrated education and the role of the federal government."
9   *Board of Education of Oklahoma City Public Schools v. Dowell*, 498 U.S. 237 (1991).
10 Orfield et al., "Brown at 60"; Gary Orfield et al., "'Brown' at 62: School Segregation by
    Race, Poverty and State," *University of California Civil Rights Project* (2016).
11 Sean F. Reardon et al., "Brown fades: The end of court-ordered school desegregation and the
    resegregation of American public schools," *Journal of Policy Analysis and Management* 31, no.
    4 (2012): 876–904.
12 Erica Frankenberg et al., "Harming our common future."
13 Kenneth T. Walsh, "50 years ago, immigration changed in America," *U.S. News*, October 2,
    2015, https://www.usnews.com/news/articles/2015/10/02/50-years-ago-immigration
    -changed-in-america.
14 William H. Frey, "Less than half of US children under 15 are white, census shows,"
    Brookings, June 24, 2019, https://www.brookings.edu/research/less-than-half-of-us-children
    -under-15-are-white-census-shows/.
15 Erica Frankenberg et al., "Harming our common future."
16 Erica Frankenberg et al., "Harming our common future."
17 "Racial/Ethnic Enrollment in Public Schools," *National Center for Education Statistics*, May
    2017, https://nces.ed.gov/programs/coe/indicator_cge.asp.
18 Sean F. Reardon et al., "Brown fades."
19 Erica Frankenberg et al., "Harming our common future."
20 Erica Frankenberg et al., "Harming our common future."
21 John Kucsera and Gary Orfield, "New York State's extreme school segregation: Inequality,
    inaction and a damaged future," *The Civil Rights Project at the University of California* (2014),
    https://civilrightsproject.ucla.edu/research/k-12-education/integration-and-diversity/ny
    -norflet-report-placeholder/Kucsera-New-York-Extreme-Segregation-2014.pdf.
22 Toby L. Parcel and Andrew J. Taylor, *The End of Consensus: Diversity, Neighborhoods, and the
    Politics of Public School Assignments* (University of North Carolina Press Books, 2015); Erica
    Frankenberg and Gary Orfield, eds., *The Resegregation of Suburban Schools: A Hidden Crisis
    in American Education* (Harvard Education Press, 2012); Susan Eaton, "Not your father's
    suburb: Race and rectitude in a changing Minnesota community," *One Nation Indivisible*
    (2012).
23 Toby L. Parcel and Andrew J. Taylor, *The End of Consensus: Diversity, Neighborhoods, and
    the Politics of Public School Assignments*; Erica Frankenberg and Gary Orfield, eds., *The
    Resegregation of Suburban Schools: A Hidden Crisis in American Education*; Susan Eaton, "Not
    your father's suburb: Race and rectitude in a changing Minnesota community."

24 Sean F. Reardon and Ann Owens, "60 years after Brown: Trends and consequences of school segregation," *Annual Review of Sociology* 40 (2014).

25 Sean F. Reardon et al., "Brown fades."

26 "Non-white school districts get $23 billion less than white districts, despite serving the same number of students," *EdBuild.org*, 2019.

27 Individual conversation with author, 2019.

28 Charles T. Clotfelter, Helen F. Ladd, and Jacob Vigdor, "Who teaches whom? Race and the distribution of novice teachers," *Economics of Education Review* 24, no. 4 (2005): 377–392.

29 Clotfelter, Ladd, and Vigdor, "Who teaches whom?"

30 Russell W. Rumberger and Gregory J. Palardy, "Does segregation still matter? The impact of student composition on academic achievement in high school," *Teachers College Record* 107, no. 9 (2005): 1999; Caroline Hoxby, "Peer effects in the classroom: Learning from gender and race variation," *National Bureau of Economic Research*, no. w7867 (2000); Janet W. Schofield, "Ability grouping, composition effects and the achievement gap," *Migration Background, Minority-Group Membership and Academic Achievement* (2007).

31 Linsey Edwards, "Homogeneity and inequality: School discipline inequality and the role of racial composition," *Social Forces* 95, no. 1 (2016): 55–76.

32 Rucker C. Johnson and Robert F. Schoeni, "The influence of early-life events on human capital, health status, and labor market outcomes over the life course," *The BE Journal of Economic Analysis & Policy* 11, no. 3 (2011).

33 K. N. Bolick and B. Rogowsky, "Ability grouping is on the rise, but should it be?" *Journal of Education and Human Development* 5, no. 2 (2016): 40–51.

34 "The resurgence of ability grouping and persistence of tracking: Part II of the 2013 brown center report on American education," *Brookings*, March 18, 2013, https://www.brookings.edu/research/the-resurgence-of-ability-grouping-and-persistence-of-tracking/.

35 Doug Archbald and Julia Keleher, "Measuring conditions and consequences of tracking in the high school curriculum," *American Secondary Education* (2008): 26–42.

36 Harriet R. Tenenbaum and Martin D. Ruck, "Are teachers' expectations different for racial minority than for European American students? A meta-analysis," *Journal of Educational Psychology* 99, no. 2 (2007): 253.

37 Amine Ouazad, "Assessed by a teacher like me: Race and teacher assessments," *Education Finance and Policy* 9, no. 3 (2014): 334–372.

38 Ouazad, "Assessed by a teacher like me."

39 McKown and Weinstein, "The development and consequences of stereotype consciousness in middle childhood."

40 Christia Spears Brown and Hui Chu, "Discrimination, ethnic identity, and academic outcomes of Mexican immigrant children: The importance of school context," *Child Development* 83, no. 5 (2012): 1477–1485.

41 Carol Goodenow, "Classroom belonging among early adolescent students: Relationships to motivation and achievement," *The Journal of Early Adolescence* 13, no. 1 (1993): 21–43; Gladys E. Ibañez et al., "Cultural attributes and adaptations linked to achievement motivation among Latino adolescents," *Journal of Youth and Adolescence* 33, no. 6 (2004): 559–568.

42 Christia Spears Brown et al., "Perceptions of discrimination predict retention of college students of color: Connections with school belonging and ethnic identity," *National Conference on Undergraduate Research*, 2020.

43 Abigail W. Geiger, "America's public school teachers are far less racially and ethnically diverse than their students," *Pew Research Center*, August 27, 2018, https://www.pewresearch.org/fact-tank/2018/08/27/americas-public-school-teachers-are-far-less-racially-and-ethnically-diverse-than-their-students/.

44 Roslyn Arlin Mickelson, "Subverting Swann: First-and second-generation segregation in the Charlotte-Mecklenburg schools," *American Educational Research Journal* 38, no. 2 (2001): 215–252; Doug Archbald, Joseph Glutting, and Xiaoyu Qian, "Getting into honors or not: An analysis of the relative influence of grades, test scores, and race on track placement in a comprehensive high school," *American Secondary Education* (2009): 65–81.

45 Mickelson, "Subverting Swann"; Tenenbaum and Ruck, "Are teachers' expectations different for racial minority than for European American students?"

46 Maureen T. Hallinan, "Race effects on students' track mobility in high school," *Social Psychology of Education* 1, no. 1 (1996): 1–24.

47 For more information about inequities in tracking, see Sean Kelly and Heather Price, "The correlates of tracking policy: Opportunity hoarding, status competition, or a technical-functional explanation?" *American Educational Research Journal* 48, no. 3 (2011): 560–585; Donna M. Harris and Celia Rousseau Anderson, "Equity, mathematics reform and policy: The dilemma of 'opportunity to learn,'" *Equity in Discourse for Mathematics Education* (Springer, 2012), 195–204; Jacob Werblow, Angela Urick, and Luke Duesbery, "On the wrong track: How tracking is associated with dropping out of high school," *Equity & Excellence in Education* 46, no. 2 (2013): 270–284.

48 "Employment projections: Education pays," *Bureau for Labor Statistics*, 2019, https://www.bls .gov/emp/chart-unemployment-earnings-education.htm.

49 Janet W. Schofield and Leslie R.M. Hausmann, "The conundrum of school desegregation: Positive student outcomes and waning support," *University of Pittsburgh Law Review* 66 (2004): 83; Roslyn Arlin Mickelson, Martha Cecilia Bottia, and Richard Lambert, "Effects of school racial composition on K–12 mathematics outcomes: A metaregression analysis," *Review of Educational Research* 83, no. 1 (2013): 121–158.

50 Rumberger and Palardy, "Does segregation still matter?"

51 Aprile D. Benner and Robert Crosnoe, "The racial/ethnic composition of elementary schools and young children's academic and socioemotional functioning," *American Educational Research Journal* 48, no. 3 (2011): 621–646.

52 Koji Ueno, "Same-race friendships and school attachment: Demonstrating the interaction between personal network and school composition," *Sociological Forum* 24, no. 3 (2009): 515–537.

53 James Moody, "Race, school integration, and friendship segregation in America," *American Journal of Sociology* 107, no. 3 (2001): 679–716.

54 Brown and Chu, "Discrimination, ethnic identity, and academic outcomes of Mexican immigrant children."

55 Jaana Juvonen, Adrienne Nishina, and Sandra Graham, "Ethnic diversity and perceptions of safety in urban middle schools," *Psychological Science* 17, no. 5 (2006): 393–400.

56 Eleanor K. Seaton and Sara Douglass, "School diversity and racial discrimination among African-American adolescents," *Cultural Diversity and Ethnic Minority Psychology* 20, no. 2 (2014): 156.

57 Jochem Thijs and Maykel Verkuyten, "School ethnic diversity and students' interethnic relations," *British Journal of Educational Psychology* 84, no. 1 (2014): 1–21; Linda R. Tropp and Mary A. Prenovost, "The role of intergroup contact in predicting children's interethnic attitudes: Evidence from meta-analytic and field studies," *Intergroup Attitudes and Relations in Childhood Through Adulthood*, ed. Sheri R. Levy and Melanie Killen (Oxford University Press, 2008), 236–248.

58 Thomas F. Pettigrew and Linda R. Tropp, "A meta-analytic test of intergroup contact theory," *Journal of Personality and Social Psychology* 90, no. 5 (2006): 751.

59 Sandra Graham, "Race/ethnicity and social adjustment of adolescents: How (not if) school diversity matters," *Educational Psychologist* 53, no. 2 (2018): 64–77.

60 Vladimir T. Khmelkov and Maureen T. Hallinan, "Organizational effects on race relations in schools," *Journal of Social Issues* 55, no. 4 (1999): 627–645.

61 Linda R. Tropp and Thomas F. Pettigrew, "Relationships between intergroup contact and prejudice among minority and majority status groups," *Psychological Science* 16, no. 12 (2005): 951–957.

62 Alaina Brenick et al., "Perceptions of discrimination by young diaspora migrants," *European Psychologist* (2012).

63 Christopher K. Marshburn and Belinda Campos, "Seeking just us: A mixed methods investigation of racism-specific support among Black college students," *Journal of Black Psychology* (2021).

64 Rebecca Kang McGill, Niobe Way, and Diane Hughes, "Intra-and interracial best friendships during middle school: Links to social and emotional well-being," *Journal of Research on Adolescence* 22, no. 4 (2012): 722–738.

65 Rodolfo Mendoza-Denton and Elizabeth Page-Gould, "Can cross-group friendships influence minority students' well-being at historically white universities?" *Psychological Science* 19, no. 9 (2008): 933–939.

66 Sandra Graham, Race/Ethnicity and Social Adjustment of Adolescents: How (Not if) School Diversity Matters, *Educational Psychologist* 53, no. 2 (2018): 64–77, doi:10.1080 /00461520.2018.1428805.

67 Monica Anderson and Jingjing Jiang, "Teens, Social Media & Technology 2018," *Pew Research Center*, May 31, 2018, https://www.pewresearch.org/internet/2018/05/31/teens -social-media-technology-2018/.

68 Monica Anderson and Jingjing Jiang, "Teens' Social Media Habits and Experiences," *Pew Research Center*, November 28, 2018, https://www.pewresearch.org/internet/2018/11/28 /teens-and-their-experiences-on-social-media/.

69 Brendesha M. Tynes et al., "Online racial discrimination and psychological adjustment among adolescents," *Journal of Adolescent Health* 43, no. 6 (2008): 565–569.

70 Tynes et al., "Online racial discrimination and psychological adjustment among adolescents."

71 Brendesha M. Tynes et al., "Online racial discrimination and the protective function of ethnic identity and self-esteem for African American adolescents," *Developmental Psychology* 48, no. 2 (2012): 343.

72 Jesse Washington, "Why did Black Lives Matter protests attract unprecedented white support? The cruelty of George Floyd's killing resonated in the pandemic lockdown," *The Undefeated*, June 18, 2020, https://theundefeated.com/features/why-did-black-lives-matter -protests-attract-unprecedented-white-support/.

73 Brendesha M. Tynes et al., "Race-related traumatic events online and mental health among adolescents of color," *Journal of Adolescent Health* 65, no. 3 (2019): 371–377.

74 Joshua Schuschke and Brendesha M. Tynes, "Online community empowerment, emotional connection, and armed love in the Black Lives Matter Movement," in *Emotions, Technology, and Social Media* (Academic Press, 2016), 25–47.

75 Bianca Bosker, "'Tweet,' 'Social Media' Added to Merriam-Webster Dictionary," *HuffPost*, October 25, 2011, https://www.huffpost.com/entry/tweet-social-media-merriam-webster -dictionary_n_937180?guccounter=1&guce_referrer=aHR0cHM6Ly93d3cuZ29vZ2 xlLmNvbS8&guce_referrer_sig=AQAAAEjYftk0noI_PesAPDKsuUwrTILjWu7zoc8Q3 sbKglaxUPPSenqB4xxZY88zu6IXgryydcohoGaWJf59RcJHIN3R0GyWI7OFy3UlHO YOZwRZqhu1c5J57eC_mJT-2-hDR_YrrapX1No5tFyThvnIH9IjOd_QrNXhS2s9jmaL uAT1/.

76 Fay Sudweeks and Susan Herring, *Culture, Technology, Communication: Towards an Intercultural Global Village* (Suny Press, 2014).

CHAPTER 8: BORDER WALLS, TRAVEL BANS, AND GLOBAL PANDEMICS

1   Lizzy Gurdus, "Trump: 'We have some bad hombres and we're going to get them out,'" *CNBC*, October 29, 2016, https://www.cnbc.com/2016/10/19/trump-we-have-some-bad -hombres-and-were-going-to-get-them-out.html.

2   Sarah Larimer, "Middle schoolers chant 'build that wall' during lunch in aftermath of Trump win," *Washington Post*, November 10, 2016, https://web.archive.org/ web/20190107072532/https://www.washingtonpost.com/news/education/wp/2016/11/10/ middle-schoolers-chant -build-that-wall-during-lunch-in-aftermath-of-trump-win/.

3   Maureen B. Costello, "After election day: The Trump effect: The impact of the 2016 presidential election on our nation's schools," *Southern Poverty Law Center*, 2016, https:// www.spl center.org/sites/default/files/the_trump_effect.pdf.

4   Francis L. Huang and Dewey G. Cornell, "School teasing and bullying after the presidential election," *Educational Researcher* 48, no. 2 (2019): 69–83.

5   Huang and Cornell, "School teasing and bullying after the presidential election."

6   Christia Spears Brown, "American elementary school children's attitudes about immigrants, immigration, and being an American," *Journal of Applied Developmental Psychology* 32, no. 3 (2011): 109–117.

7   Thierry Devos and Hafsa Mohamed, "Shades of American identity: Implicit relations between ethnic and national identities," *Social and Personality Psychology Compass* 8, no. 12 (2014): 739–754; Thierry Devos and Mahzarin R. Banaji, "American = white?" *Journal of Personality and Social Psychology* 88, no. 3 (2005): 447.

8   Tiane L. Lee and Susan T. Fiske, "Not an outgroup, not yet an ingroup: Immigrants in the stereotype content model," *International Journal of Intercultural Relations* 30, no. 6 (2006): 751-768; Robert Short, "Justice, politics, and prejudice regarding immigration attitude," *Current Research in Social Psychology* 9, no. 14 (2004): 193–208.

9   Frances E. Aboud, "The formation of in-group favoritism and out-group prejudice in young children: Are they distinct attitudes?" *Developmental Psychology* 39, no. 1 (2003): 48.

10   Brown, "Elementary school children's attitudes about immigrants, immigration, and being an American."

11   Kimberly Costello and Gordon Hodson. "Exploring the roots of dehumanization: The role of animal–human similarity in promoting immigrant humanization," *Group Processes & Intergroup Relations* 13, no. 1 (2010): 3–22.

12   Jeanne Batalova, Mary Hanna, and Christopher Levesque, "Frequently requested statistics on immigrants and immigration in the United States," *Migration Policy Institute*, February 11, 2021, https://www.migrationpolicy.org/article/frequently-requested-statistics -immigrants-and-immigration-united-states.

13   Norma E. Werner and Idella M. Evans, "Perception of prejudice in Mexican-American preschool children," *Perceptual and Motor Skills* 27, no. 3_suppl (1968): 1039–1046.

14   "Modern Immigration Wave Brings 59 Million to U.S., Driving Population Growth and Change Through 2065," *Pew Research Center*, September 28, 2015, https://www.pewresearch .org/hispanic/2015/09/28/modern-immigration-wave-brings-59-million-to-u-s-driving -population-growth-and-change-through-2065/.

15   Joanna Dreby, "The burden of deportation on children in Mexican immigrant families," *Journal of Marriage and Family* 74, no. 4 (2012): 829–845.

16   Christia Spears Brown (2017). *Discrimination in Childhood and Adolescence*; Aprile D. Benner and Sandra Graham, "Latino adolescents' experiences of discrimination across the first 2 years of high school: Correlates and influences on educational outcomes," *Child Development* 82, no. 2 (2011): 508–519.

17   Brown et al., "Ethnicity and gender in late childhood and early adolescence: Group identity and awareness of bias."

18   Elena Flores et al., "Perceived racial/ethnic discrimination, posttraumatic stress symptoms, and health risk behaviors among Mexican American adolescents," *Journal of Counseling Psychology* 57, no. 3 (2010): 264.

19   Szalacha et al., "Discrimination and Puerto Rican children's and adolescents' mental health."

20   Fisher, Wallace, and Fenton, "Discrimination distress during adolescence," *Journal of Youth and Adolescence* 29, no. 6 (2000): 679–695; Susan Rakosi Rosenbloom and Niobe Way, "Experiences of discrimination among African American, Asian American, and Latino adolescents in an urban high school," *Youth & Society* 35, no. 4 (2004): 420–451.

21   Greene, Way, and Pahl, "Trajectories of perceived adult and peer discrimination among Black, Latino, and Asian American adolescents: patterns and psychological correlates"; Umaña-Taylor and Updegraff, "Latino adolescents' mental health: Exploring the interrelations among discrimination, ethnic identity, cultural orientation, self-esteem, and depressive symptoms."

22   Jeffrey C. Wayman, "Student perceptions of teacher ethnic bias: A comparison of Mexican American and non-Latino White dropouts and students," *The High School Journal* 85, no. 3 (2002): 27–37.

23   Tiffany Yip et al., "Moderating the association between discrimination and adjustment: A meta-analysis of ethnic/racial identity," *Developmental Psychology* 55, no. 6 (2019): 1274.

24   Dreby, "The burden of deportation on children in Mexican immigrant families."

25   Cecilia Ayón, "Economic, social, and health effects of discrimination on Latino immigrant families," *Migration Policy Institute* (2015).

26   Nicole L. Novak, Arline T. Geronimus, and Aresha M. Martinez-Cardoso, "Change in birth outcomes among infants born to Latina mothers after a major immigration raid," *International Journal of Epidemiology* 46, no. 3 (2017): 839–849.

27   Courtney Crowder and MacKenzie Elmer, "Postville raid anniversary: A timeline of events in one of America's largest illegal immigration campaigns," *The Des Moines Register,* May 10, 2018, https://www.desmoinesregister.com/story/news/investigations/2018/05/10/postville-raid-anniversary-timeline-aaron-rubashkin-agriprocessors-postville-iowa-immigration-raid/588025002/.

28   Novak, Geronimus, and Martinez-Cardoso, "Change in birth outcomes among infants born to Latina mothers after a major immigration raid."

29   Randy Capps, Michael Fix, and Jie Zong, "A profile of US children with unauthorized immigrant parents," *Migration Policy Institute,* 2016.

30   Stephanie Potochnick, Jen-Hao Chen, and Krista Perreira, "Local-level immigration enforcement and food insecurity risk among Hispanic immigrant families with children: National-level evidence," *Journal of Immigrant and Minority Health* 19, no. 5 (2017): 1042–1049.

31   Potochnick, Chen, and Perreira, "Local-level immigration enforcement and food insecurity risk among Hispanic immigrant families with children: National-level evidence."

32   Gary Claxton et al., "Kaiser Family Foundation," *Health Research & Educational Trust* (2016).

33   Ashley M. Groh et al., "Attachment in the early life course: Meta-analytic evidence for its role in socioemotional development," *Child Development Perspectives* 11, no. 1 (2017): 70–76.

34   Groh et al., "Attachment in the early life course: Meta-analytic evidence for its role in socioemotional development."

35   Wyatt Clarke, Kimberly Turner, and Lina Guzman, "One quarter of Hispanic children in the United States have an unauthorized immigrant parent," *National Research Center on Hispanic Children & Families,* October 4, 2017, https://www.hispanicresearchcenter.org/research-resources/one-quarter-of-hispanic-children-in-the-united-states-have-an-unauthorized-immigrant-parent/.

36   Dreby, "The burden of deportation on children in Mexican immigrant families."

37   Dreby, "The burden of deportation on children in Mexican immigrant families."

38 Jongyeon Ee and Patricia Gándara, "The impact of immigration enforcement on the nation's schools," *American Educational Research Journal* 57, no. 2 (2020): 840–871.

39 Costello, "The Trump effect."

40 Johayra Bouza et al., "The science is clear: Separating families has long-term damaging psychological and health consequences for children, families, and communities," *Society for Research in Child Development* 20 (2018).

41 Amy K. Marks, John L. McKenna, and Cynthia Garcia Coll, "National immigration receiving contexts: A critical aspect of native-born, immigrant, and refugee youth well-being," *European Psychologist* 23, no. 1 (2018): 6.

42 Besheer Mohamed, "New estimates show U.S. Muslim population continues to grow," *Pew Research Center*, January 3, 2018, https://www.pewresearch.org/fact-tank/2018/01/03/new-estimates-show-u-s-muslim-population-continues-to-grow/.

43 Arab American Institute Foundation Demographics, https://censuscounts.org/wp-content/uploads/2019/03/National_Demographics_SubAncestries-2018.pdf.

44 Capucine Le Tarnec, "Children: The primary victims of the refugee crisis," *Humanium*, October 4, 2017, https://www.humanium.org/en/children-the-primary-victims-of-the-refugee-crisis/#:~:text=In%202015%2C%20about%20337%2C000%20asylum,which%2088%2C300%20were%20unaccompanied%20minors.&text=Many%20children%20are%20forced%20to,died%20in%20the%20Mediterranean%20Sea.

45 Nick Cumming-Bruce, "Number of people fleeing conflict is highest since World War II, U.N. says," *The New York Times*, June 19, 2019, https://www.nytimes.com/2019/06/19/world/refugees-record-un.html.

46 "Most Say 'No' to Syrian Refugees in Their State," *Rasmussen Reports*, November 19, 2015, https://www.rasmussenreports.com/public_content/politics/current_events/israel_the_middle_east/most_say_no_to_syrian_refugees_in_their_state.

47 United Nations Refugee Agency (2015). https://www.unhcr.org/refugee-statistics/download/?url=p9M8.

48 Jenna Johnson and Abigail Hauslohner, "'I think Islam hates us': A timeline of Trump's comments about Islam and Muslims," *The Washington Post*, May 20, 2017, https://www.washingtonpost.com/news/post-politics/wp/2017/05/20/i-think-islam-hates-us-a-timeline-of-trumps-comments-about-islam-and-muslims/.

49 "Rubio to Trump: 'I Want to Be Correct,' Not Politically Correct – Newsy," Newsy Politics, YouTube video, 0:10, March 10, 2016, https://www.youtube.com/watch?v=-xZRb86Drrw&t=8s&ab_channel=NewsyPolitics.

50 "Rubio to Trump: 'I Want to Be Correct,' Not Politically Correct – Newsy," Newsy Politics.

51 Carol Morello, January 27, 2017, "Trump signs order temporarily halting admission of refugees, promises priority for Christians," *The Washington Post*, https://www.washingtonpost.com/world/national-security/trump-approves-extreme-vetting-of-refugees-promises-priority-for-christians/2017/01/27/007021a2-e4c7-11e6-a547-5fb9411d332c_story.html.

52 Jessica Taylor, "Trump calls for 'total and complete shutdown of Muslims entering' U.S.," *NPR*, December 7, 2015, https://www.npr.org/2015/12/07/458836388/trump-calls-for-total-and-complete-shutdown-of-muslims-entering-u-s.

53 "CAIR-NY Reports 74% Increase in Anti-Muslim Hate Crimes Since Trump's Election," *Council on American-Islamic Relations*, March 5, 2018, https://www.cair-ny.org/news/2018/3/5/cair-ny-reports-74-increase-in-anti-muslim-hate-crimes-since-trumps-election.

54 Travis L. Dixon and Charlotte L. Williams, "The changing misrepresentation of race and crime on network and cable news," *Journal of Communication* 65, no. 1 (2015): 24–39.

55 Brown et al., "U.S. children's stereotypes and prejudicial attitudes toward Arab Muslims."

56 Kathleen M. Cain, Gail D. Heyman, and Michael E. Walker, "Preschoolers' ability to make dispositional predictions within and across domain," *Social Development* 6, no. 1 (1997): 53–75.

57 Ashley Fantz, Steve Almasy, and AnneClaire Stapleton, "Muslim teen Ahmed Mohamed creates clock, shows teachers, gets arrested," *CNN*, September 16, 2015, https://www.cnn.com/2015/09/16/us/texas-student-ahmed-muslim-clock-bomb/index.html.

58 Karen J. Aroian, "Discrimination against Muslim American adolescents," *The Journal of School Nursing* 28, no. 3 (2012): 206–213; Selcuk R. Sirin and Michelle Fine, "Hyphenated selves: Muslim American youth negotiating identities on the fault lines of global conflict," *Applied Development Science* 11, no. 3 (2007): 151–163.

59 Aroian, "Discrimination against Muslim American adolescents."

60 Aroian, "Discrimination against Muslim American adolescents."

61 "2019 Bullying Report," *Council on American-Islamic Relations California*, 2019, https://ca.cair.com/publications/2019-bullying-report/.

62 Siham Elkassem et al., "Growing up Muslim: The impact of Islamophobia on children in a Canadian community," *Journal of Muslim Mental Health* 12, no. 1 (2018): 3–18.

63 Laura Wray-Lake, Amy K. Syvertsen, and Constance A. Flanagan, "Contested citizenship and social exclusion: Adolescent Arab American immigrants' views of the social contract," *Applied Development Science* 12, no. 2 (2008): 84–92.

64 Elkassem et al., "Growing up Muslim."

65 "2019 Bullying Report," *Council on American-Islamic Relations California*.

66 Thomas and Blackmon, "The influence of the Trayvon Martin shooting on racial socialization practices of African American parents."

67 Michael Hameleers, Linda Bos, and Claes H. De Vreese, ""They did it": The effects of emotionalized blame attribution in populist communication," *Communication Research* 44, no. 6 (2017): 870–900.

68 Allan Smith, "Photo of Trump remarks shows 'corona' crossed out and replaced with 'Chinese' virus," *NBC News*, March 19, 2020, https://www.nbcnews.com/politics/donald-trump/photo-trump-remarks-shows-corona-crossed-out-replaced-chinese-virus-n1164111.

69 Wenei Philimon, "Black Americans report hate crimes, violence in wake of George Floyd protests and Black Lives Matter gains," *USA Today*, July 17, 2020, https://www.usatoday.com/story/news/nation/2020/07/07/black-americans-report-hate-crimes-amid-black-lives-matter-gains/3259241001/.

70 Charissa S.L. Cheah et al., "COVID-19 racism and mental health in Chinese American families." *Pediatrics* 146, no. 5 (2020).

71 Belle Liang, Jennifer M. Grossman, and Makiko Deguchi, "Chinese American middle school youths' experiences of discrimination and stereotyping," *Qualitative Research in Psychology* 4, no. 1–2 (2007): 187–205.

72 Su Yeong Kim et al., "Accent, perpetual foreigner stereotype, and perceived discrimination as indirect links between English proficiency and depressive symptoms in Chinese American adolescents," *Developmental Psychology* 47, no. 1 (2011): 289.

73 Desiree Baolian Qin, Niobe Way, and Meenal Rana, "The 'model minority' and their discontent: Examining peer discrimination and harassment of Chinese American immigrant youth," *New Directions for Child and Adolescent Development* 2008, no. 121 (2008): 27–42.

74 Qin, Way, and Rana, "The 'model minority' and their discontent."

75 Qin, Way, and Rana, "The 'model minority' and their discontent."

76 Qin, Way, and Rana, "The 'model minority' and their discontent."

77 Angela Kim and Christine J. Yeh, "Stereotypes of Asian American students," *ERIC Digest* (2002).

78 Qin, Way, and Rana, "The 'model minority' and their discontent."

79 "Executive Order 9066 of February 19, 1942, Authorizing the Secretary of War to Prescribe Military Areas," *National Archives*, https://www.archives.gov/historical-docs/todays-doc/?dod-date=219.

80 "Japanese Internment," *History.com*, last updated April 20, 2021, https://www.history.com/topics/world-war-ii/japanese-american-relocation.

81 Ryan D. King and Darren Wheelock, "Group threat and social control: Race, perceptions of minorities and the desire to punish," *Social Forces* 85, no. 3 (2007): 1255–1280.

82 Kamala Kelkar, "How a shifting definition of 'white' helped shape U.S. immigration policy," *PBS*, September 16, 2017, https://www.pbs.org/newshour/nation/white-u-s-immigration -policy.

83 Christopher Wray, "Worldwide Threats to the Homeland," Statement before the House Homeland Security Committee, 116th Congress, 2nd session, September 17, 2020.

84 Seth G. Jones et al., "The war comes home: The evolution of domestic terrorism in the United States," *Center for Strategic & International Studies*, October 22, 2020, https://www. csis.org /analysis/war-comes-home-evolution-domestic-terrorism-united-states.

85 Walter Stephan and Cookie White Stephan, *Improving Intergroup Relations* (Routledge, 1996).

86 Carola Suárez-Orozco and Marcelo M. Suárez-Orozco, *Transformations: Immigration, Family Life, and Achievement Motivation Among Latino Adolescents* (Stanford University Press, 1995).

CHAPTER 9: GENDER GAPS, #METOO, AND TOXIC MASCULINITY

1 David A. Cotter, "CCF BRIEF: Patterns of progress? Changes in gender ideology 1977– 2016," *Council on Contemporary Families*, April 3, 2018, https://contemporaryfamilies.org /genderideology1977-2016/.

2 Claire Cain Miller, "Americans value equality at work more than equality at home," *The New York Times*, December 3, 2018, https://www.nytimes.com/2018/12/03/upshot/americans -value-equality-at-work-more-than-equality-at-home.html.

3 "Athletics," *The National Coalition for Women and Girls in Education*, last updated June 20, 2017, https://www.ncwge.org/athletics.html.

4 "Women in Politics: 2019," *United Nations Entity for Gender Equality and Empowerment of Women*, January 1, 2019, https://www.unwomen.org/-/media/headquarters/attachments /sections/library/publications/2019/women-in-politics-2019-map-en.pdf?la=en&vs=3303.

5 Juliana Menasce Horowitz and Ruth Igielnik, "A century after women gained the right to vote, majority of Americans see work to do on gender equality," Pew Research Center, July 7, 2020, https://www.pewresearch.org/social-trends/2020/07/07/a-century-after-women- gained -the-right-to-vote-majority-of-americans-see-work-to-do-on-gender-equality/.

6 Susan Jones and Debra Myhill, "'Troublesome boys' and 'compliant girls': Gender identity and perceptions of achievement and underachievement," *British Journal of Sociology of Education* 25, no. 5 (2004): 547–561.

7 Sean F. Reardon et al., "Gender achievement gaps in US school districts. CEPA Working Paper No. 18-13," *Stanford Center for Education Policy Analysis* (2018).

8 Christia Spears Brown, Sharla D. Biefeld, and Nan Elpers. "A bioecological theory of sexual harassment of girls: Research synthesis and proposed model," *Review of General Psychology* 24, no. 4 (2020): 299–320.

9 Lin Bian, Sarah-Jane Leslie, and Andrei Cimpian, "Gender stereotypes about intellectual ability emerge early and influence children's interests," *Science* 355, no. 6323 (2017): 389–391.

10 Seth Stephens-Davidowitz, "Google, tell me. Is my son a genius?" *The New York Times*, January 18, 2014, https://www.nytimes.com/2014/01/19/opinion/sunday/google-tell-me-is -my-son-a-genius.html.

11 Janet S. Hyde et al., "Gender similarities characterize math performance," *Science* 321, no. 5888 (2008): 494–495.

12 Hyde et al., "Gender similarities characterize math performance."

13 Alicia Chang, Catherine M. Sandhofer, and Christia S. Brown, "Gender biases in early number exposure to preschool-aged children," *Journal of Language and Social Psychology* 30, no. 4 (2011): 440–450; Kevin Crowley et al., "Parents explain more often to boys than to girls during shared scientific thinking," *Psychological Science* 12, no. 3 (2001): 258–261.

14 Harriet R. Tenenbaum and Campbell Leaper, "Parent-child conversations about science: The socialization of gender inequities?" *Developmental Psychology* 39, no. 1 (2003): 34.

15 Chang, Sandhofer, and Brown, "Gender biases in early number exposure to preschool-aged children"; K. Crowley, M. A. Callanan, H. R. Tenenbaum, and E. Allen, "Parents explain more often to boys than to girls during shared scientific thinking," *Psychological Science* 12, no. 3 (2001): 258–261; Tenenbaum and Leaper, "Parent-child conversations about science."

16 Penelope Espinoza, Ana B. Arêas da Luz Fontes, and Clarissa J. Arms-Chavez, "Attributional gender bias: Teachers' ability and effort explanations for students' math performance," *Social Psychology of Education* 17, no. 1 (2014): 105–126.

17 Ruchi Bhanot and Jasna Jovanovic, "Do parents' academic gender stereotypes influence whether they intrude on their children's homework?" *Sex Roles* 52, no. 9-10 (2005): 597–607; Sandra D. Simpkins, Chara D. Price, and Krystal Garcia, "Parental support and high school students' motivation in biology, chemistry, and physics: Understanding differences among Latino and Caucasian boys and girls," *Journal of Research in Science Teaching* 52, no. 10 (2015): 1386–1407.

18 Dario Cvencek, Andrew N. Meltzoff, and Anthony G. Greenwald, "Math-gender stereotypes in elementary school children," *Child Development* 82, no. 3 (2011): 766–779; Barbara Muzzatti and Franca Agnoli, "Gender and mathematics: Attitudes and stereotype threat susceptibility in Italian children," *Developmental Psychology* 43, no. 3 (2007): 747; Melanie C. Steffens, Petra Jelenec, and Peter Noack, "On the leaky math pipeline: Comparing implicit math-gender stereotypes and math withdrawal in female and male children and adolescents," *Journal of Educational Psychology* 102, no. 4 (2010): 947; Emma M. Mercier, Brigid Barron, and K. M. O'Connor, "Images of self and others as computer users: The role of gender and experience," *Journal of Computer Assisted Learning* 22, no. 5 (2006): 335–348; Ursula Kessels, "Fitting into the stereotype: How gender-stereotyped perceptions of prototypic peers relate to liking for school subjects," *European Journal of Psychology of Education* 20, no. 3 (2005): 309–323.

19 David I. Miller et al., "The development of children's gender-science stereotypes: a meta-analysis of 5 decades of US draw-a-scientist studies," *Child Development* 89, no. 6 (2018): 1943–1955.

20 Melanie C. Steffens and Petra Jelenec, "Separating implicit gender stereotypes regarding math and language: Implicit ability stereotypes are self-serving for boys and men, but not for girls and women," *Sex Roles* 64, no. 5-6 (2011): 324–335.

21 Christia Spears Brown and Campbell Leaper, "Latina and European American girls' experiences with academic sexism and their self-concepts in mathematics and science during adolescence," *Sex Roles* 63, no. 11-12 (2010): 860–870.

22 Jennifer M. Grossman and Michelle V. Porche, "Perceived gender and racial/ethnic barriers to STEM success," *Urban Education* 49, no. 6 (2014): 698–727.

23 Josh Trapani and Katherine Hale, "Higher Education in Science and Engineering," *Science and Engineering Indicators 2020: National Science Foundation*, 2020, https://ncses.nsf.gov/pubs/nsb20197/.

24 "SWE research update: Women in engineering by the numbers," *Society of Women Engineers*, September 11, 2018, https://alltogether.swe.org/2018/09/swe-research-update-women-in-engineering-by-the-numbers/.

25 "Real-time insight into the market for entry-level STEM jobs," *Burning Glass*, February 2014, https://www.burning-glass.com/wp-content/uploads/Real-Time-Insight-Into-The-Market-For-Entry-Level-STEM-Jobs.pdf.

26 Jones and Myhill, "'Troublesome boys' and 'compliant girls.'"

27 Jon Pickering, *Raising Boys' Achievement* (Continuum Education, 1997).

28   Russell J. Skiba et al., "The color of discipline: Sources of racial and gender disproportionality in school punishment," *The Urban Review* 34, no. 4 (2002): 317–342.

29   Barbara Bleyaert, "Disproportional high school suspension rates by race and ethnicity: Research brief," *Education Partnerships, Inc.* (2009).

30   Patricia Kearney et al., "Experienced and prospective teachers' selections of compliance-gaining messages for "common" student misbehaviors," *Communication Education* 37, no. 2 (1988): 150–164.

31   Anne Gregory, Russell J. Skiba, and Kavitha Mediratta, "Eliminating disparities in school discipline: A framework for intervention," *Review of Research in Education* 41, no. 1 (2017): 253–278.

32   Emily Arcia, "Achievement and enrollment status of suspended students: Outcomes in a large, multicultural school district," *Education and Urban Society* 38, no. 3 (2006): 359–369.

33   Harris O'Malley, "The difference between toxic masculinity and being a man," *The Good Men Project*, June 27, 2016, https://goodmenproject.com/featured-content/the-difference-between -toxic-masculinity-and-being-a-man-dg/.

34   Robyn Fivush, "Gender and emotion in mother-child conversations about the past," *Journal of Narrative and Life History* 1, no. 4 (1991): 325–341.

35   Lotte D. van der Pol et al., "Fathers' and mothers' emotion talk with their girls and boys from toddlerhood to preschool age," *Emotion* 15, no. 6 (2015): 854.

36   Sarah M. Coyne, Mark Callister, and Tom Robinson, "Yes, another teen movie: Three decades of physical violence in films aimed at adolescents," *Journal of Children and Media* 4, no. 4 (2010): 387–401.

37   "If he can see it, will he be it? Representations of masculinity in boys' television," *Geena Davis Institute*, 2020, https://seejane.org/wp-content/uploads/if-he-can-see-it-will-he-be-it -representations-of-masculinity-in-boys-tv.pdf; see also Mary Strom Larson, "Interactions, activities and gender in children's television commercials: A content analysis," *Journal of Broadcasting & Electronic Media* 45, no. 1 (2001): 41–56.

38   Carol J. Auster and Claire S. Mansbach, "The gender marketing of toys: An analysis of color and type of toy on the Disney store website," *Sex Roles* 67, no. 7 (2012): 375–388; see also Judith E. Owen Blakemore and Renee E. Centers, "Characteristics of boys' and girls' toys," *Sex Roles* 53, no. 9 (2005): 619–633.

39   Susan G. Kahlenberg and Michelle M. Hein, "Progression on Nickelodeon? Gender-role stereotypes in toy commercials," *Sex Roles* 62, no. 11 (2010): 830–847.

40   Marie Hardin et al., "'Have you got game?' Hegemonic masculinity and neo-homophobia in US newspaper sports columns," *Communication, Culture & Critique* 2, no. 2 (2009): 182–200; Michael A. Messner and Donald F. Sabo, *Sex, Violence & Power in Sports: Rethinking Masculinity* (The Crossing Press, 1994).

41   Karen E. Dill and Kathryn P. Thill, "Video game characters and the socialization of gender roles: Young people's perceptions mirror sexist media depictions," *Sex Roles* 57, no. 11 (2007): 851–864.

42   "The state of gender equality for U.S. adolescents: Full research findings from a national survey of adolescents," *Plan International*, September 12, 2018, https://www.planusa.org/docs /state-of-gender-equality-2018.pdf.

43   Matthew Oransky and Jeanne Marecek, "'I'm not going to be a girl': Masculinity and emotions in boys' friendships and peer groups," *Journal of Adolescent Research* 24, no. 2 (2009): 218–241.

44   Oransky and Marecek, "'I'm not going to be a girl.'"

45   Sarah M. Kiefer and Allison M. Ryan, "Striving for social dominance over peers: The implications for academic adjustment during early adolescence," *Journal of Educational Psychology* 100, no. 2 (2008): 417.

46 Kiefer and Ryan, "Striving for social dominance over peers"; Carlos E. Santos et al., "Gender-typed behaviors, achievement, and adjustment among racially and ethnically diverse boys during early adolescence," *American Journal of Orthopsychiatry* 83, no. 2, pt3 (2013): 252–264.

47 Edward W. Morris, *Learning the Hard Way: Masculinity, Place, and the Gender Gap in Education* (Rutgers University Press, 2012), 53.

48 Oransky and Marecek, "'I'm not going to be a girl.'"

49 Morris, *Learning the Hard Way*; Skiba et al., "The color of discipline."

50 Cheri J. Pascoe, *Dude, You're a Fag: Masculinity and Sexuality in High School* (University of California Press, 2011), 5.

51 Pascoe, *Dude, You're a Fag*, 55.

52 V. Paul Poteat et al., "Short-term prospective effects of homophobic victimization on the mental health of heterosexual adolescents," *Journal of Youth and Adolescence* 43, no. 8 (2014): 1240–1251.

53 Jennifer A. Jewell and Christia Spears Brown, "Relations among gender typicality, peer relations, and mental health during early adolescence," *Social Development* 23, no. 1 (2014): 137–156.

54 Marika Tiggemann and Amy Slater, "Contemporary girlhood: Maternal reports on sexualized behaviour and appearance concern in 4–10 year-old girls," *Body Image* 11, no. 4 (2014): 396–403.

55 "Unlimited potential: Report of the Commission of Gender Stereotypes in Early Childhood," *Fawcett Society*, December 2020, https://www.fawcettsociety.org.uk/Handlers/Download.ashx?IDMF=17fb0c11-f904-469c-a62e-173583d441c8.

56 "The state of gender equality for U.S. adolescents," *Plan International*.

57 L. M. Ward, "Media and sexualization: State of empirical research, 1995–2015," *The Journal of Sex Research* 53, no 4–5 (2016): 560–577.

58 "The state of gender equality for U.S. adolescents," *Plan International*.

59 Elizabeth McDade-Montez, Jan Wallander, and Linda Cameron, "Sexualization in US Latina and White girls' preferred children's television programs," *Sex Roles* 77, no. 1 (2017): 1–15.

60 McDade-Montez, Wallander, and Cameron, "Sexualization in US Latina and White girls' preferred children's television programs."

61 Samantha M. Goodin et al., "'Putting on' sexiness: A content analysis of the presence of sexualizing characteristics in girls' clothing," *Sex Roles* 65, no. 1–2 (2011): 1.

62 Ellen A. Stone, Christia Spears Brown, and Jennifer A. Jewell, "The sexualized girl: A within-gender stereotype among elementary school children," *Child Development* 86, no. 5 (2015): 1604–1622.

63 Kaitlin Graff, Sarah K. Murnen, and Linda Smolak, "Too sexualized to be taken seriously? Perceptions of a girl in childlike vs. sexualizing clothing," *Sex Roles* 66, no. 11 (2012): 764–775.

64 Christine R. Starr and Eileen L. Zurbriggen, "Self-sexualization in preadolescent girls: Associations with self-objectification, weight concerns, and parent's academic expectations," *International Journal of Behavioral Development* 43, no. 6 (2019): 515–522.

65 Maria Giuseppina Pacilli, Carlo Tomasetto, and Mara Cadinu, "Exposure to sexualized advertisements disrupts children's math performance by reducing working memory," *Sex Roles* 74, no. 9–10 (2016): 389–398; Sarah J. McKenney and Rebecca S. Bigler, "Internalized sexualization and its relation to sexualized appearance, body surveillance, and body shame among early adolescent girls," *The Journal of Early Adolescence* 36, no. 2 (2016): 171–197.

66 Christia Spears Brown, "Sexualized gender stereotypes predict girls' academic self-efficacy and motivation across middle school," *International Journal of Behavioral Development* 43, no. 6 (2019): 523–529.

67 Brown, "Sexualized gender stereotypes predict girls' academic self-efficacy and motivation across middle school."

68   Dorothy L. Espelage et al., "Understanding types, locations, & perpetrators of peer-to-peer sexual harassment in US middle schools: A focus on sex, racial, and grade differences," *Children and Youth Services Review* 71 (2016): 174–183.

69   Espelage et al., "Understanding types, locations, & perpetrators of peer-to-peer sexual harassment in US middle schools."

70   Lauren F. Lichty and Rebecca Campbell, "Targets and witnesses: Middle school students' sexual harassment experiences," *The Journal of Early Adolescence* 32, no. 3 (2012): 414–430.

71   Carol Lynn Martin and Diane N. Ruble, "Patterns of gender development," *Annual Review of Psychology* 61 (2010): 353–381.

72   Campbell Leaper and Christia Spears Brown, "Perceived experiences with sexism among adolescent girls," *Child Development* 79, no. 3 (2008): 685–704.

73   Debbie Chiodo et al., "Impact of sexual harassment victimization by peers on subsequent adolescent victimization and adjustment: A longitudinal study," *Journal of Adolescent Health* 45, no. 3 (2009): 246–252; James E. Gruber and Susan Fineran, "Comparing the impact of bullying and sexual harassment victimization on the mental and physical health of adolescents," *Sex Roles* 59, no. 1–2 (2008): 1; Jennifer L. Petersen and Janet Shibley Hyde, "A longitudinal investigation of peer sexual harassment victimization in adolescence," *Journal of Adolescence* 32, no. 5 (2009): 1173–1188; Lynda M. Sagrestano, Alayne J. Ormerod, and Cirleen DeBlaere, "Peer sexual harassment predicts African American girls' psychological distress and sexual experimentation," *International Journal of Behavioral Development* 43, no. 6 (2019): 492–499.

74   Chiodo et al., "Impact of sexual harassment victimization by peers on subsequent adolescent victimization and adjustment"; Sara E. Goldstein et al., "Risk factors of sexual harassment by peers: A longitudinal investigation of African American and European American adolescents," *Journal of Research on Adolescence* 17, no. 2 (2007): 285–300; Gruber and Fineran, "Comparing the impact of bullying and sexual harassment victimization on the mental and physical health of adolescents"; Petersen and Hyde, "A longitudinal investigation of peer sexual harassment victimization in adolescence"; Sagrestano, Ormerod, and DeBlaere, "Peer sexual harassment predicts African American girls' psychological distress and sexual experimentation."

75   Catherine Hill and Holly Kearl, *Crossing the Line: Sexual Harassment at School* (American Association of University Women, 2011).

76   Malachi Willis, Kristen N. Jozkowski, and Julia Read, "Sexual consent in K–12 sex education: An analysis of current health education standards in the United States," *Sex Education* 19, no. 2 (2019): 226–236.

77   Willis, Jozkowski, and Read, "Sexual consent in K–12 sex education."

78   Richard Weissbourd et al., "The talk: How adults can promote young people's healthy relationships and prevent misogyny and sexual harassment," *Harvard Graduate School of Education* 16, no. 8 (2017): 1–46.

79   Linda Charmaraman et al., "Is it bullying or sexual harassment? Knowledge, attitudes, and professional development experiences of middle school staff," *Journal of School Health* 83, no. 6 (2013): 438–444.

80   Charmaraman et al., "Is it bullying or sexual harassment?"

81   Charmaraman et al., "Is it bullying or sexual harassment?"

82   Sarah J. Rinehart and Dorothy L. Espelage, "A multilevel analysis of school climate, homophobic name-calling, and sexual harassment victimization/perpetration among middle school youth," *Psychology of Violence* 6, no. 2 (2016): 213.

83   Jennifer Jewell, Christia Spears Brown, and Brea Perry, "All my friends are doing it: Potentially offensive sexual behavior perpetration within adolescent social networks," *Journal of Research on Adolescence* 25, no. 3 (2015): 592–604.

84   Philippe Bernard et al., "Integrating sexual objectification with object versus person recognition: The sexualized-body-inversion hypothesis," *Psychological Science* 23, no. 5 (2012): 469–471.

85   Maria Giuseppina Pacilli et al., "Less human and help-worthy: Sexualization affects children's perceptions of and intentions toward bullied peers," *International Journal of Behavioral Development* 43, no. 6 (2019): 481–491.

86   Karolien Driesmans, Laura Vandenbosch, and Steven Eggermont, "Playing a video game with a sexualized female character increases adolescents' rape myth acceptance and tolerance toward sexual harassment," *Games for Health Journal* 4, no. 2 (2015): 91–94.

87   "The state of gender equality for U.S. adolescents," *Plan International*.

88   Alan M. Gross et al., "An examination of sexual violence against college women," *Violence Against Women* 12, no. 3 (2006): 288–300.

CHAPTER 10: WHEN THE AUTHENTIC IS INVISIBLE, BUT THE SLURS ARE EVERYDAY

1   Rachel H. Farr et al., "Elementary school-age children's attitudes toward children in same-sex parent families," *Journal of GLBT Family Studies* 15, no. 2 (2019): 127–150.

2   Stacey S. Horn and Larry Nucci, "The multidimensionality of adolescents' beliefs about and attitudes toward gay and lesbian peers in school," *Equity & Excellence in Education* 36, no. 2 (2003): 136–147.

3   Horn and Nucci, "The multidimensionality of adolescents' beliefs about and attitudes toward gay and lesbian peers in school."

4   Horn and Nucci, "The multidimensionality of adolescents' beliefs about and attitudes toward gay and lesbian peers in school."

5   Horn and Nucci, "The multidimensionality of adolescents' beliefs about and attitudes toward gay and lesbian peers in school."

6   "In many countries, younger generations more accepting of homosexuality," *Pew Research Center*, June 24, 2020, https://www.pewresearch.org/global/2020/06/25/global-divide-on -homosexuality-persists/pg_2020-06-25_global-views-homosexuality_0-06/.

7   Kerith J. Conron, "LGBT Youth Population in the United States," *UCLA School of Law Williams Institute*, September 2020, https://escholarship.org/content/qt18t179cz/qt18t179cz .pdf.

8   "Accelerating acceptance: A Harris Poll survey of Americans' acceptance of LGBTQ people," *GLAAD*, 2017, https://www.glaad.org/files/aa/2017_GLAAD_Accelerating_ Acceptance.pdf.

9   Jeffrey M. Jones, "LGBT identification rises to 5.6% in latest U.S. estimate," *Gallup*, February 24, 2021, https://news.gallup.com/poll/329708/lgbt-identification-rises-latest-estimate.aspx.

10   "Where we are on TV, 2018–2019," *GLAAD Media Institute*, https://glaad.org/files/WWAT /WWAT_GLAAD_2018-2019.pdf.

11   Jones, "LGBT identification rises to 5.6% in latest U.S. estimate."

12   "Disney Channel's 'Good Luck Charlie' Introduces Lesbian Couple (VIDEO)," *HuffPost*, last updated February 2, 2016, https://www.huffpost.com/entry/good-luck-charlie-lesbians _n_4675943.

13   Yomi Adegoke, "Move over, Disney! Meet the woman leading the LGBT cartoon revolution," *The Guardian*, October 1, 2019, https://www.theguardian.com/tv-and-radio /2019/oct/01/move-over-disney-meet-rebecca-sugar-the-woman-leading-the-lgbt-cartoon -revolution-steven-universe-adventure-time.

14   Briana R. Ellison, "Trending: Disney Channel just made a huge leap forward in LGBT representation," *The Washington Post*, February 10, 2019, https://www.washingtonpost.com /express/2019/02/11/trending-disney-channel-just-made-huge-leap-forward-lgbt -representation/.

15 Julie Salamon, "Culture wars pull Buster into the fray," *The New York Times,* January 27, 2005, https://www.nytimes.com/2005/01/27/arts/culture-wars-pull-buster-into-the-fray. html?.

16 Salamon, "Culture wars pull Buster into the fray."

17 Lauren B. McInroy and Shelley L. Craig, "Perspectives of LGBTQ emerging adults on the depiction and impact of LGBTQ media representation," *Journal of Youth Studies* 20, no. 1 (2017): 32–46.

18 Kristen Myers, ""Cowboy up!": Non-hegemonic representations of masculinity in children's television programming," *The Journal of Men's Studies* 20, no. 2 (2012): 125–143.

19 "Where we are on TV, 2018-2019," *GLAAD Media Institute.*

20 Kosciw et al., "The 2017 National School Climate Survey: The experiences of lesbian, gay, bisexual, transgender, and queer youth in our nation's schools," *GLSEN,* 2017.

21 Lydia A. Sausa, "Translating research into practice: Trans youth recommendations for improving school systems," *Journal of Gay & Lesbian Issues in Education* 3, no. 1 (2005): 15–28.

22 Kosciw et al., "The 2019 National School Climate Survey."

23 "Educational exclusion: Drop out, push out, and school-to-prison pipeline among LGBTQ youth," *GLSEN,* 2016, https://www.glsen.org/sites/default/files/2019-11/Educational_ Exclusion_2013.pdf.

24 Kosciw et al., "The 2019 National School Climate Survey."

25 Department for Education and Skills, "Stand up for us: Challenging homophobia in schools," 2004, https://dera.ioe.ac.uk/6243/7/stand_up_for_us_04_Redacted.pdf.

26 Kosciw et al., "The 2011 National School Climate Survey."

27 James Norman, Miriam Galvin, and G. McNamara, "Straight talk: An investigation of attitudes and experiences of homophobic bullying in second-level schools," *Dublin, Ireland: Department of Education and Science Gender Equality Unit* (2006).

28 Jennifer Pearson, Chandra Muller, and Lindsey Wilkinson, "Adolescent same-sex attraction and academic outcomes: The role of school attachment and engagement," *Social Problems* 54, no. 4 (2007): 523–542; Stephen T. Russell, Hinda Seif, and Nhan L. Truong, "School outcomes of sexual minority youth in the United States: Evidence from a national study," *Journal of Adolescence* 24, no. 1 (2001): 111–127.

29 GLSEN. 2015 National School Climate Survey. https://www.glsen.org/research/2015 -national-school-climate-survey.

30 Bryan Alexander, "The bullying of Seth Walsh: Requiem for a small-town boy," *Time Magazine,* October 2, 2010, http://content.time.com/time/nation/article/0,8599,2023083,00 .html.

31 Alexander, "The bullying of Seth Walsh."

32 Karin A. Martin, "Normalizing heterosexuality: Mothers' assumptions, talk, and strategies with young children," *American Sociological Review* 74, no. 2 (2009): 190–207.

33 Anthony R. D'Augelli, Arnold H. Grossman, and Michael T. Starks, "Families of gay, lesbian, and bisexual youth: What do parents and siblings know and how do they react?" *Journal of GLBT Family Studies* 4, no. 1 (2008): 95–115.

34 Anthony R. D'Augelli et al., "Predicting the suicide attempts of lesbian, gay, and bisexual youth," *Suicide and Life-Threatening Behavior* 35, no. 6 (2005): 646–660.

35 Caitlin Ryan et al., "Family acceptance in adolescence and the health of LGBT young adults," *Journal of Child and Adolescent Psychiatric Nursing* 23, no. 4 (2010): 205–213.

36 Ryan et al., "Family acceptance in adolescence and the health of LGBT young adults."

37 Rachel H. Farr, Stephen L. Forssell, and Charlotte J. Patterson, "Parenting and child development in adoptive families: Does parental sexual orientation matter?" *Applied Developmental Science* 14, no. 3 (2010): 164-178; Rachel H. Farr, Samuel T. Bruun, and Charlotte J. Patterson, "Longitudinal associations between coparenting and child adjustment among lesbian, gay, and heterosexual adoptive parent families," *Developmental Psychology* 55, no. 12 (2019): 2547.

38 Rachel H. Farr, Stephen L. Forssell, and Charlotte J. Patterson, "Parenting and child development in adoptive families."

39 Rachel H. Farr et al., "Microaggressions, feelings of difference, and resilience among adopted children with sexual minority parents," *Journal of Youth and Adolescence* 45, no. 1 (2016): 85–104.

40 Selby Frame, "Charlotte Patterson, at the forefront of LGBTQ family studies," *American Psychological Association,* June 26, 2017, https://www.apa.org/members/content/patterson -lgbtq-research.

CHAPTER 11: UNRAVELING BIAS CAN START AT HOME

1 D. M. Amodio, "The neuroscience of prejudice and stereotyping," *Nature Reviews Neuroscience* 15, no. 10 (2014): 670–682.

2 P. G. Devine, P. S. Forscher, A. J. Austin, and W. T. Cox, "Long-term reduction in implicit race bias: A prejudice habit-breaking intervention," *Journal of Experimental Social Psychology* 48, no. 6 (2012): 1267–1278.

3 Devine et al., "Long-term reduction in implicit race bias."

4 Joshua Correll et al., "The police officer's dilemma: Using ethnicity to disambiguate potentially threatening individuals," *Journal of Personality and Social Psychology* 83, no. 6 (2002): 1314.

5 Devine et al., "Long-term reduction in implicit race bias."

6 Chloë FitzGerald et al., "Interventions designed to reduce implicit prejudices and implicit stereotypes in real world contexts: a systematic review," *BMC Psychology* 7, no. 1 (2019): 1-12.

7 Devine et al., "Long-term reduction in implicit race bias."

8 Michael A. Olson and Russell H. Fazio, "Implicit and explicit measures of attitudes: The perspective of the MODE model," in *Attitudes: Insights from the New Implicit Measures*, ed. Richard E. Petty, Russell H. Fazio, and Pablo Briñol (Psychology Press, 2008), 19–63.

9 Adam Lueke and Bryan Gibson, "Brief mindfulness meditation reduces discrimination," *Psychology of Consciousness: Theory, Research, and Practice* 3, no. 1 (2016): 34.

10 Marta Miklikowska, "Empathy trumps prejudice: The longitudinal relation between empathy and anti-immigrant attitudes in adolescence," *Developmental Psychology* 54, no. 4 (2018): 703.

11 V. Paul Poteat, "When prejudice is popular: Implications for discriminatory behavior," *Social Development* 24, no. 2 (2015): 404–419.

12 Frances E. Aboud et al., "Interventions to reduce prejudice and enhance inclusion and respect for ethnic differences in early childhood: A systematic review," *Developmental Review* 32, no. 4 (2012): 307–336.

13 Jellie Sierksma, Jochem Thijs, and Maykel Verkuyten, "In-group bias in children's intention to help can be overpowered by inducing empathy," *British Journal of Developmental Psychology* 33, no. 1 (2015): 45–56.

14 Veronica Ornaghi, Jens Brockmeier, and Ilaria Grazzani, "Enhancing social cognition by training children in emotion understanding: A primary school study," *Journal of Experimental Child Psychology* 119 (2014): 26–39.

15 Miao K. Qian et al., "A long-term effect of perceptual individuation training on reducing implicit racial bias in preschool children," *Child Development* 90, no. 3 (2019): e290-e305.

16 Wen S. Xiao et al., "Individuation training with other-race faces reduces preschoolers' implicit racial bias: A link between perceptual and social representation of faces in children," *Developmental Science* 18, no. 4 (2015): 655–663.

17 Xiao et al., "Individuation training with other-race faces reduces preschoolers' implicit racial bias."

18 Farr et al., "Elementary school-age children's attitudes toward children in same-sex parent families."; Brown et al., "U.S. children's stereotypes and prejudicial attitudes toward Arab Muslims."

19 Patricia G. Devine et al., "The regulation of explicit and implicit race bias: The role of motivations to respond without prejudice," *Journal of Personality and Social Psychology* 82, no. 5 (2002): 835.

20 Perry et al., "Initial evidence that parent-child conversations about race reduce racial biases among white U.S. children."

21 Meagan M. Patterson et al., "Toward a developmental science of politics," *Monographs of the Society for Research in Child Development* 84, no. 3 (2019): 7–185.

22 Bigler and Liben, "Developmental Intergroup Theory."

23 Yip et al., "Moderating the association between discrimination and adjustment."

24 Yip et al., "Moderating the association between discrimination and adjustment."

25 Campbell Leaper, Christia Spears Brown, and Melanie M. Ayres, "Adolescent Girls' Cognitive Appraisals of Coping Responses to Sexual Harassment," *Psychology in the Schools* 50, no. 10 (2013): 969–986.

26 Dana J. Stone and Megan Dolbin-MacNab, "Racial socialization practices of White mothers raising Black-White biracial children," *Contemporary Family Therapy* 39, no. 2 (2017): 97–111.

27 Tiffany Yip et al., "Racial disparities in sleep: Associations with discrimination among ethnic/racial minority adolescents," *Child Development* 91, no. 3 (2020): 914–931.

28 Yijie Wang and Tiffany Yip, "Sleep facilitates coping: Moderated mediation of daily sleep, ethnic/racial discrimination, stress responses, and adolescent well-being," *Child Development* 91, no. 4 (2020): e833–e852.

CHAPTER 12: HOW SCHOOLS AND THE COMMUNITY CAN HELP

1 Casey A. Knifsend and Jaana Juvonen, "Extracurricular activities in multiethnic middle schools: Ideal context for positive intergroup attitudes?" *Journal of Research on Adolescence* 27, no. 2 (2017): 407–422.

2 Richard A. Fabes, Erin Pahlke, Carol Lynn Martin, and Laura D. Hanish, "Gender-segregated schooling and gender stereotyping," *Educational Studies* 39, no. 3 (2013): 315–319.

3 Justin E. Heinze, and Stacey S. Horn, "Intergroup contact and beliefs about homosexuality in adolescence," *Journal of Youth and Adolescence* 38, no. 7 (2009): 937–951.

4 Jewell, Brown, and Perry, "All my friends are doing it."

5 Maarten Herman Walter Van Zalk et al., "Xenophobia and tolerance toward immigrants in adolescence: Cross-influence processes within friendships," *Journal of Abnormal Child Psychology* 41, no. 4 (2013): 627–639.

6 Van Zalk et al., "Xenophobia and tolerance toward immigrants in adolescence."

7 Aboud et al., "Interventions to reduce prejudice and enhance inclusion and respect for ethnic differences in early childhood."

8 Joshua R. Polanin, Dorothy L. Espelage, and Therese D. Pigott, "A meta-analysis of school-based bullying prevention programs' effects on bystander intervention behavior," *School Psychology Review* 41, no. 1 (2012): 47–65.

9 Juliet E. Hart Barnett et al., "Promoting upstander behavior to address bullying in schools," *Middle School Journal* 50, no. 1 (2019): 6–11.

10 Brown and Chu, "Discrimination, ethnic identity, and academic outcomes of Mexican immigrant children."

11 Brown and Chu, "Discrimination, ethnic identity, and academic outcomes of Mexican immigrant children."

12 Brooke Seipel, "Six teen girls who met on Twitter were behind Nashville's massive Black Lives Matter protest," *The Hill*, June 5, 2020, https://thehill.com/homenews/state-watch/501450-six-teen-girls-who-met-on-twitter-were-behind-nashvilles-massive-black.

13 Juan Carlos Guerrero, "California dreaming: Protest leads young California BLM activist on journey to family's past," *ABC News*, February 17, 2021, https://abc7news.com/black-lives-matter-protest-california-social-activism-tiana-day-blm-rodney-king/10345634/.

CHAPTER 13: CHANGING THE BIGGER PICTURE

1 Peter A. Leavitt et al., ""Frozen in time": The impact of Native American media representations on identity and self-understanding," *Journal of Social Issues* 71, no. 1 (2015): 39–53.

2 "CCBC 2017 multicultural statistics," *Cooperative Children's Book Center*, February 22, 2018, http://ccblogc.blogspot.com/2018/02/ccbc-2017-multicultural-statistics.html.

3 Lindsey Cameron et al., "Changing children's intergroup attitudes toward refugees: Testing different models of extended contact," *Child Development* 77, no. 5 (2006): 1208–1219.

4 Christia Spears Brown and Sharla Biefeld, "Evaluating school policy efficacy to prevent sexual and youth violence," University of Kentucky (forthcoming).

5 Hill and Kearl, *Crossing the Line;* Kosciw et al., "The 2019 National School Climate Survey," GLSEN.

6 Mikki Kendall, "Why dress codes can't stop sexual assault," *The Washington Post*, April 13, 2016, https://www.washingtonpost.com/posteverything/wp/2016/04/13/why-dress-codes-cant-stop-sexual-assault/.

7 Li Zhou, "The sexism of school dress codes," *The Atlantic*, October 20, 2015, https://www.theatlantic.com/education/archive/2015/10/school-dress-codes-are-problematic/410962/.

8 Roman Stubbs, "A wrestler was forced to cut his dreadlocks before a match. His town is still looking for answers," *The Washington Post*, April 17, 2019, https://www.washingtonpost.com/sports/2019/04/17/wrestler-was-forced-cut-his-dreadlocks-before-match-his-town-is-still-looking-answers/.

9 Phillip Atiba Goff et al., "The essence of innocence: Consequences of dehumanizing Black children," *Journal of Personality and Social Psychology* 106, no. 4 (2014): 526.

10 Eileen Poe-Yamagata and Michael A. Jones, *And Justice for Some: Differential Treatment of Minority Youth in the Justice System* (Youth Law Center, 2000); "Child population by race in the United States," *Kids Count Data Center*, https://datacenter.kidscount.org/data/tables/103-child-population-by-race#detailed/1/any/false/1729,37,871,870,573,869,36,868,867,133/68,69,67,12,70,66,71,72/423,424.

11 Maria Trent, Danielle G. Dooley, and Jacqueline Dougé, "The impact of racism on child and adolescent health," *Pediatrics* 144, no. 2 (2019).

12 Ilana Sherer et al., "Affirming gender: Caring for gender-atypical children and adolescents," *Contemporary Pediatrics* 32, no. 1 (2015).

Index

About the Author

Christia Spears Brown, PhD, is the Lester and Helen Milich Professor of Children at Risk in the Department of Psychology, and founding director of the Center for Equality and Social Justice, at the University of Kentucky (previously at UCLA). She earned her PhD in Developmental Psychology at The University of Texas at Austin. Her research focuses on how children and teens develop gender and ethnic stereotypes, how they are shaped by discrimination, and how that process can be disrupted. In addition to peer-reviewed journal articles and book chapters, she co-edited the *Wiley Handbook of Group Processes in Children and Adolescents* and has written two other books, one for an academic audience, *Discrimination in Childhood and Adolescence*, and one for parents, *Parenting Beyond Pink and Blue: How to Raise Children Free of Gender Stereotypes*. She frequently speaks to and consults with parent groups, schools, toy and media companies, and professional organizations about reducing the impact of stereotypes and discrimination, is regularly featured in national and international media outlets, and has served as an expert witness for the ACLU on cases of gender discrimination in schools. She has been a scholar-in-residence for Society for Research in Child Development, is on the Anti-Racism Task Force of the Society for Research on Adolescence, and is a fellow of the Association of Psychological Science. She lives with her husband, Kris Kearns, her two daughters, Maya and Grace, and her elderly boxer, Coco. When she's not working or hanging out with her family, she spends time reading, running, or watching British cop shows.